AA

TOURING ENGLAND

THE NORTH COUNTRY

THE COMPLETE TOURING GUIDE

Cover picture:
Packhorse bridge at Ashness Bridge, Derwent Water, Cumbria.

Produced by the Publishing Division of the Automobile Association
Editor Allen Stidwill
Designer Neil Roebuck
Picture Researcher Wyn Voysey
Index by D Hancock

Tours compiled and driven by the Publications Research Unit of
the Automobile Association.

Photographs by British Tourist Authority, Woodmansterne Picture
Library, Jarrold Colour Library, J Allen Cash Photolibrary,
C Molyneux, J Sumner, G M Player, S & O Mathews, Yorkshire &
Humberside Tourist Board, AA Photolibrary, V Patel.

All maps by the Cartographic Department, Publishing Division of
the Automobile Association. Based on the Ordnance Survey Maps,
with the permission of the Controller of HM Stationery Office.
Crown Copyright Reserved.

Town plans produced by the AA's Cartographic Department.
©The Automobile Association.

Filmset by Senator Graphics, Great Suffolk St, London SE1
Printed and bound by New Interlitho SPA, Milan, Italy

Published by the Automobile Association, Fanum House,
Basing View, Basingstoke, Hampshire RG21 2EA

ISBN 0 86145 502 9
AA Reference 51952

Touring the North Country

CONTENTS

The jagged, timeless ruins of Whitby Abbey, founded by St Hilda in 657, rise majestically above the town on the East Cliff and provide an impressive landmark for miles along the coast.

INTRODUCTION

The North is rich in variety and contrasts, an area of huge industrial conurbations and of vast tracts of land of outstanding natural beauty. There are the beautiful Yorkshire Dales and Moors, and the magnificent Lake District of Wordsworth, with its dramatic panoramas. To the far north-east the Northumberland countryside is quite magnificent too, as its land rolls away in exhilarating freedom to the Scottish border. Here, faint echoes of Border Battles still linger around towering fortresses that rise majestically about the sea.

The region's cities are equally exquisite: York with its medieval walls and graceful Minster or the lovely Chester, with its unique 'Rows'. In complete contrast to these are the holiday playgrounds of the north, those utterly English traditional seaside resorts such as Blackpool and Morecambe.

This book reveals these treasures and more through its carefully planned motoring tours which provide the ideal way to explore this fascinating region. Each self-contained circular tour can be completed within a day and includes magnificent colour pictures to give a foretaste of what is to come.

As well as the tours the book includes 31 pages of invaluable town plans to guide you around the North's popular towns. There is also a large scale, 3 miles to the inch atlas of the region.

Touring The North Country is just one in a series of six colourful *Regional Guides* which embrace the rich history and varied countryside of Britain. The other five guides in the series are: *Touring the West Country, Touring South and South East England, Touring Wales, Touring Central England and East Anglia* and *Touring Scotland*. The six geographical regions covered by the series are shown on the adjacent map.

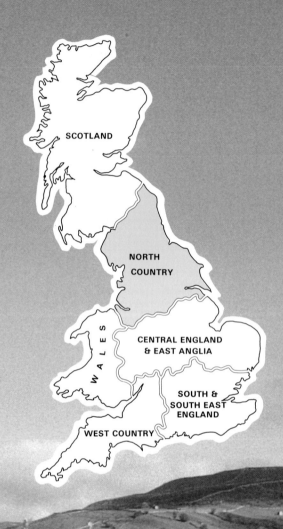

ABOUT THE TOURS

The tours in this guide have been designed for clarity. Each tour occupies two pages and has a clear map accompanying the text. All the places described in the text are shown in **black** on the tour maps and are described as they occur on the road, linked in sequence by route directions. This precise wayfinding information is set in *italic*.

Castles, stately homes and other places of interest described in the tours are not necessarily open to the public or may be open only at certain times. It is therefore advisable to check the opening times of any place before planning a stop there. Properties administered by the National Trust, National Trust for Scotland and the Ancient Monument Scheme (NT, NTS and AM) are generally open most of the year, but this should be checked with the relevant organisation, as should precise opening times.

The Automobile Association's guide *Stately Homes, Museums, Castles and Gardens in Britain* is the most comprehensive annual publication of its kind and describes over 2,000 places of interest, giving details of opening times and admission prices, including many listed in this book.

The tranquility of a traditional hay meadow at Muker in Upper Swaledale contrasts with the spectacular scenery of its setting in the remote Yorkshire Dales.

HOW TO FIND THE TOURS

All the motor tours in the book are shown on the key map below and identified by the towns where they start. The tours are arranged in the book in alphabetical order by start town name. Page numbers are also given on page vii. Each tour begins at a well-known place, but it is possible to join or leave at any point if more convenient.

MAPS					TEXT	
Main Tour Route		Marshland			AM	Ancient Monument
Detour/Diversion from Main Tour Route		Memorial/Monument	m		c	circa
Motorway		Miscellaneous Places of			NT	National Trust
Motorway Access		Interest & Route Landmarks	■		NTS	National Trust for Scotland
Motorway Service Area		National Boundary			OACT	Open at Certain Times
Motorway and Junction Under Construction		National Trust Property	NT		PH	Public House
A-class Road	A68	National Trust for Scotland Property	NTS		RSPB	Royal Society for the
B-class Road	B700	Non-gazetteer Placenames	Thames /Astwood			Protection of Birds
Unclassified Road	unclass	Notable Religious Site	✝		SP	Signpost (s) (ed)
Dual Carriageway	A70	Picnic Site	(PS)			
Road Under Construction	= = = =	Prehistoric Site	ʰ			
Airport	✈	Racecourse	⬭			
Battlefield	✕	Radio/TV Mast				
Bridge	⌣	Railway (BR) with Station				
Castle	♙	Railway (Special) with Station				
Church as Route Landmark	✝	River & Lake				
Ferry	(V)	Woodland Area				
Folly/Tower		Scenic Area				
Forestry Commission Land	♠	Seaside Resort	⌘			
Gazetteer Placename	Zoo /Lydstep	Stately Home	⌂			
Industrial Site (Old & New)	⌗	Summit/Spot Height	KNOWE HILL 209 ▲			
Level Crossing	LC		KNOWE HILL 209 ▲			
Lighthouse	⚲	Viewpoint	☀			

TOURING
THE NORTH COUNTRY

Motor Tours
Pages 2-65

2

ALNWICK, Northumb
This attractive and historic town is a convenient touring centre situated in attractive countryside only 4 miles from the coast. Its splendid castle was once a stronghold of the dukes of Northumberland, and over hundreds of years has been extended to cover some 7 acres of ground. It was founded by the Percy family in the 12th century, but was ruined during a particularly violent phase of border warfare and was not restored to military effectiveness until the 14th century. The major features of its design date from this time, although a great deal of maintenance work was carried out in the 18th and 19th centuries, and today it ranks as one of the most magnificent buildings of its type in the country. The gateway is guarded by an impressive barbican, and the outline of its massive keep, walls and towers completely dominates the town's horizon. Parts of the castle open to visitors are the armoury in Constable's Tower, a museum of British and Roman antiquities in the Postern Tower, the keep, and many of its beautifully furnished state rooms. The town itself has several good churches and several good Georgian buildings. St Michael's echoes the castle with its battlemented tower and is said to preserve some of the best 15th-century workmanship in the county. Among the treasures inside are numerous fine monuments and a Flemish carved chest that dates from the 14th century. Remains of Alnwick Abbey stand on the northern outskirts of the town and include a well-preserved 14th-century gatehouse. The 18th-century Town Hall has shops in its arcaded ground floor. The annual Alnwick fair is held on the last Sunday in June, when the townsfolk dress in period costumes. The fair lasts for 7 days. Some 3 miles north-west of Alnwick in Hulne Park are the remains of 13th-century Hulne Priory.

Follow SP 'Morpeth', then 'Bamburgh B1340' and cross the River Aln via Denwick Bridge. Pass through Denwick, turn right on to an unclassified road SP 'Longhoughton', and after $2\frac{1}{2}$ miles turn left to join the B1339. Enter Longhoughton, then after another 1 mile turn right and in $\frac{1}{2}$ mile drive forward on to an unclassified road SP 'Howick'. Continue for 1 mile to pass the entrance to Howick Hall, then turn right and after another $\frac{1}{2}$ mile keep left to reach the edge of Howick.

HOWICK, Northumb
Situated where the Great Whin Sill outcrop meets the sea in 120ft cliffs of black rock, this hamlet is also a good base from which to tour the fine 18th-century mansion (open) standing in beautiful grounds (open).

In 1¼ miles meet crossroads and turn right through an archway to the fishing village of Craster.

AN UNDISCOVERED COAST

Much of Northumberland's coast is unvisited and unspoiled. North of Alnwick it is designated an Area of Outstanding Natural Beauty, while to the south the lovely River Coquet meets the sea after winding past the religious foundations and mighty castles of bygone ages.

Crabbing boats at Craster are still built to the traditional Northumbrian design.

CRASTER, Northumb
Craster is known for its oak-smoked kippers and splendid cliff scenery. The former can be sampled at many places in the district, and the latter is best appreciated from a $1\frac{1}{4}$-mile walk leading to Dunstanburgh Castle. Above the village is the Georgian house of Craster Tower, which incorporates the remains of a medieval building from which it takes its name.

DUNSTANBURGH CASTLE, Northumb
The great rocky promontory that juts into the sea here would be impressive in any circumstances, but crowned with the picturesque ruins of Dunstanburgh Castle it is magnificent. Remains of this essentially 14th-century structure (AM, NT) cover 11 acres of ground and are enclosed by massive defensive walls. This particular section of coast is in a designated area of outstanding natural beauty.

Return from Craster for $\frac{1}{2}$ mile and turn right SP 'Embleton'. In another $\frac{3}{4}$ mile meet a T-junction and turn right for Embleton.

Restoration in the 19th century preserved Bamburgh Castle's imposing presence on the Whin Sill outcrop.

EMBLETON, Northumb
One of the main buildings in this pretty village is the 14th-century fortified vicarage, which incorporates a pele tower. Military precautions in buildings ideologically devoted to peace are not uncommon in this area which was racked by war between Scots and English for centuries.

Keep left and drive to the church, then turn right on to the B1339. In $1\frac{1}{4}$ miles keep forward on to the B1340, and $1\frac{1}{4}$ miles farther turn right. In another $1\frac{1}{2}$ miles meet crossroads and turn right again for Beadnell.

BEADNELL, Northumb
Close to this small fishing village are several 18th-century lime kilns (NT). Safe bathing and a sandy beach make it attractive as a resort, and the surrounding countryside is beautiful.

Continue to Seahouses.

SEAHOUSES, Northumb
During the late 19th century a harbour was built here to serve north Sunderland, and the village that grew up to house the port workers has changed little to the present day. It is a pretty place with plenty of boat traffic, including a service that runs to the offshore Farne Islands.

FARNE ISLANDS, Northumb
It is said that St Aidan came to this group of 25 small islands (NT) to meditate in the 7th century, and that St Cuthbert stayed in a little hermitage here until he was reluctantly persuaded to become Bishop of Lindisfarne in the same period. Nowadays the group is best known for its bird sanctuary, and ornithologists of the Bird Observatory study from a converted 16th-century pele tower.

At Seahouses turn right, reach a war memorial, and turn left to follow the coast road to Bamburgh.

BAMBURGH, Northumb
Grace Darling was born in this unspoilt fishing village in 1815, and is buried in the graveyard of the mainly 13th-century church. She became instantly famous in 1838 when she sailed with her father from a lighthouse on Longstone Island, in the teeth of a gale, to rescue survivors from the wrecked ship *Forfarshire*. The RNLI has founded a local museum to her memory. Immediately obvious to the visitor is Bamburgh's huge Norman castle (open), once the seat of the kings of Northumbria now restored to its original magnificence, it includes the Armstrong Museum of Industrial Archaeology. During the 18th century it became a charitable institution, with schools, accommodation for shipwrecked sailors, and a hospital.

Branch right on to the B1342 SP 'Belford' and in 2½ miles meet a T-junction. Turn left, then after another 1¾ miles reach Belford Station and drive over a level crossing. In 1 mile cross over the A1 on to the B6349 for Belford.

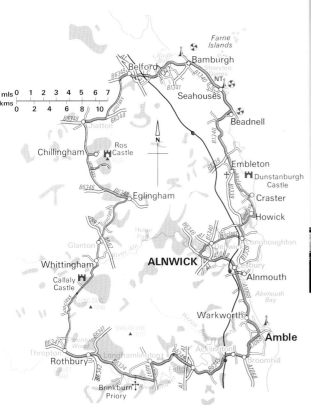

Statues guard the barbican at Alnwick Castle.

ROTHBURY, Northumb
The Victorian Cragside House was the first house in the world to be lit by electricity generated by water power (open), it stands in a 900-acre country park. The surrounding area is rich in various prehistoric remains.

Keep forward and in ½ mile bear right on to the B6334 SP 'Morpeth'. After 3½ miles it is possible to take a short detour from the main route by turning right to Brinkburn Priory.

BRINKBURN PRIORY, Northumb
Beautifully set in a loop of the River Coquet, and is surrounded by rhododendrons in a wooded setting, this 12th-century foundation was created by Augustinian Canons and has one of the best priory buildings (AM) in the country. This status is largely due to sensitive 19th-century restorers.

On the main route, continue for 1½ miles and turn left on to the A697 SP 'Coldstream'. Reach the edge of Longframlington and turn right on to the B6345, then continue to Felton. Cross the River Coquet, keeping on the B6345 SP 'Amble'. After another 1¾ miles turn left and continue through Acklington. Turn left again at Broomhill village on to the A1068 for Amble.

AMBLE, Northumb
North of this attractive little resort is a stretch of coast that has been designated an area of outstanding natural beauty. Eider ducks breed on Coquet Island, which lies offshore from Amble.

Turn left and follow SP 'Alnwick', then in 1¾ miles meet a T-junction and turn right into Warkworth.

WARKWORTH, Northumb
At the top of the main street in Warkworth are the impressive remains of a 12th-century and later castle (AM) that was probably built by the 1st Earl of Northumberland. Its keep, gatehouse, and hall are particularly notable. The view along the main street as it climbs towards the ruins between buildings of many periods is unforgettable. The mainly Norman Church of St Lawrence has an outstanding stone spire which is one of only two ancient examples to be found in the county, and the famous Warkworth Hermitage is a rock-cut chapel (AM) dating from the 14th century.

In 3¼ miles meet a roundabout and drive forward. A short diversion can be made from the main route by taking the 3rd exit from the roundabout and visiting Alnmouth.

ALNMOUTH, Northumb
This holiday resort was once a major grain-shipping port, but nowadays it deals mainly with yachtsmen and other small-boat sailors.

On the main drive, return along the A1068 via Lesbury to Alnwick.

BELFORD, Northumb
In coaching days this small market town on the Great North Road was a popular stop where passengers could stretch their legs and take refreshment at local inns. Belford Hall (not open) is a large building designed by James Paine in 1756.

Continue on the B6349 SP 'Wooler', and after another ¾ mile turn left again on to an unclassified road SP 'Chatton'. In 3 miles meet a T-junction and turn right on to the B6348, then descend from Chatton Moor to reach Chatton village. Drive to the end of the village and turn left on to an unclassified road SP 'Chillingham'. After another 1¼ miles reach Chillingham Post Office and turn left; cross a ford into the village.

CHILLINGHAM, Northumb
During the summer months the grounds of 14th- and 17th-century Chillingham Castle (not open) are accessible for people wishing to see the remarkable Chillingham wild cattle. The animals in this herd are the descendants of wild oxen believed to have been trapped when the park was created in 1220.

Return to Chillingham Post Office and turn left, then pass an unclassified left turn leading to Ros Castle. This offers a pleasant detour from the main route.

ROS CASTLE, Northumb
Local people will insist, with some justice, that the views from this 1,036ft hill (NT) are better than any others in the county. The magnificent panorama stretches east to the coast and the Farne Islands, west to the Cheviot Hills, and embraces the romantic medieval outlines of both Bamburgh and Dunstanburgh Castles.

On the main tour, continue for 3 miles and drive forward to join the B6346 for Eglingham.

EGLINGHAM, Northumb
The multi-period church in Eglingham is a charming, if heavily restored, asset to the villagescape. Eglingham Hall (not open) dates from the early 18th century.

On the nearside of Eglingham turn right on to an unclassified road SP 'Beanley' and 'Powburn', then in 1 mile bear left SP 'Glanton'. After another 2½ miles cross a main road for Glanton, then turn right and take the next turning left for Whittingham.

Atlantic seals bask under Longstone lighthouse in the Farne Islands, offshore from Bamburgh.

WHITTINGHAM, Northumb
Attractively grouped on both banks of the River Aln, this pretty village was once famous as the location of a large fair. A lovely stone bridge spans the river, and the local church shows evidence of Saxon origins in its tower and nave. A 15th-century pele tower survives here.

Cross the River Aln, turn right SP 'Callalay', and after 2 miles skirt the grounds of Callalay Castle.

CALLALAY CASTLE, Northumb
The Callalays are the last of three families to have successively owned this estate since Saxon times, and the manor house is one of the best in the county. Most of the present building (open) dates from the 17th to 19th centuries, but the 15th-century pele tower which it incorporates is evidence of a much earlier building.

In 2½ miles turn left SP 'Thropton', ascend, then descend into Coquet Dale at the edge of Thropton. Meet a T-junction and turn left on to the B6341 for Rothbury.

AMBLESIDE, Cumbria

This popular tourist centre of grey slate houses stands near the northern end of Lake Windermere and is popular with anglers, fell walkers, and climbers. The waters of the lake are alive with fish large enough to satisfy the most discriminating fishermen, and the rugged countryside of the Coniston Fells is only 3 miles away. The beautiful scenery of the lake shores is best appreciated from the water, and regular boat tours can be joined at Waterhead. In the town library are various relics discovered on the site of a 2nd- to 4th-century Roman fort excavated in Borrans Park. Tiny 18th-century Bridge House contains a National Trust information centre. About 1 mile south of Ambleside is the enchanting woodland garden of Stagshaw (NT) (open) with superb views of the lake from informal surroundings. In early times the floors of domestic and public buildings were covered with dried rushes that were replaced as they became soiled, and every July the town has a rush-bearing ceremony as a reminder of the days when everybody in the community collected rushes for the church floor. This very practical idea may have stemmed from Roman harvest thanksgiving celebrations.

Leave Ambleside with SP 'Keswick' to join the A591 and drive through pleasant mountain scenery to reach Rydal, near the Rydal Water.

RYDAL, Cumbria

Close to Rydal is the little River Rothay, which links the east end of peaceful Rydal Water with the vast expanse of Lake Windermere. The poet William Wordsworth lived at Rydal Mount (open) from 1815 until his death in 1850, and must have been inspired by the glorious views over two beautiful lakes that can be enjoyed from the 4½-acre gardens. Nowadays the house is a sort of historical shrine to the poet, preserving many personal relics from his lifetime. Dora's Field was given by Wordsworth to his daughter, and is famous for its daffodils. Nearby Nab Cottage is associated with the writers Thomas de Quincey and Hartley Coleridge. The whole area is dominated by the rugged heights of Nab Scar and Loughrigg Fell.

Leave Rydal and drive past the shores of Rydal Water and Grasmere, with Rydal Fell rising to the right. Continue for ¼ mile beyond Grasmere to reach Dove Cottage.

DOVE COTTAGE, Cumbria

After William Wordsworth had lived in this tiny 17th-century cottage from 1799 to 1808 it became the home of the writer Thomas de Quincey, who occupied it for 26 years. A Wordsworth Museum which now adjoins the house preserves several manuscripts and first editions of the poet's work.

Leave Dove Cottage and turn left on to the B5287 to reach Grasmere.

HIGH LAKELAND PASSES

Fell and dale scenery at its most impressive can be enjoyed from this route, but it should be remembered that the roads in this part of Lakeland are particularly severe. Hard Knott and Wrynose passes have gradients up to 1 in 3 and should not be attempted unless both car and driver are fit.

GRASMERE, Cumbria

The idyllic setting for this tiny stone village is between the tranquil waters of Grasmere Lake and the jagged heights of Helm Crag and Nab Scar. Close by is a beautiful natural arena where the famous Grasmere Sports are staged every August, perpetuating such traditional events as Lakeland wrestling and the guides footrace. The latter follows an arduous course up a steep crag and along a ridge before descending through rough country to end in the arena. Important sheepdog trials are held in the village at about the same time, and the two events make a colourful high spot to the summer. A local rush-bearing ceremony involves the carrying of elaborately decorated bundles of rushes to the church, after which each of the bearers is rewarded with a piece of delicious local gingerbread.

Tranquil Rydal Water contrasts with the constant bustle and activity of Lake Windermere. Both waters are renowned for their excellent fishing, and are the homes of many wildfowl.

In Grasmere turn left on to an unclassified road SP 'Langdale' and follow a winding, bumpy road along the west side of Grasmere Lake. In 1¼ miles begin the ascent of Red Bank passing through woodland, and climb to the summit. Turn right here, descend through picturesque moorland, and at Chapel Stile bear right SP 'Dungeon Ghyll' to join the B5343. Drive along Great Langdale, passing through magnificent mountain scenery below cliffs that tower high above the road. Ahead are Langdale Pikes.

Dove Cottage in Grasmere, once the simple home of poet William Wordsworth, is now a museum containing examples of his work and various personal belongings.

Among the many traditions preserved in Grasmere is that of gingerbread making.

LANGDALE PIKES, Cumbria

Harrison Stickle and Pike O'Stickle soar to respective heights of 2,403ft and 2,323ft above the secluded green dales and sparkling little tarns of the area. Collectively known as Langdale Pikes, they are separated by a deep cleft which contains the roaring waters of Dungeon Ghyll Force. This spectacular Lakeland feature is well worth a visit and can be easily reached by footpath from the New Hotel.

Drive ¾ mile beyond the New Hotel and turn sharp left on to an unclassified road. Continue through a narrow pass with several steep climbs and a number of hairpin bends. Views from the road extend back to Great Langdale, and the lovely waters of Blea Tarn can be seen from the summit of the pass. Descend steeply, with views of the picturesque Little Langdale Valley, then turn very sharp right to climb the steep Wrynose Pass.

WRYNOSE PASS, Cumbria

All around this high pass are the steep sloping peaks of the Cumbrian Mountains. Just below the 1,281ft summit is the Three Shires Stone, where the boundaries of Lancashire, Cumberland, and Westmorland used to meet before the national county reorganization. The summit itself affords spectacular views over the surrounding hills and moors.

CUMBRIAN MOUNTAINS, Cumbria

Lakeland's highest passes cross the ancient Cumbrian Mountains, a range made up of several major groups separated by deep lake and river-filled valleys. At the geographical centre of the district are 3,210ft Scafell Pike, which is the highest mountain in England, the 3,162ft bulk of Sca Fell, and 2,960ft Bow Fell. To the north-west rise the Great Gable and Pillar groups, and Langdale Pikes to the east. Climbing parties test their skills on many of the peaks, and the high country holds many scenic rewards for the energetic fell walker.

Descend sharply from the summit of Wrynose Pass. Views ahead extend over the valley to Hard Knott Pass, where the mountain road can be seen snaking across ridges and dropping away into hidden folds in the landscape. Continue along Wrynose Bottom alongside the River Duddon, with steep scree slopes on either side.

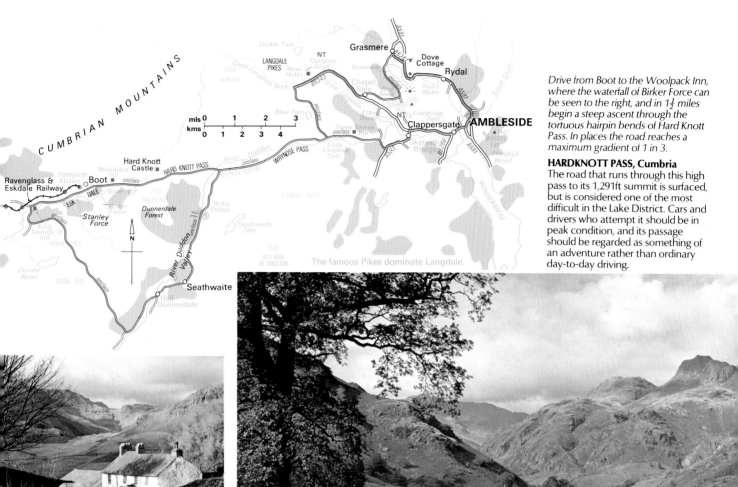

The famous Pikes dominate Langdale.

Drive from Boot to the Woolpack Inn, where the waterfall of Birker Force can be seen to the right, and in 1¼ miles begin a steep ascent through the tortuous hairpin bends of Hard Knott Pass. In places the road reaches a maximum gradient of 1 in 3.

HARDKNOTT PASS, Cumbria
The road that runs through this high pass to its 1,291ft summit is surfaced, but is considered one of the most difficult in the Lake District. Cars and drivers who attempt it should be in peak condition, and its passage should be regarded as something of an adventure rather than ordinary day-to-day driving.

A typical Lakeland cottage at Blea Tarn, one of the wilder and less frequented areas of Lakeland.

RIVER DUDDON VALLEY, Cumbria
Close to the Three Shires Stone in Wrynose Pass is the source of the River Duddon, a beautiful water that chatters down to Wrynose Bottom, through Seathwaite and the Dunnerdale villages to Ulpha. Its entire course is through attractive scenery immortalized by Wordsworth in no less than 35 individual sonnets.

In 2 miles turn left SP 'Broughton, Duddon Valley', with 2,129ft Harter Fell prominent to the right. Continue past a deep river gorge on the right. Pass the Dunnerdale Picnic Area, with the 2,631ft Old Man of Coniston to the left, and continue to Seathwaite.

DUNNERDALE FOREST, Cumbria
Walks from a riverside carpark provided by the Forestry Commission lead through the lovely and secluded countryside of Dunnerdale Forest, a haven for many different species of wildlife. A particularly scenic path leads to 2,129ft Harter Fell, providing excellent views over the Duddon Valley, Eskdale, and the Hard Knott Pass from its high route. Just below Birk's Bridge the Duddon flows through an impressive gorge.

SEATHWAITE, Cumbria
A remote Dunnerdale village in attractive surroundings, Seathwaite is well known as a walking centre and was beloved of the poet Wordsworth. His *Excursion* describes both the village and its 18th-century parson Robert Walker, whose grave can be seen in the local churchyard. About ½ mile north of Seathwaite is the Walna Scar Track, which leads 5 miles across the fells to Coniston.

Leave Seathwaite and continue, passing the peak of 1,735ft Caw on the left, to reach Hall Dunnerdale. At Hall Dunnerdale turn right and drive under a thickly wooded ridge, then in 1¼ miles at Ulpha turn right with SP 'Eskdale' and ascend through more thick woodland. Follow a narrow winding road over Birker Fell for magnificent views to Sca Fell, Scafell Pike, Bow Fell, and the cone-shaped bulk of Harter Fell. Reach the King George IV Inn and turn sharp right with SP 'Boot, Langdale'. Follow the picturesque valley of Eskdale to reach Dalegarth Station, on the Ravenglass and Eskdale Railway.

RAVENGLASS AND ESKDALE RAILWAY, Cumbria
Established in 1875 to carry iron ore, this fascinating little narrow-gauge railway has been revived to carry passengers through 7 miles of enchanting countryside between Dalegarth in Eskdale to Ravenglass, on the coast. Other stations allow the line to be joined at Eskdale Green and Beckfoot. The railway operates both steam and diesel locomotives, and provides a very convenient way by which to enjoy some of the district's best scenery.

ESKDALE AND STANLEY FORCE, Cumbria
At its lower end this beautiful valley has a pastoral aspect, with bankside footpaths following the course of the River Esk through gentle farmlands. Beyond the villages of Eskdale Green and Boot it turns north and becomes wilder as it forges between the rocky flanks of Sca Fell and Bow Fell. Opposite Dalegarth Station is the starting point for the Stanley Gill Nature Trail, which leads to a lush valley and the stunning 60ft cascade of Stanley Force. Many of the paths in the dale are more suited to climbing than walking.

Leave Dalegarth Station and continue on an unclassified road to Boot.

BOOT, Cumbria
A good starting point for walks along the heathery foothills of Eskdale, this beautifully situated village is surrounded by some of the highest mountains in the Lake District. Lovely Dalegarth Hall is a quaint old farmhouse with round chimney stacks that were once typical of the Lakeland region in general.

HARDKNOTT CASTLE, Cumbria
Just before the summit of Hardknott Pass are the remains of a Roman fort (AM) known as Hardknott Castle. Built in the 2nd century AD, the ruins include surviving fragments of corner watchtowers and a bath house. It was sited in this improbable and isolated position to guard a route from the port of Ravenglass.

Begin the steep descent from the summit of the pass, negotiating very sharp hairpin bends, and in 1 mile bear left and drive along Wrynose Bottom before climbing over the steep Wrynose Pass. Descend, with excellent views over Little Langdale, and follow the valley with Little Langdale Tarn visible to the right. Pass the Three Shires Inn and in 1 mile meet a T-junction and turn right SP 'Coniston'. In ¼ mile turn left on to the A593 SP 'Ambleside', and drive through Skelwith Bridge to reach Clappersgate.

CLAPPERSGATE, Cumbria
Magnificent views are afforded by the White Craggs Garden (limited opening) in Clappersgate, and in the gardens are splendid displays of heathers, rhododendrons, azaleas and many other plants.

Leave Clappersgate and cross the river bridge, then turn left for the return to Ambleside.

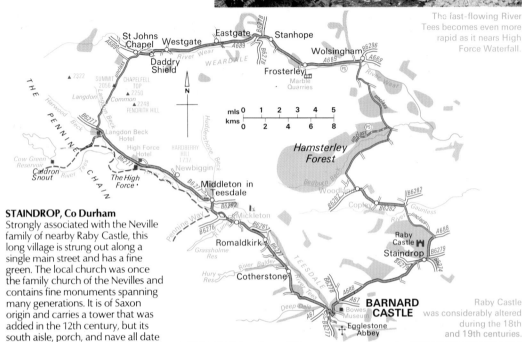

THROUGH WEARDALE AND TEESDALE

Deep in the wooded outriders of the eastern Pennines are beautiful river valleys and spectacular waterfalls, attractive little dales villages, and the stream-fed waters of placid reservoirs. Everywhere is the sound of water falling from ledges, tumbling over boulders, and cascading down hillsides.

The fast-flowing River Tees becomes even more rapid as it nears High Force Waterfall.

BARNARD CASTLE, Co Durham

The town of Barnard Castle stands in a picturesque setting on a clifftop overlooking the River Tees and is an ideal base from which to explore the lovely countryside of Teesdale. The first castle to stand here was built in the 12th century by Guy de Balliol, but this was rebuilt by his nephew Bernard – hence the Barnard element of the town name – and adapted throughout the centuries by various owners. During the Civil War it fell to the Cromwellian army, after which it was left to crumble away in peace. Today the site covers 6½ acres, and the extensive remains (AM) include the 3-storey keep and parts of a 14th-century great hall. In the town itself is a medieval bridge that is still in use, and many old houses and inns. It is thought that Charles Dickens may have written *Nicholas Nickleby* while staying here. Close to the town is the fascinating Bowes Museum of Art and the local countryside is dotted with picturesque little villages.

A short detour before the main route begins can be taken to Egglestone Abbey by driving south on the B6277 and turning off with SP on an unclassified road.

Egglestone Abbey is now a romantic ruin.

EGGLESTONE ABBEY, Co Durham

These lovely ruins (AM) date from the 12th century and occupy a beautiful rural site beside the River Tees. Close by the Thorsgill Beck is spanned by a medieval packhorse bridge and an attractive 18th-century road bridge.
On the main tour, leave Barnard Castle with SP 'Bishop Auckland' and at the edge of the town turn left to follow the A688 to Staindrop.

STAINDROP, Co Durham

Strongly associated with the Neville family of nearby Raby Castle, this long village is strung out along a single main street and has a fine green. The local church was once the family church of the Nevilles and contains fine monuments spanning many generations. It is of Saxon origin and carries a tower that was added in the 12th century, but its south aisle, porch, and nave all date from the 15th century. Inside is the only pre-Reformation screen surviving in County Durham.
Turn left by Staindrop Church and after 1 mile reach the entrance to Raby Castle.

RABY CASTLE, Co Durham

This impressive pile stands in a 270-acre deer park and exactly matches the popular conception of what a castle should look like, right down to its moat and nine great towers. It is known to have been in existence in one form or another from 1016, but its present distinctive appearance is largely due to 14th-century rebuilding and extension. Over the centuries Raby has played a major role in the politics of Britain. The huge Baron's Hall was the scene of plotting aimed at putting Mary Queen of Scots on the English throne instead of Elizabeth I, but when the scheme failed the castle was forfeited and passed into the hands of the Neville family. Later it became the property of the Vanes, Lords of Barnard; nowadays it is a valuable national asset which attracts many visitors each year. Inside are fine collections of furniture, paintings and ceramics, and among the many fine chambers is a curious octagonal drawing room. The kitchens display 14th-century rib vaulting and preserve a smoke-driven spit, while outside in the stables is a collection of carriages.

Raby Castle was considerably altered during the 18th and 19th centuries.

Leave Raby Castle and continue along the A688 for ½ mile. Turn left on to an unclassified road SP 'Cockfield' and after ½ mile keep straight on SP 'Butterknowle'. After another 2¼ miles turn left on to B6282 for Copley and continue to Woodland. Meet a T-junction and turn left, then after 300 yards turn right on to an unclassified road SP 'Hamsterley'. Descend, with good views over Hamsterley Forest.

HAMSTERLEY FOREST, Co Durham

Fast becoming known as one of the most beautiful countryside recreation areas in the county, this large state forest is crossed by a road that is open to motorists. It can be explored via dozens of footpaths, and parking space is virtually limitless. Visitors are catered for with three picnic sites, drinking water, forest picnic furniture, and a visitors' centre. A special woodland trail has been laid out to help children identify various species of plants and animals, and the glades away from the busy areas are the homes of roe, fallow, and red deer.

After 3 miles turn left SP 'Wolsingham' and descend, then in ¾ mile meet a T-junction and turn left again to cross Bedburn Beck. After a short distance pass a left turn that gives access to Hamsterley Forest, and drive through woodland before emerging into open countryside and descending into Weardale. Cross the River Wear and continue to the edge of Wolsingham.

WOLSINGHAM, Co Durham

A good base from which to explore beautiful Weardale, this typical Durham town of stone-built houses holds a precarious balance between the needs of industry and the preservation of its charm. The result is the type of contrast seen between giant steelworks on the outskirts and the historic 12th-century tower of St Mary's Church, more towards the centre of the town. North of Wolsingham is the lovely Tunstall Reservoir, which was formed by the constriction of Waskerley Beck and has become the home of many water birds and other wild creatures with a liking for aquatic surroundings.

Turn left on to the A689 SP 'Stanhope' and continue to Frosterley.

FROSTERLEY, Co Durham

A local stone known as Frosterley marble is much prized for building and monumental sculpture, but centuries of quarrying have almost exhausted the supply. What little is left is being saved for purposes considered important enough for such a rare material. Many of the county's churches have fonts, memorials, pillars, and various other features fashioned from the stone, which is not really marble but a grey limestone that becomes black and reveals hundreds of tiny fossils when polished. A particularly fine example of the material can be seen near the door of the local church, bearing the inscription 'This Frosterley marble and limestone, quarried for centuries in this parish, adorns cathedrals and churches throughout the world'.

Leave Frosterley and continue along the A689 to Stanhope.

An unusual feature of Stanhope Churchyard is the fossilized stump of a tree.

STANHOPE, Co Durham

Stanhope churchyard features the fossilized stump of a tree that grew some 150 million years ago. The church itself dates from 1200 and contains a number of fascinating relics, including a Saxon font, two wooden plaques and a painting all thought to be Flemish. Close to the churchyard gate is the old town cross. West of Stanhope, in the high Weardale moorland, is a wooded gorge containing the famous Heathery Burn Cave. Bronze-age weapons and various artefacts proving the early domestication of horses were found here, and are now on display in London's British Museum.

Leave Stanhope on the A689 'Alston' road and continue to Eastgate.

The drama of Caldron Snout is well worth the difficult approach.

EASTGATE, Co Durham

Attractive Frosterley marble is shown to advantage by the font in Eastgate's 19th-century parish church. A feature of the beautiful moorland countryside around the village is the Low Linn Falls, where a burn tumbles over rocks in an area that is of particular interest to geologists and botanists.

Leave Eastgate and continue along the A689 beside the River Wear to reach Westgate.

WESTGATE, Co Durham

Both Westgate and Eastgate derived their names from the entrances to Old Park, which was once the hunting residence of the bishops of Durham. The village has a 19th-century church and an attractive watermill, and was once well known as a cock-fighting centre. Nowadays it has a strange claim to fame as the only place where a medieval thimble has been found.

Continue to Daddry Shield.

The high moorland of Weardale is within easy reach of Stanhope.

DADDRY SHIELD, Co Durham

Another old centre of cock fighting, this attractive Weardale village stands just north of a mountain rescue post.

Continue to St John's Chapel.

ST JOHN'S CHAPEL, Co Durham

This ancient market centre takes its name from the Church of St John the Baptist. The original foundation was probably created many hundreds of years ago, but the present building dates from 1752.

Turn left on to an unclassified road SP 'Middleton-in-Teesdale' and climb to 2,056ft on Langdon Common, part of the Pennine Chain.

THE PENNINE CHAIN

Popularly known as the Backbone of England, this great upland mass of hills, moorland, and mountains stretches north from Kinder Scout in Derbyshire to the Cheviot foothills on the Scottish border. A 250-mile footpath known as the Pennine Way traverses the range from end to end.

Descend into Teesdale, meet a T-junction, and turn left on to the B6277. In $\frac{1}{4}$ mile reach the Langdon Beck Hotel, where a short detour can be made from the main route by turning right and driving along a rough track to the picnic area at Cow Green Reservoir. A private road (locked) and footpath (open) lead from here to the waterfall of Caldron Snout.

CALDRON SNOUT, Co Durham

More of a tiered cascade than a proper waterfall, beautiful Caldron Snout tumbles 200ft down a natural staircase formed by a hard rock known as dolerite. It used to be fed by a long winding pool called the Well, but this has now been incorporated in the Cow Green Reservoir. Downstream from the cascade is the spectacular High Force waterfall, and between the two are the remains of a slate mill.

Continue along the B6277 and after 2½ miles meet the High Force Hotel. A footpath opposite the hotel leads to the High Force waterfall.

HIGH FORCE, Co Durham

Here one of England's loveliest waterfalls plunges 70ft over the menacing black cliff of the Great Whin Sill, to be caught in a deep pool surrounded by shrubs and rocks.

Continue along the B6277 through Newbiggin to reach the town of Middleton-in-Teesdale

MIDDLETON-IN-TEESDALE, Co Durham

Strong Quaker influence is evident in the no-frills orderliness of this stern little town. This is because local lead mines, the mainstay of Middleton's economy until they were closed at the start of this century, were run by that denomination. The local church dates from the 19th century and shares its churchyard with various remains of a predecessor.

Leave Middleton-in-Teesdale and turn right on to a road SP 'Scotch Corner'. Cross the River Tees and in ½ mile keep left SP 'Barnard Castle'. Continue for ¾ mile, rejoin the B6277, and continue through Mickleton and attractive Romaldkirk.

ROMALDKIRK, Co Durham

The attractive houses of this perfect little Teesdale village are interspersed with greensward that transforms an already good villagescape into a splendid one.

Leave Romaldkirk and continue along the B6277 to Cotherstone.

COTHERSTONE, Co Durham

Beautiful and dramatic scenery surrounds this pleasant village, which stands at the junction of Balder Beck and the River Tees. Close to the watersmeet are slight remains of a Norman castle.

Leave Cotherstone, recross the River Tees, and return to Barnard Castle.

AMONG THE BORDER FORESTS

The fascinating remains of Hadrian's Wall can be seen at their best over the vast coniferous plantations and wild moorlands of the Kielder and Redesdale Forests, parts of the Border Forest Park. Special Forestry Commission roads allow motorists to enjoy this area right up to the Scottish Border.

Bewcastle's ancient cross is decorated with intricate carvings and Runic inscriptions.

BELLINGHAM, Northumb
The focus of life in North Tynedale, this small market town once had a flourishing iron industry but nowadays is best known as a gateway to the great moors and forests of Nortumberland. Its ancient Church of St Cuthbert has a unique roof, barrel vaulted with six-sided stone ribs instead of the usual timber, probably as a precaution against fire. In the churchyard is a well whose waters are traditionally held to have healing powers.

Leave Bellingham on the B6320 with SP 'Hexham', and in ¼ mile turn left and cross a river bridge. Take the next turning right on to an unclassified road SP 'Kielder', then drive through picturesque North Tynedale.

NORTHUMBERLAND NATIONAL PARK, Northumb
Extending from Hadrian's Wall in the south to the Cheviot Hills in the north, this 400-square-mile national park occupies the whole western corner of Northumberland and joins the Border Forest Park along its western boundary. Much of the district is high moorland, with rugged hills and summits that afford superb views of the local countryside, but towards the east its character changes to a gentler landscape where the valleys of the Coquet, Redesdale, and North Tyne meander through beautiful woodland. Walking and pony-trekking are two popular ways in which visitors explore the park.

Continue for 4 miles, cross a river bridge, then turn right and continue to Stannersburn. After a while enter the Kielder Forest and drive to Kielder Reservoir.

KIELDER FOREST, Northumb
Really part of the Border Forest Park, this great sea of conifers blankets the slopes of the Cheviot Hills with the varied greens of larch, spruce, Scots pine, and lodgepole pine. It was planted by the state to meet the needs of industry and has matured as a valuable addition to the Northumbrian landscape.

BORDER FOREST PARK, Northumb, Borders
So called because it crosses the border into Scotland, this vast area of woodland incorporates three forests and is the largest area of its type in Britain. In the east its vast landscapes merge with the open moorland horizons of the Northumberland National Park, making a staggering 600 square miles

of beautiful, wild, and essentially unspoiled countryside in all. Both parks are crossed by the 250-mile Pennine Way footpath, and the Kielder, Redesdale, and Wauchope forests offer many planned walks and nature trails. Various leisure activities are catered for.

KIELDER RESERVOIR, Northumb
The largest reservoir in Western

Europe, situated in the heart of the Border Forest Park, offers a variety of activities. Within Tower Knowe is a Water Authority's Information Centre.

Continue through the Kielder Forest to the village of Kielder.

Much of the Border Forest Park has been planted with softwood species to supply the timber industries. Their dark ranks echo the forests of the past.

KIELDER, Northumb
This and several other villages were developed as the area's forestry industry became established, and nowadays they make handy bases from which to explore the local countryside. Kielder Castle is an 18th-century shooting lodge that now serves as a Border Forest Park information centre and a Forest Museum.

Continue for 3 miles and cross the Scottish border, then in 3¼ miles turn left on to the B6357 SP 'Newcastleton' and follow the attractive Liddel Water. In 6¼ miles reach a junction with the B6399. A detour from the main route to Hermitage Castle can be made by turning right on to the B6399, driving for 4 miles, then turning left on to an unclassified road.

HERMITAGE CASTLE, Borders
Romantically associated with Mary Queen of Scots, this brooding castle (AM) punctuates the desolate moorland landscape with four great towers and grim walls that entirely suit their windswept situation. It was a stronghold of the Douglas family in the 14th century, and much later became the property of Mary's lover Bothwell.

On the main route, bear left with the B6357 to reach Newcastleton.

NEWCASTLETON, Borders

Before the forestry industry became such an important influence on local life this attractive village was a flourishing weaving centre. Its position affords views of beautiful Liddesdale from almost anywhere in or around the village, and beyond Newcastleton Forest are the magnificent 1,678ft Larriston Fells. This part of the Border Forest Park was planted in 1921.

Drive to the far end of the village and turn left on to an unclassified road (no SP). Cross a river bridge and turn right SP 'Brampton', then after 3 miles cross Kershope Burn to enter the English county of Cumbria. Ascend a winding road through the Kershope Forest, then after ¾ mile reach the Dog and Gun Inn and turn left SP 'Carlisle'. In 4 miles turn right, and in another ¾ mile drive forward on to the B6318. Take the next turning left on to an unclassified road and drive to Bewcastle.

BEWCASTLE, Cumbria

Several ancient remains can be seen in the bleak open moorland that surrounds Bewcastle. Materials from a Roman fort that was once an outpost of Hadrian's Wall were used to build a castle (AM) here, but this too has succumbed to the ravages of time and cottage builders, leaving just a few fragments. In the village churchyard is the famous Bewcastle Cross, which dates from the 7th century and is intricately carved with Runic inscriptions and patterns.

At Bewcastle turn right (no SP) and cross a river bridge. In 5 miles cross the B6318, and in 2½ miles meet a T-junction. Turn left SP 'Birdoswald' and follow the line of Hadrian's Wall for ¼ mile to reach Banks.

HADRIAN'S WALL, Northumb, Cumbria

This mighty engineering achievement was built in the 2nd century AD and is the most impressive monument to the Roman occupation in Britain. It runs for 73 miles across the entire width of northern England and is remarkably well preserved along several sections. It was part of a complex defence system designed to keep the marauding Scottish tribes out of the Romanized south, and included two broad ditches and a series of milecastles interspersed with turrets and signal towers. The Romans finally abandoned the wall in AD 383, but it survived in a reasonably complete state until quarried by road builders in the 18th century. Well-preserved forts can be seen at Chesters, Housesteads, Vindolanda, and Birdoswald, while the most complete section of wall stands to the west of the River North Tyne. Walks along the wall are most enjoyable and can be very instructive.

The northern frontier of Roman Britain still forms a barrier as it follows the high ridges of Whin Sill.

One of the best-preserved of the original 17 Hadrian's Wall forts has been excavated at Housesteads, revealing many facets of Roman life.

BANKS, Northumb

A turret (AM) on the Roman wall here was once manned by troops garrisoned at the nearest milecastle. A footpath leads east to the Pike Hill signal tower, part of a beacon system by which a warning of attack could be sent the length of the wall with surprising speed. One mile south west lies the Augustinian, Lanercost Priory (AM) which was founded in 1166 and its nave is still in use. In the rebuilt Abbey Mill, is a craft workshop for the handicapped.

Continue to Birdoswald.

BIRDOSWALD, Cumbria

Large and impressive outer defences of a Roman fort (AM) known as *Camboglanna* can be seen here beside the River Irthing, and well-preserved sections of Hadrian's Wall (AM) extend east and west. Close by are the substantial remains of Harrow's Scar Milecastle (AM).

In ½ mile ascend, then turn right on to the B6318 SP 'Gilsland' and in 1 mile turn right to reach Gilsland.

GILSLAND, Northumb

Sulphur and chalybeate springs brought brief fame to this small place as a spa resort, but it is much better known for its excellent Roman remains. Hadrian's Wall runs south of the village and includes the Poltross Burn Milecastle (AM), a fascinating and well-preserved survivor from the occupation. Close to the village is an attractive waterfall.

From Gilsland turn left along the B6318 and in 2 miles meet a junction and turn left to enter Greenhead.

GREENHEAD, Northumb

Close to Greenhead is a dramatic series of ravines known as the Nine Nicks of Thirlwall. Near by are the ruins of Thirlwall Castle, which was built in the 14th century, and the route of a Roman track known as the Maiden Way runs through the area.

Turn left on the B6318, ascend, and in 5 miles reach the Twice Brewed Inn.

TWICE BREWED INN, Northumb

Slightly away from the site of the original building, this famous inn now houses a useful Northumberland National Park information centre. Close by, at Winshields, the Roman wall (AM) reaches its highest point of 1,230ft above sea level.

Continue along the B6318 to reach Housesteads, where there is a reasonable carpark.

HOUSESTEADS, Northumb

The best-preserved fort (AM, NT) on Hadrian's Wall can be seen here. Once known as *Vercovicium*, it follows the typical Roman pattern of rectangular walls with rounded corners, and was built to house up to 1,000 infantrymen. Relics found during excavations in the area are displayed in a well laid-out museum, and close to Housesteads the wall itself reaches its highest point as it follows the high ridges of the Great Whin Sill rock outcrop. Marvellous views from the ridge extend west and take in several little lakes, including the lovely Crag Lough.

Continue for 5 miles to reach Carrawborough.

CARRAWBOROUGH, Northumb

One of the very few Mithraic temples to be found in Britain has been excavated here. Probably dating from the 3rd century, it was a very small building containing three dedicatory altars to the deity Mithras, and a figure of the Mother Goddess. Close by is the Roman fort known as *Brocolitia*.

Continue along the B6318 to reach Chollerford.

CHOLLERFORD, Northumb

Housesteads may be the best preserved of the Roman wall's forts, but *Cilurnum* (or Chesters) is by far the most interesting and best excavated. It was a large stronghold housing 500 troops. Digging has revealed fascinating details of the fort itself, plus the remains of a bath house and central heating system. Relics from this and other sites can be seen in the interesting local museum, and traces of the Tyne bridge that the fort was built to guard have been found downstream of the present 18th-century crossing.

Meet a roundabout and take the 1st exit on to the B6320 SP 'Wark, Bellingham'. Enter the North Tyne Valley to reach Wark.

WARK, Northumb

Access to this picturesque huddle of cottages and houses is by an iron bridge over the River North Tyne. The woodlands of Wark Forest stretch away to the west.

Continue along the B6320 for the return to Bellingham.

PEACE IN THE BORDER LANDS

Green rounded hills and unspoilt miles of coastline betray nothing of the centuries of human violence that once made this lovely area a place to avoid. Now the only battles are between nesting gulls, and the only invasions are of migrant birds seeking the haven of a largely unpopulated countryside.

BERWICK-UPON-TWEED, Northumb

A busy seaport and now England's northernmost town, Berwick was alternately held by Scottish and English forces during the bitter border struggles that began with the Romans and persisted until the 15th century. Remains of a castle built here by the Normans in the 12th century include three towers and ancient sections of wall that were later incorporated in the medieval town defences. During Elizabethan times the town walls (AM) were restored to full defensive effectiveness, and they have survived as a complete 2-mile circuit round old Berwick. Their rebuilding was done with gun warfare very much in mind, and in their present condition they represent the earliest examples of their type in northern Europe. The approach to the town itself is dominated by three famous and attractive bridges over the River Tweed. Berwick Bridge dates from the 17th century and has 15 elegant arches, the Royal Border Bridge of 1880 was built to carry a railway into the town, and the Tweed Road Bridge is a good example of modern architecture dating from 1928. It is said that the town has more buildings scheduled for preservation than any other place of comparable size in England, and a walk round the lovely old streets would certainly seem to confirm that. The parish church, one of the few to be built during Cromwell's Commonwealth, is of exceptional architectural interest and was extended in the 19th century. In 1717 Vanbrugh built Britain's earliest barracks here, and today these incorporate the well laid out Museum of the King's Own Scottish Borderers. The Georgian period is represented by the Town Hall (open by arrangement) and several fine houses attractively sited by the quay. Relics from the town's past can be seen with collections of paintings and ceramics in Berwick Museum, and the lovely local countryside includes a coastal area of outstanding natural beauty. Every May Day the traditional ceremony of Riding the Bounds, reaffirming the parish boundaries, takes place here.

Leave Berwick on the A1167 with SP 'Edinburgh', and in ½ mile bear left on the A6105 SP 'Kelso'. In a further ½ mile turn left A1 then after ½ mile turn right B6461 after 1 mile enter the old Scottish county of Berwickshire. In ¾ mile keep left, and after another 1½ miles turn left on to an unclassified road SP 'Norham'. Later cross the River Tweed by the Union Suspension Bridge and re-enter Northumbeland. In ½ mile meet a T-junction and turn right, then in 1¼ miles turn right again and continue to Norham.

Berwick's 17th-century bridge was built across the estuary in 1611 to connect the town with Tweedmouth.

NORHAM, Northumb

One of the two triangular greens in this attractive village features a 19th-century cross, and together they form a focal point for the solid little stone-built houses that surround them. At the east end of the main street the massive Norman keep of a 12th-century castle (AM) towers above the River Tweed from a rocky outcrop, proclaiming a strength that resisted the efforts of Scottish forces for many hundreds of years. The army of Robert the Bruce unsuccessfully assaulted its walls for nearly a year, and 12 months later the castle resisted a siege that was immortalized by Sir Walter Scott in the poem *Marmion*. The hero of the occasion was Sir William Marmion, an English knight who accepted a lady's challenge to take command of the most dangerous place in Great Britain as proof of his love. On February 13 the opening of the salmon season is marked by a ceremony known as the Blessing of the Nets, after which the Tweed can be fished for salmon by anyone with the right or money to do so.

Leave Norham, meet a main road, and turn left on to the B6470 SP 'Cornhill'. In ⅓ mile turn right on to an unclassified road, then in ¾ mile turn right again on to the A698. After a further 2 miles cross (with care) the picturesque Twizel Bridge.

The keep of Norham Castle dates from c1160.

TWIZEL BRIDGE, Northumb

This beautiful 15th-century bridge spans the River Till with a single elegant arch of 90ft. Views from the bridge into the deep wooded glen are enchanting, and the ivy-covered folly of Twizel Castle enhances the scene from a nearby ridge. Many such 18th-century conceits were left unfinished, but this was genuinely never completed.

Leave Twizel Bridge and continue to Cornhill-on-Tweed.

CORNHILL-ON-TWEED, Northumb

The Scottish poet and folk hero Robert Burns entered England for the first time when he crossed the River Tweed here in 1787. This and other events are recorded on a plaque at nearby Coldstream.

A detour can be made from the main route to Flodden Field from Cornhill: meet a roundabout in the village and take the 1st exit on to the A697, then after 1½ miles turn right on to an unclassified road and proceed to Branxton for Flodden Field.

FLODDEN FIELD, Northumb

In 1513 one of the bloodiest battles ever witnessed on English soil was fought at Flodden Field, just a few hundred yards south of Branxton village. A monument inscribed 'To the brave of both nations' now marks the spot where James IV of Scotland was killed when the English army of 26,000 defeated a huge invading force of 40,000. Both sides suffered appalling casualties, with as many as 1,600 deaths between them.

A second detour from the main route at Cornhill to the village of Coldstream can be followed by taking the 2nd exit at the roundabout on to the A697 and driving for 1¾ miles.

COLDSTREAM, Borders

John Smeaton built the 5-arched bridge over the River Tweed here in 1766 to replace a ford that had been used for many hundreds of years, often by the armies of Scotland and England. A plaque on the bridge records the poet Burns' first crossing of the river into England, and one near the market commemorates the raising of the Coldstream Guards to fight in Cromwell's New Model Army.

On the main tour, meet the roundabout in Cornhill and take the 2nd exit on to the A697. Take the first turning left on to an unclassified road SP 'Learmouth', then in 1¼ miles meet crossroads and drive forward. Take the 2nd turning left SP 'Yetholm' and in 2⅓ miles meet crossroads. Turn left on to the B6352 SP 'Wooler' and in ⅓ mile bear right to follow the Bowmont Water, then 2 miles farther turn right on to the B6351. Cross a river bridge, meet a T-junction, and turn left to follow the foot of the Cheviot Hills. Pass the edge of Kilham and drive to Kirknewton.

KIRKNEWTON, Northumb

Kirknewton's church has a chancel and south transept that were obviously built for defensive as well as religious purposes, a reminder of the centuries of unrest suffered by this and many other border villages. The valley of the College Burn leads from the village to the 2,676ft summit of The Cheviot via a narrow constriction known as Hen Hole. The lovely countryside hereabouts is best appreciated on foot.

Continue along the B6351 to Yeavering.

YEAVERING, Northumb

The Saxon King Edwin had his capital here in the 7th century, and excavations in a field near the River Glen have revealed traces of wooden halls and amphitheatres from his ancient town. It was Edwin who, according to tradition, allowed the monk Paulinus to convert the people of Northumbria to Christianity. One of the largest hillforts in the border country can be seen to the south of the village, on the 1,182ft summit of Yeavering Bell.

From Yeavering continue along the foot of the Cheviot Hills.

Winter in the Cheviot Hills can be a beautiful but lonely season.

THE CHEVIOT HILLS, Northumb

Much of this lonely range forms the border between Scotland and England. Its grassy flanks and mountainous summits are cropped smooth by the famous Black Face and Cheviot sheep, hardy breeds that can find food in the most unlikely places and survive with the minimum of interference from man. The countryside between the hills and Hadrian's Wall forms part of the Northumberland National Park, and the arduous northern section of the 250-mile Pennine Way brings the footpath to an end here. North-east of the great mass that is The Cheviot itself lies the picturesque College Valley, and the equally attractive Harthope Valley lies to the east. Auchope Cairn, rising to 2,382ft, straddles the border between England and Scotland.

After 1¼ miles turn right on to the A697 to reach the edge of Wooler.

WOOLER, Northumb

Situated north-east of the Cheviot, this attractive little place makes a natural base from which to explore the open landscapes of the Cheviot Hills. Close to the village is a stone which commemorates the Battle of Hamildon Hill, when an English army led by Henry Percy defeated a huge Scottish army under the command of the Earl of Douglas.

Leave Wooler, turn left on to the B6525 SP 'Berwick' and continue to the village of Doddington.

The Priory at Holy Island was an important religious centre for centuries.

DODDINGTON, Northumb

Features of this village include a ruined pele tower of 1584 and a 13th-century church containing a Norman font. The local countryside is very rich in prehistoric remains, including earthworks and stones bearing the enigmatic cup-and-ring marks of ancient cultures. South is the iron-age hillfort of Dod Law, where a natural crag known as the Lateral Stone features curious carvings and vertical grooves. Below this is a cave known as Cudy's Camp; Rowting Lyn Camp is situated in a miniature gorge near by.

Leave Doddington and drive forward for 5 miles, then branch right on to the B6353 to reach Lowick. Pass Fenwick, meet the A1, and turn left to reach the Plough Hotel in West Mains; a detour from the main route can be taken by following a side road to the right by the hotel and driving to the village of Beal.

BEAL, Northumb

Most of the beautiful coastline near Beal is included in a national nature reserve, and the horizon to the south-west is dominated by the low summits of the gentle Kyloe Hills. A causeway exposed at low tide leads to Holy Island, but visitors should take careful note of the tide tables displayed all round the village to avoid being cut off.

To continue the detour, cross to the Holy Island of Lindisfarne via a causeway that is exposed for about 2 hours before and from approximately 3½ hours after high tide.

HOLY ISLAND (LINDISFARNE), Northumb

Historically known as Lindisfarne, this Cradle of Christianity is only an island at high tide but offered sufficient isolation to please the missionaries who were led here from Iona by St Aidan in the 7th century. About 150 years later their monastic foundation was sacked and destroyed by Danish marauders, but in 1082 the Benedictine order built a fine priory on the same site. Its gaunt ruins (AM) still stand today, and various relics found during excavations can be seen in a local museum. The island's restored 16th-century castle (NT) contains antique oak furniture. Examples of the needlework for which the islanders are justly famous can be seen in the 13th-century parish church. Christianity has been at Lindisfarne for a long time, but a reminder of more ancient days is the Petting Stone. A legend attached to this was that brides who jumped over the stone would have a happy marriage – a tradition with more than a hint of paganism. The nature reserve on Holy Island is an important haven for an enormous variety of wildfowl and wading birds.

On the main tour, leave the Plough Hotel in West Mains and continue along the A1. Passing Scremerston, at roundabout take 2nd exit A1167 and return to Berwick-upon-Tweed.

BEVERLEY, Humberside

The gothic completeness of medieval Beverley Minster has won it acclaim as one of the most beautiful churches in Europe. Its lovely twin bell towers can be seen for miles across the flat Humberside pastures, and its interior is packed with the monumental art of some 700 years. Here can be seen the full blossoming of the 14th-century stonemason's skill in the magnificent Percy Tomb, the ingenuity of 15th-century glassmakers in the great east window, and the craft of local men in the rich extravagance of carved wood. At the far end of the Main Street is St Mary's Church, a beautiful building that was started in the 12th century as a chapel for its more famous neighbour. Over the years it has been enlarged, with a wealth of excellent architectural detail, and is now independent. One of its more notable features is a 15th-century ceiling painting of the English kings. In early times the town was an important market centre and the capital of the East Riding of Yorkshire, a status that it had to defend with a stout wall pierced by five gates. Subsequent periods saw the community outgrow these confines, and all that remains today is the 15th-century North Bar. Evidence that much of the expansion was in the 18th and 19th centuries can be seen in the many Georgian houses and shopfronts that survive. The ornate market cross dates from c1714, and the Guildhall of 1762 displays a wealth of plasterwork and wood carving by local men. Inside 18th-century Lairgate Hall (open), which houses the council offices, is a Chinese Room with hand-painted wallpaper. Beverley's Art Gallery and Museum displays pictures and relics of local interest.

Leave Beverley and follow SP 'Hessle, A164'. Later reach Skidby Windmill.

SKIDBY WINDMILL, Humberside

Well-preserved Skidby Windmill was built in 1821 and is the only example to have remained intact north of the River Humber and east of the Pennine Chain. Its black-tarred tower and white cap form a striking combination that makes it a prominent local landmark. An agricultural museum has been established inside (open).

At the windmill turn left on to an unclassified road SP 'Cottingham'. Later turn right on to the B1233 to reach Cottingham.

COTTINGHAM, Humberside

Several halls of residence for the students from Hull University are established in this village, which is grouped round a large square. Inside the local church is a fine brass dating from the 14th century.

Continue along the B1233 and drive over a level crossing. Keep forward through 2 roundabouts, then ½ mile beyond the University of Hull turn right on to the A1079. Proceed to the centre of Hull.

HUMBERSIDE AND HOLDERNESS

Between the River Humber and the sea is a flat peninsula famous for its magnificent churches, whose towers and spires stand high above the surrounding countryside of marshlands and drainage canals. Fishing fleets put out from Hull, and many of the coastal villages have become holiday resorts.

HULL, Humberside

This major industrial and commercial centre is an international port and a fishing base for deep-sea vessels. As such it suffered badly in World War II, but its rebuilding has included a fine shopping precinct scattered with flowerbeds and interspersed with parks and gardens. Docks stretch for a full 7 miles along the north side of the Humber, joined here by the little River Hull, and one of the world's longest suspension bridges at 4,626ft/1,410m — The Humber Bridge. Despite these extensive new developments the city centre still has a few old buildings untouched by bombs or town planning, including the largest parish church in England and 18th-century Maister House (NT). An early 17th-century mansion in which the MP and anti-slavery campaigner William Wilberforce was born in 1759 is now preserved as the William Wilberforce Historical Museum. The Town Docks Museum relates to fishing and shipping, and the Transport Museum has a collection of vehicles including a steam Train Locomotive of 1882. The Archaeology and Natural History Museum has several interesting displays and contains The Hasholme Boat, the biggest surviving prehistoric logboat in the country.

St Patrick's Church in Patrington has the grandeur of a small cathedral.

Leave Hull on the A165 with SP 'Hornsea' and 'Bridlington'. In 3¼ miles reach a roundabout. Keep forward to another roundabout and take the 3rd exit on to the B1238 SP 'Aldbrough'. Continue for 1¼ miles and keep forward to reach Sproatley.

SPROATLEY, Humberside

This village is in the heart of the Holderness area, where vast fields, golden with corn in summer, stretch flatly to the horizon or lap the fringes of small copses. Its 19th-century church, given an air of mystery by a cloak of ivy, contains an inscribed coffin lid of the 13th century.

Bear right, drive to the end of the village, and turn left on to an unclassified road to reach Burton Constable Hall.

BURTON CONSTABLE HALL, Humberside

Grand 18th-century state rooms and 200 acres of parkland enchantingly landscaped by Capability Brown are features of this attractive Elizabethan house (open). Lakes covering some 22 acres provide plenty of scope for boating, venue for several rallies and fairs during the summer months.

Return to Sproatley and turn right to return along the B1238. Meet a war memorial and branch left on to the B1240 to Preston. At Preston turn left again to reach Hedon.

The Proud Pharisee is one of many carvings in the nave of magnificent Beverley Minster.

HEDON, Humberside

At one time this small town was a major port connected to the Humber Estuary by canals. It was rich enough to start building the magnificent King of Holderness in the 12th century, and subsequent work on this church shows the prosperity to have lasted at least until the 15th century. Trade has long since filtered away to Hull, but the huge pinnacled tower of the 'King' remains in all its glory. Near by, the Ravenspur Cross commemorates a long vanished village of that name, where Bolingbroke (later Henry IV) landed in 1399 to claim the English throne for the House of Lancaster.

Turn left on to the A1033 SP 'Withernsea'. Pass through flat agricultural countryside crisscrossed by drainage canals to reach Keyingham.

KEYINGHAM, Humberside

An attractive medieval church can be seen in this village, and just to the north west is a tower that was once a windmill.

Drive through Ottringham and continue to the edge of Winestead.

WINESTEAD, Humberside

Features from the Norman and Jacobean periods jostle for attention with others less easy to define in Winestead Church. A good 16th-century brass can be seen inside.

Continue to Patrington.

PATRINGTON, Humberside

Hedon's superb church has a rival here in the Queen of Holderness, a magnificent cruciform building in the decorated style of architecture. Its tower and spire are considered outstanding, and excellent craftsmanship of many kinds can be seen inside. At one time the village was an important market town in the manor administered by the archbishops of York.

A pleasant detour can be taken from the main route by following the B1445 from Patrington to Easington (where there is a natural gas pipe terminal), and continuing through Kilnsea to Spurn Head and the Humber Shore.

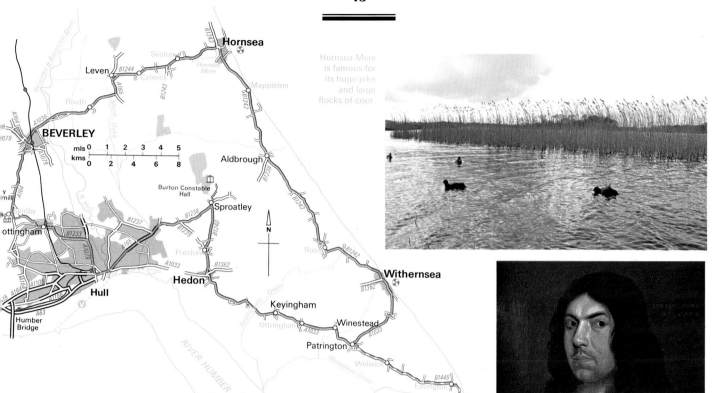

Hornsea Mere is famous for its huge pike and large flocks of coot.

The poet Andrew Marvell was MP for Kingston upon Hull from 1658 until his death in 1678.

SPURN HEAD, Humberside
Between the North Sea and the Humber estuary is Spurn Head, a narrow hook of sand and shingle that lengthens by about a yard each year as silt from the Humber and aggregate from the Holderness cliffs is deposited at its tip. At present it is about 3½ miles long and is gradually being stabilized by the tough roots of marram grass. Many migrant species of bird rest in the sanctuary at the end of the peninsula, and their comings and goings are watched from a special observatory Centuries ago a beacon was burned here to guide shipping through the Humber estuary, but nowadays the steady beam of a lighthouse provides a more dependable warning. A road stretches for about three-quarters of the peninsula's length; the rest, except parts of the bird sanctuary, can be explored on foot.

On the main route, drive from Patrington on the A1033 and continue to Withernsea.

Spurn Head Nature Reserve attracts huge numbers of migrant birds, as well as flocks of waterfowl and waders.

WITHERNSEA, Humberside
This quiet resort offers donkey rides, a reasonable sand and shingle beach, paddling and boating pools, a playground, and various amusement arcades – in fact, many of the diversions associated with family seaside holidays. Sports facilities include bowling greens, a putting course, and an open-air swimming pool. Inland the white 127ft bulk of a disused 19th-century lighthouse rises from a street of houses, and a quirky castellated gateway survives from a pier that stood here in the Victorian heyday of seaside holidays.

Drive to the Spread Eagle (PH) in Withernsea and turn left into Hull Road. Drive to the old lighthouse and turn right on to the B1242 SP 'Roos' and 'Hornsea'. Pass through Roos and in ½ mile turn left. Continue for a further ¼ mile, then turn right and proceed to Aldbrough.

Withernsea lighthouse is now disused but still provides a focal point in this small resort.

ALDBROUGH, Humberside
About 1½ miles from this small village is a pleasant sand and shingle beach backed by small eroded cliffs. In the village itself is a 13th- to 15th-century church with a Norman arch and a sundial bearing a Saxon inscription.

Continue along a flat, winding road and pass through Mappleton to reach Hornsea.

HORNSEA, Humberside
Hornsea has become very well known through its fine pottery, which is made in Rolston Road and can be bought from a seconds shop. More can be learned about the processes and skills involved from a conducted tour, and the company has a special playground and mini-zoo for the children. The resort itself is popular with families and offers excellent sands divided from gardens and amusements by the fine Promenade. Behind the narrow streets and clustered houses of the old village is Hornsea Mere, a 2-mile lagoon formed during the ice ages. Today it is a popular boating venue with a reserve for wildfowl and a 5-mile walk round its wood and reed-fringed banks.

Skirt Hornsea Mere on the B1244 with SP 'Beverley'. Pass through Seaton and Catwick to reach Leven.

LEVEN, Humberside
Between Leven and the River Hull is a 3-mile stretch of canal built in 1802. At one end of the waterway is the Canal House, a fine 3-bay building which incorporates a grand Georgian doorway from a house at Hull. Inside the dignified village church is the shaft of a Saxon cross.

Turn left on to the A165 then after 1 mile meet a roundabout and take the 2nd exit on to the A1035 SP 'Beverley'. Pass through rather featureless countryside and cross the River Hull, and the adjacent Beverley and Barmston drain; re-enter Beverley.

BEACHES AND THE BOWLAND FELLS

Blackpool is more than the most popular holiday resort in the north; it is also an ideal place from which to tour the rolling, windmill-dotted landscape of the Fylde, its austere little villages, and the high wild moors of the Forest of Bowland.

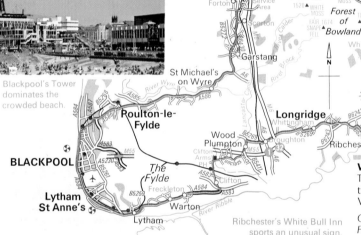

The packhorse bridge near Hurst Green.

Blackpool's Tower dominates the crowded beach.

BLACKPOOL, Lancs

Every summer Lancashire shuts down its industry for the annual wake, or holiday, and for a brief period Blackpool's resident population of about 152,000 is swelled by an influx of 8 million trippers eager to be entertained. Until the seaside-holiday vogue of the 18th century the town was little more than a cluster of cottages, but it has developed from these small beginnings to become one of the premier resorts in Great Britain. Everything is geared up to the boisterous, fun-fair atmosphere of high summer, and the natural asset of a beautiful sandy beach is supplemented by three fine piers and the splendid dominance of the famous 519ft tower. In the latter are a ballroom that is often the scene of dance festivals and beauty contests, undersea world, amusements, and various facilities for children. The traditional heart of the 7-mile Promenade is the famous Golden Mile, a bewildering collection of novelty shops, ice-cream vendors, and seafood stalls. Blackpool Zoo is one of the most modern in Britain, featuring a unique free-flight bird hall. Some of the other animal enclosures can be visited by miniature railway, and the entire complex is laid out to the best advantage of both visitors and animals. The East Drive area is well known for its richly-planted gardens, and the town's many other parks and public open spaces are green islands of peace amongst the bustle and noise of streets packed with tourist and local traffic. Sporting events held here every year include county cricket, league football, and various other championships associated with the amenities available.

Leave Blackpool and follow the A584 SP 'Lytham St Anne's' along the coast to reach Lytham St Anne's.

LYTHAM ST ANNE'S, Lancs

No less than four championship courses make this popular seaside resort a mecca for golfing enthusiasts. Sand yachting and safe bathing are offered by 6 miles of sandy beach, and the British Sand Yachting Championships are held here every May. The residential part of the resort is laid out on garden-city lines, with many beautiful parks and gardens between streets of pleasant houses. Ashton Gardens and Lowther Gardens are of particular note, and the fascinating Alpine Gardens offer fine walks in landscaped surroundings where little bridges span water and cool hollows. In and between these gardens are many good half-timbered buildings, including the attractive 18th-century structure of Lytham Hall.

Drive through the town to Lytham.

LYTHAM, Lancs

Lytham and St Anne's are incorporated in the borough of Lytham St Anne's, but this is where the similarity stops. The former is a quiet residential town with few of the holiday amusements and entertainments offered by the St Anne's area. A white windmill on picturesque Lytham Green near the shore is typical of many that once operated in the area.

Ribchester's White Bull Inn sports an unusual sign.

THE FYLDE, Lancs

Between the Wyre estuary north of Blackpool and the Ribble estuary in the south is a flat, wind-blown area of land known as the Fylde. This area was once known for its many windmills, and several of these fascinating old structures have survived intact.

Continue along the A584 SP 'Preston' to reach Warton.

WARTON, Lancs

There is a small aerodrome here, and the town has a good church of Victorian date.

Continue along the A584 to Freckleton, then in 2¾ miles meet traffic signals and turn left on to the A583. Take the first turning right on to an unclassified road SP 'Clifton'. Skirt Clifton, and in 2 miles reach the Clifton Arms (PH). Turn right SP 'Broughton' and cross the Lancaster Canal. In 1¼ miles meet a T-junction and turn right, then after another ¼ mile turn left. In 1¼ miles join the B5411 and continue to Woodplumpton.

WOODPLUMPTON, Lancs

The 20th-century navigator Henry Foster was born in this village, and his memorial can be seen in the local church. This warm, honey-coloured building is mainly of 15th- to 19th-century date.

Drive to the end of the village and turn right SP 'Broughton', then in a short distance turn right again on to the B5269. Continue to Broughton, meet traffic signals, and drive forward SP 'Longridge'. Proceed through Whittingham to Longridge.

LONGRIDGE, Lancs

High above the roof tops of this pleasant village is the fine steeple of 19th-century St Wilfrid's Church, a symmetrical counterpoint to the nearby craggy bulk of 1,148ft Longridge Fell.

Leave Longridge on the B6243 SP 'Clitheroe' and in ½ mile turn right with the B6245 SP 'Blackburn'. Later bear left into Ribchester.

RIBCHESTER, Lancs

In Roman times the wild country hereabouts was guarded by a fort that stood on this site for 300 years. Known as *Bremetennacum*, its large remains have been excavated and many of the finds installed in the local Museum of Roman Antiquities. A model displayed here shows what the building must have looked like in its complete state, and among the exhibits are gold coins, pieces of pottery, brooches, oil lamps, and a rare bronze parade helmet. Other remains from the same period have been incorporated in some of the village buildings. Two Roman columns support the oak gallery in 13th-century St Wilfred's Church, and the pillars at the entrance of the White Bull Inn are said to have come from a Roman temple. Just to the north of Ribchester is the Norman Stydd Chapel and a neat row of attractive 18th-century almshouses.

A detour from the main route can be made to Longridge Fell by leaving the centre of Ribchester on an unclassified road SP 'Chipping', then driving for 3½ miles to the excellent road summit and viewpoint of the fell. On the main tour, leave Ribchester by continuing along the B6254 and in ½ mile turn left on to an unclassified road SP 'Hurst Green'. In 1¾ miles reach the top of an ascent and turn right on to the B6243 'Clitheroe' road and continue to Hurst Green.

HURST GREEN, Lancs

An attractive feature of this village is the Church of St John the Evangelist, which was built in 1838 and has a castellated tower in keeping with the romantic leanings of the period. In magnificent grounds close to Hurst Green is the imposing building of Stonyhurst, a famous school that was founded in the 16th century.

Leave Hurst Green and continue along the B6243. In 1¾ miles cross the River Hodder, with a 16th-century packhorse bridge visible to the right. In 1¼ miles meet a junction with the unclassified 'Bashall Eaves' road. A short detour can be taken from the main route to Clitheroe by turning right here and driving along the B6243.

CLITHEROE, Lancs

After the Civil War the small Norman keep of Clitheroe Castle (open) was presented to General Monk, and today it still stands in a dominant position on a limestone knoll above the town. Inside is an important collection of fossils from the surrounding district. The town itself is an industrial centre that grew to prosperity through cotton, and at one time it was full of the clatter and noise of textile milling. Sinister Pendle Hill, associated with the notorious trial of several Lancashire women who were said to be witches and accordingly executed, rises to 1,831ft on the east side of Clitheroe. Ironically the founder of the Society of Friends claims to have drawn his inspiration from the same hill.

Refreshing solitude is discovered near Blaze Moss in the Trough of Bowland.

On the main tour, keep forward at the junction and follow the unclassified road to Bashall Eaves. After 1 mile drive over crossroads and follow the Hodder Valley, with Longridge Fell on the left. To the right are views of 1,296ft Waddington Fell and 1,300ft Easington Fell. At Bashall Eaves keep forward, then after 1 mile reach Browsholme Hall.

BROWSHOLME HALL, Lancs

Altered and extended during the 18th century, this basically Tudor mansion contains fascinating collections of tapestry work, armour, furniture, and pictures. It is open by appointment and stands in beautiful gardens that were landscaped in honour of the Prince Regent and Mrs Fitzherbert.

Continue for 1 mile and turn right SP 'Whitewell' via Hall Hill. After ¼ mile an unclassified right turn offers a short detour which ascends for 1 mile to a 960ft viewpoint.

VIEWPOINT, Lancs

One of the best parts of the tour, this high road summit affords magnificent views south to the Hodder Valley, Longridge Fell, and Pendle Hill, with the dark peaks of the Pennine Range in the distance. North and west are the hills of the Forest of Bowland, with 1,629ft Totridge Fell and 1,415ft Burn Fell particularly prominent.

On the main tour, climb to a road summit of 750ft and descend into the Hodder Valley at Whitewell. Turn right SP 'Lancaster' and enter the Forest of Bowland.

FOREST OF BOWLAND, Lancs

In the days when the word 'forest' meant 'hunting ground' this area was the preserve of the kings of England, who regarded the local deer as their own property and were particularly hard on anybody caught poaching. Today the forest is a largely treeless expanse of moorland and steep-sided fells which has been designated as being of outstanding natural beauty. It lies partly in Lancashire and partly in what used to be the West Riding of Yorkshire, and offers excellent riverside walks.

Cross the River Hodder and Langden Brook. Drive through Dunsop Bridge into a deep, narrow valley and climb to the Trough of Bowland.

TROUGH OF BOWLAND, Lancs

Here the road climbs to more than 1,000ft above sea level via steep gradients (1 in 6) through lonely moorland that was once the haunt of highwaymen. Views from the summit encompass 1,383ft Blaze Moss to the south, 1,651ft Whin Fell in the north-east, and 1,567ft Hawthornthwaite Fell in the distance.

Descend from the road summit of the Trough of Bowland to reach the village of Marshaw. After 1¾ miles reach a chapel and turn left on to the 'Preston' road and descend (1 in 5) to Abbeystead. Follow SP 'Preston' and in 3¼ miles reach Dolphinholme. After ¼ mile reach a church and bear right, then in 1¼ miles meet a T-junction and turn left SP 'Garstang'. The revolving restaurant tower of Forton Service Area can be seen on the left as the route reaches Forton village. After the village drive for 1½ miles and turn left on to the A6 SP 'Preston', then continue for 2¼ miles. A detour from the main route to Garstang can be made by turning left here on to the B6430 and driving into the town itself.

The Forest of Bowland is a lonely area of great beauty.

GARSTANG, Lancs

Among the fine Georgian buildings in this little town, which stands on the Lancaster Canal, are the Town Hall and elegant St Thomas' Church.

On the main tour, continue along the A6 for another 2½ miles and turn right on to the A586 SP 'Blackpool'. Follow the course of the River Wyre to St Michael's-on-Wyre.

ST MICHAEL'S-ON-WYRE, Lancs

Situated at the junction of the Rivers Calder, Brock, and Wyre, this pleasant village has a lovely church which preserves fragments of 14th-century wall paintings. The rural nature of the community is emphasized by a shearing scene in the church's 16th-century stained-glass window.

Continue along the A586 to reach Poulton-le-Fylde.

POULTON-LE-FYLDE, Lancs

Old fish stones where the prices of fish caught by local boats were once fixed survive here, and the old market place features a set of stocks. Alongside the latter is a whipping post and a stepped Jacobean pillar. Georgian St Chad's Church features a beautiful carved screen and chairs that are prime examples of the wood craftsman's art.

Continue along the A586 to re-enter Blackpool.

THE NORTH WOLDS

In this area of North Yorkshire and Humberside, lush green meadows, rich in wildlife and scattered with tiny villages, slope gently seawards beyond the resorts of Filey and Bridlington to the chalky cliffs of Flamborough Head

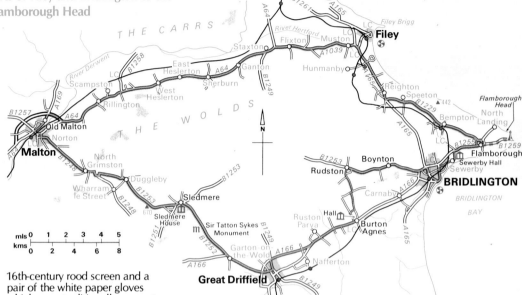

BRIDLINGTON, Humberside

Bridlington has less of the 'genteel' Yorkshire resort atmosphere of days gone by, but it is still a very popular seaside town boasting an attractive and historically interesting centre. The main point of interest in old Bridlington is the Priory Church of St Mary, which is particularly noted for its nave — the remains of an Augustinian priory founded here in the 12th century. The richly-decorated north porch, the 14th-century south aisle and the beautiful west doorway are also of note. Across the green is the priory's Bayle Gate which was built in 1388 and has, at various times since, served as the prior's courtroom, a sailors' prison, a barracks and a school, before being used in its present role of museum. Stones from the old priory were used in the building of 2 piers in the harbour which still services a small fishing fleet. The long stretches of fine sandy beach to the north and south of the harbour, on Bridlington Bay, enjoys a sheltered location protected by the great headland of Flamborough.

Leave by the Promenade for Flamborough Road. In 1¼ miles, at the roundabout, take the 3rd exit into Sewerby Road. Go over the level-crossing into Sewerby for Sewerby Hall.

SEWERBY HALL, Humberside

Sewerby Hall (OACT) was built between 1714 and 1720 and is surrounded by a fine park of 50 acres, which sweeps down to striking cliffs overlooking Bridlington Bay. The mansion has been turned into a museum, and included in this is the Amy Johnson Room, where many of the pilot's momentoes are kept. The grounds are also open to the public, and a miniature golf course, croquet lawns, a putting green and a children's corner provide entertainment.

At the entrance to the Hall keep left. In ½ mile turn right on to the B1255 (no SP) then bear right for Flamborough.

FLAMBOROUGH, Humberside

About 1,000 years ago the area around Flamborough was taken by the Vikings, and is still sometimes called 'Little Denmark'. The sprawling village stands 2 miles inland from Flamborough Head and the lighthouse, and boasts a much restored but delightful church, in which there is a fine

16th-century rood screen and a pair of the white paper gloves which were traditionally worn at the funeral of a maiden. There is also a monument of a man with his heart bared; he is Sir Marmaduke Constable who died in 1520, because, it is said, a toad which he swallowed ate his heart. Flamborough Head is where the Yorkshire Wolds meet the sea in glistening white 400ft cliffs. From here onlookers watched John Paul Jones, the Scottish-born American sailor who performed a number of daring naval exploits during his career, win a sea battle with 2 British men-of-war. The cliffs between Flamborough and Bempton are famous as a valuable breeding ground for seabirds, and here the only mainland gannetry in Britain is to be found.

Continue on the B1229, SP 'Filey', and at the end of the village turn right. Pass through Bempton, then in 4¼ miles turn right on to the A165, SP 'Scarborough', and enter Reighton. In 3 miles a detour along the A1039 (right) leads into Filey.

FILEY, N Yorks

Filey is now a popular holiday town, standing mostly on the cliff tops overlooking the bay. The old village has quaint streets and several houses dating from the 17th century, and the modern town boasts a fine promenade, a sandy beach and well-kept gardens. A lovely wooded road called the Ravine leads down to the beach, and at the top of it stands St Oswald's Church. The oldest parts are 12th century, and the great square medieval tower bears not a weathercock, but a 'weatherfish'. One of the windows commemorates all the Filey men

Cobles — open-decked fishing boats — run holiday fishing trips from Bridlington's harbour which is also still a working port

lost at sea. A great attraction nearby is Filey Brigg, a mile-long reef jutting out from the Carr Naze headland with caves, coves, cliffs and rock pools which are a delight to explore.

The main tour continues on the A165 for ¼ mile and turns left on to the A1039, SP 'Malton'. Pass through Flixton, then in 1 mile at the roundabout join the A64, SP 'York'. After 14 miles join the Malton Bypass and in 1¼ miles branch left, SP 'Malton B1257'. At the roundabout turn left for Old Malton and Malton.

MALTON, N Yorks

Malton is actually divided in half by the site of a Roman station which lies in between. New Malton is the busy market town serving a large farming community and its large market square is

always a hive of activity. The 18th-century town hall around the corner from the market square bears a plaque recording the fact that Edmund Burke was Malton's MP from 1780 to 1794. Other buildings of interest include the Cross Keys Inn in Wheelgate, which has a medieval crypt, and the former Hospital of St Mary Magdalene. The quaint old-fashioned cottages and inns of Old Malton lie a mile north-east of the town. Here, the Church of St Mary was built on the remains of a Gilbertine priory founded in the 12th century. South-east of Malton, at Langton Wold, is a famous training ground for race horses.

Above: the cliffs of Flamborough Head

Left: the elegant furnishings of King James's bedroom at Burton Agnes Hall are shown off by the Jacobean panelling

GT DRIFFIELD, Humberside
Driffield is a busy agricultural town on the edge of the Yorkshire Wolds, boasting an annual show and a regular Thursday cattle market. Anglers come to Driffield to fish for trout in the numerous streams which flow down from the Wolds.

Leave by the Bridlington road A166 to reach Burton Agnes.

BURTON AGNES, Humberside
The magnificent Elizabethan mansion, Burton Agnes Hall (OACT), is the main attraction in this sleepy village. The mellow redbrick exterior with stone trim is an impressive sight, distinguished by semi-octagonal bays on the south front. Octagonal towers are a feature of the gatehouse which was built a little later than the house. It provides an elegant entrance-way to the house via velvet lawns complemented by almost 100 clipped yew trees. The Hall is still owned by the Griffith family, whose ancestor, Sir Henry Griffith, built it more than 350 years ago. The splendid interior is just as impressive as the outside and visitors may require more than one trip to absorb all details of the richly-furnished rooms. Of special note are the stone and alabaster chimneypiece and oak and plaster screen of the great hall, the massive staircase and the beautifully-restored long gallery. The house also contains a fine collection of paintings.

The main tour turns left on to an unclassified road for Rudston.

RUDSTON, Humberside
In 1933 a ploughman uncovered a Roman villa at Rudston, and 3 fine mosaic pavements from the site are now on view in the Hull Transport Museum. The largest pavement measures 13ft by 10ft 6in and depicts a voluptuous Venus with flying hair, holding an apple and a mirror and surrounded by leopards, birds and hunters. An enormous monolith, a relic of earlier times, stands in the churchyard at Rudston.

At the far end of the village turn right on to the B1253, SP 'Bridlington'. In 2½ miles skirt the village of Boynton.

BOYNTON, Humberside
This small, picturesque village of whitewashed houses is set amidst woods on the slopes of the Gypsey Race valley. The Stricklands of Boynton Hall (not open) are thought to have introduced the turkey to England from America and there are monuments to the family in the church, rebuilt during the 18th century. Their family crest includes a turkey and a portrait.

Remain on the B1253 for 2 miles, then turn left on to the A165 for the return to Bridlington.

main road in the village stand 2 remarkable war memorials. One, known as the Waggoners' Memorial, is a tribute to the 1,200 men from the Wolds who died in World War I, and the other is a replica of the nationally famous Eleanor Crosses. The elegant 18th-century mansion, Sledmere House, was burnt down in 1911 but was rebuilt later in the same style. A great attraction at Sledmere is the beautifully-landscaped park designed by Capability Brown. A church within the park is reputedly one of the loveliest parish churches in England. Arguably the most famous member of the Sykes family was Sir Tatton. Born in 1823 and a legend in his own time, he excelled in the skills of farming, hunting, racing, boxing, building schools and breeding sheep. He also established the Sledmere stud before he died at the age of 91. Just outside the village, on Garton Hill, is a great spire dedicated to the celebrated Sir Tatton, which has a carving on the front depicting the great man on horseback. Garton Hill is a good vantage point from which to view the magnificence of the Wolds.

Continue on the B1252 Driffield road, and in 2¼ miles pass Sir Tatton Sykes's monument. After another 2 miles turn left on to the A166 for Great Driffield.

Leave Malton on the B1248, SP 'Beverley'. Cross the River Derwent then the level-crossing and keep left. In almost ½ mile turn right, still SP 'Beverley', then at the T-junction turn left. Beyond North Grimston ascend, then branch left on to the B1253, SP 'Driffield'. At Duggleby, bear right, then cross the Wolds to enter Humberside. In 2 miles turn left into Sledmere.

SLEDMERE, Humberside
This neat little village forms part of the Sledmere estate of which Sledmere House (OACT) is the centre. The estate is the property of the Sykes family who were largely responsible for the development of the Wolds from bare open wasteland into the richly-wooded agricultural land that exists here today. Beside the

BUXTON, Derbys

Situated just outside the boundaries of the national park, this is the highest town in England and an ideal base from which to tour the moors and dales of the Peak District. It is sheltered by hills even higher than its 1,007ft site, yet is able to offer gentle scenery more typical of the lowlands alongside sedate reaches of the lovely River Wye. Grinlow Woods lie to the south of the town, Corbar Woods are a mere $\frac{1}{2}$ mile away, and 1 mile east is the enchanting valley of Ashwood Dale. The town itself is built round a spa whose medicinal properties were discovered by the Romans and exploited to the benefit of the town towards the end of the 18th century, when Buxton rivalled the elegant supremacy of Somerset's Bath. The growth of the town during this period was largely due to the efforts of the 5th Duke of Devonshire, who built the beautiful Crescent and Pump Rooms opposite the town's hot springs. The pale blue mineral water of the area still bubbles up from a mile underground at a rate of $\frac{1}{4}$ million gallons per day and a constant temperature of 82 degrees Fahrenheit and now feeds the local swimming pool. The Pavilion concert hall, theatre, and ballroom stand in 23 acres of lovely gardens featuring a boating lake, bowling and putting greens, tennis courts, and a children's play area. Spa treatment is available from the Devonshire Royal Hospital, which was originally built as the Great Stables and has a superb dome that was added in 1879. The former Pump Rooms now house the Micrarium, a unique opportunity to explore the world of nature using special microscopes. Poole's Cavern is an interesting show cave within the Buxton Country Park.

Leave Buxton on the A6 with SP 'Matlock' and descend through the wooded limestone gorge of the River Wye. Climb away from the valley, with Great Rocks Dale to the left, to reach the edge of Taddington. It is

THE PEAK DISTRICT DALES

Here the great River Wye and its tributaries have carved deep gorges in the soft limestone hills, making secluded pockets of outstanding beauty where the severity of naked rock is softened by water and foliage. The dales themselves are only accessible by foot.

possible to visit this village by turning right from the main route on to an unclassified road.

TADDINGTON, Derbys

Taddington stands at an altitude of 1,130ft in attractive limestone country and is one of the highest villages in England. The slopes of Taddington Wood (NT) face lovely Monsal Dale some $1\frac{1}{2}$ miles east, and to the south-west Taddington Moor rises to 1,500ft at the highest point in the hills south of the River Wye. Close to the summit of the moor is the Five Wells Tumulus, an unusual barrow with two burial chambers. Various interesting prehistoric remains can be found on the moors.

Descend wooded Taddington Dale, with Monsal Dale on the left, and pass Great Shacklow Wood and river valley on right. Take next junction, unclassified road, to enter Ashford-in-the-Water.

Buxton built its reputation as a spa, but today it provides facilities for all tastes. The Pavilion Gardens offer a varied and relaxing landscape which enhance the town's appeal.

ASHFORD-IN-THE-WATER, Derbys

Two ancient bridges span the Wye in this delightful village, one dated 1664 and the other complete with a sheep-dipping enclosure at one end. An interesting well-dressing ceremony is held here on the Saturday before Trinity Sunday. Ashford marble was quarried near by.

Drive to the end of the village and turn right on to the B6465 then at T-junction turn right A6020 after a short distance rejoin the A6 to reach Bakewell.

Dramatic scenery found in the Peak District can be explored from Buxton by following the River Wye as it runs south through spectacular Chee Dale.

BAKEWELL, Derbys

A busy cattle market and the largest town in the national park, Bakewell stands on the wooded banks of the Wye and is sheltered by hills on three sides. Many of its attractive brownstone buildings bear witness to a historic past, and its beautiful 12th-century church is famous for the superb Saxon cross (AM) preserved in its churchyard. The 5-arched medieval bridge (AM) that spans the river was widened in the 19th century, but is basically one of the oldest structures of its type in Britain. Holme Hall and the Market Hall both date back to the 17th century, and the Old House Museum is an early-Tudor house with wattle-and-daub interior walls. Inside the latter are exhibitions of costumes and domestic utensils. The name of the town will always be associated with the Bakewell tart, a dish apparently created by accident when a harassed cook in the Rutland Arms mistakenly poured the egg mixture meant for the pastry of a jam tart into the jam. The unusual dish was very well received by guests, and the cook was instructed to continue making her delicious mistake.

Leave Bakewell on the A6 'Matlock' road to pass Haddon Hall.

HADDON HALL, Derbys

Although originally a fortified dwelling, exquisite 12th- to 15th-century Haddon Hall (open) was never fought over and survives as one of the finest examples of medieval architecture extant. Its peaceful history is reflected in its lovely wood and parkland setting on the River Wye, and its beauty is enhanced by the enchanting rose gardens that ornament its grounds. The romantic feeling of the place is supported by its history, for it was from here that Dorothy Vernon eloped with Sir John Manners in the 16th century.

Continue along the A6 and cross the Wye to enter Rowsley.

ROWSLEY, Derbys

This charming little greystone village stands on a tongue of land at the confluence of the rivers Wye and Derwent. The actual waters' meet is a delightful spot beloved of artists and anglers alike. Sir Joseph Paxton designed the earlier of two obsolete but charming station buildings here, and the beautiful old Peacock Inn was originally a 17th-century manor house.

Pass the Peacock Inn on the left, then in a short distance turn left on to the B6012 SP 'Baslow'. Continue to Beeley.

BEELEY, Derbys

From ancient times this little community was known for the grindstones fashioned by its craftsmen from the local hard grit. A tributary of the River Derwent, which is famous for its trout, runs close to the village.

CALVER, Derbys
Anglers come here for the fine Derwent trout, and the village boasts a good 18th-century cotton mill.

In Calver meet traffic signals and turn left on to the B6001 'Bakewell' road. Continue to Hassop.

HASSOP, Derbys
Situated at the edge of wild Longstone Moor, this little village has a Jacobean hall that was the home of the Earls of Newburgh until 1853. Much of the local countryside has the tended appearance of parkland.

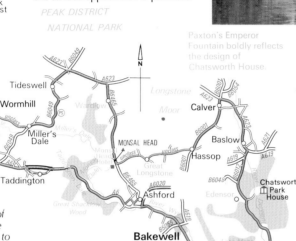

Paxton's Emperor Fountain boldly reflects the design of Chatsworth House.

Beyond Beeley skirt the grounds of Chatsworth House, then cross the River Derwent and enter the park to pass Chatsworth House itself.

CHATSWORTH HOUSE, Derbys
Popularly known as the Palace of the Peak, this magnificent mansion (open) stands in a superb park on the River Derwent and is backed by beautifully wooded slopes. It was built in the 17th century for the 1st Duke of Devonshire and is noted particularly for its superb state apartments and great art collection. An earlier house that stood on the same site was partly designed by the 1st Duke's ancestress Bess of Hardwick, and was occasionally visited by Mary Queen of Scots. Remains of the original Elizabethan park layout can be seen in the old Hunting Tower, which vies as the major focal point with a fountain that is the tallest in Britain. Features of the magnificent park include mature chestnut avenues and the charm of ornamental waters.

Beyond Chatsworth Park join the A619 and enter Baslow.

BASLOW, Derbys
This characteristic gritstone village stands on the River Derwent and is partly built round an old triangular goose green. Most through traffic is taken across the river by a recent bridge, but the old hump-backed crossing survives – complete with tollhouse.

In Baslow turn left SP 'Chapel-en-le-Frith' to join the A623. Continue to the village of Calver.

In Hassop turn right on to an unclassified road and drive to a T-junction in Great Longstone. Turn right for Monsal Head and continue to the Monsal Head Hotel, then turn right again on to the B6465 to pass a magnificent vantage point offering panoramic views across Monsal Dale.

MONSAL HEAD, Derbys
This great rocky prominence affords superb views into Monsal Dale, where the River Wye threads its way between lush slopes punctuated by rocky crags and overhangs of weathered stone. The head and dale together form one of the national park's loveliest beauty spots.

Continue through Wardlow, turn left on to the A623, and in 1¼ miles turn left again to join the B6049. Continue into Tideswell.

TIDESWELL, Derbys
Although this ancient town was granted a market as early as the 13th century, the only notable building to have survived the centuries is the superb Church of St John the Baptist. This is considered the finest building of its type in the county and is popularly known as The Cathedral of the Peak. Local wells and springs are dressed in a traditional ceremony held in Wakes Week, on the Saturday nearest June 24.

Continue with the 'Buxton' road, and after 1 mile pass the Tideswell picnic area (left). Descend into Miller's Dale.

MILLER'S DALE, Derbys
Threaded by a narrow road to Litton Mill, this part of the Wye Valley is enclosed by craggy limestone cliffs that rise high above the river behind dense screens of shrub and woodland. The mill was once used for processing silk.

Beyond a railway viaduct and just before a bridge over the Wye turn sharp right on to an unclassified road for Wormhill. Pass Chee Dale on the left and continue to Wormhill.

WORMHILL, Derbys
Situated high above the river curve that includes Chee Dale, this village is excellently situated for fine views across the River Wye and is popular with walkers. Narrow Chee Dale is only accessible on foot, but it is worth the exercise. One of the village's most notable buildings is a 17th-century hall with mullioned windows.

Pass Wormhill and bear left SP 'Peak Dale'. Continue for ¼ mile and turn right for the village of Peak Forest.

PEAK FOREST, Derbys
The name of the medieval hunting ground that covered most of northern Derbyshire is preserved in this attractive little village. A chapel founded here in 1657 was extra-parochial and could issue marriage licences to anybody who applied. Before the building was demolished, Peak Forest gained something of a Gretna Green reputation as a goal for eloping couples. North of the village on the south side of Eldon Hill is a sheer-sided pothole known as Eldon Hole. For many years this was reputed to be bottomless, but modern potholers have discovered it to be a 186ft limestone shaft leading to two caverns which radiate from the bottom. On no account should an attempt be made to descend the hole without proper equipment.

Turn left on to the A623 SP 'Chapel-en-le-Frith', keep left at Sparrowpit, and within 1¼ miles turn left on to the A6. Proceed towards Buxton, passing limestone quarries on the left at Dove Holes. Black Edge rises to the right of the road.

DOVE HOLES, Derbys
Not to be confused with a natural rock formation of the same name north-west of Tissington, this area is the site of vast limestone workings that extend some 4 miles south-east along Doveholes Dale, Peak Dale, and Great Rocks Dale. The quarries are 1,086ft above sea level. A railway tunnel penetrates 1½ miles through bedrock deep beneath the main road here.

BLACK EDGE, Derbys
This high prominence rises to 1,662ft and affords excellent views over much of the national park's finest countryside.

Descend and return to Buxton.

BOUNDARY OF AN ANCIENT EMPIRE

Here the monumental ruins of Hadrian's Wall undulate across the rocky spine of Britain, still proclaiming the might of the Roman Empire many centuries after its collapse. South are the soft woodlands of the beautiful South Tyne Valley, the heart of rural Northumberland.

Carlisle Cathedral is impressive but small

CARLISLE, Cumbria

During the Roman occupation Carlisle, then known as *Luguvalium*, was a strategic centre of the frontier that separated the largely Romanized peoples of the south from the wild northern tribes. Continued excursions from Scotland prompted William Rufus to build the town's sturdy castle (AM) in 1092; Queen Mary's Tower contains a fascinating museum devoted to the Border Regiments. During the Civil War the six western bays of Carlisle's small medieval cathedral were demolished to repair the town wall, but two surviving bays of the nave display Norman workmanship. The choir was restored in the 13th century and features a magnificent east window. In the cathedral grounds is a 13th-century pele tower known as the Prior's Tower. A museum occupies Tullie House a fine Jacobean mansion and contains exhibits relating to Hadrian's Wall.

Leave the centre of Carlisle with SP 'The South' on the A6 and in 3 miles reach the M6 junction roundabout. Take the 2nd exit SP 'Wetheral', and 1 mile beyond Cumwhinton pass a right turn leading to Wetheral Abbey. After a short distance enter the pleasant village of Wetheral.

WETHERAL, Cumbria

An ancient abbey gatehouse in this attractive village faces across the River Eden to the impressive pile of Corby Castle. Fine monuments by the sculptor Nollekens can be seen inside the local church.

Follow the main road through Wetheral village and in 1¼ miles meet a T-junction. Turn right on to the A69 SP 'Newcastle' and cross the Eden. A detour from the main route to Corby Castle can be made by turning right immediately after the bridge on to an unclassified road and driving through pleasant countryside for 1⅓ miles.

CORBY CASTLE, Cumbria

In 1611 the local Howard family extended the old pele tower that had been guarding Great Corby since the 13th century, adding a long range that transformed it into a great L-shaped house. The present aspect of the building, set amid lovely grounds (open) in a particularly scenic area, owes much to further extension work carried out in the 19th century.

On the main tour, continue along the A69, skirt the grounds of Holme Eden Abbey, and enter Warwick Bridge.

WARWICK BRIDGE, Cumbria

The two small communities of Warwick and Warwick Bridge are separated by a fine bridge of 1837. Most of the notable buildings are off the main route in Warwick, including a superb Norman church with an outstanding 12th-century apse.

Leave Warwick Bridge and after a short distance meet crossroads. Turn right on to an unclassified road SP 'Castle Carrock' and in 50 yards turn left. Follow a quiet by-road and in 1 mile pass Toppin Castle, which incorporates a pele tower. In a further 1¼ miles branch left SP 'Talkin', and 1 mile farther keep left, pass under a railway viaduct, and meet crossroads with the B6413. Drive forward over the main road and pass Talkin Fell on the right before entering Talkin.

TALKIN, Cumbria

Close to the high fells whose ownership was so hotly disputed for many centuries, this village has a lovely little church that has managed to preserve surprising evidence of its Norman origins. Work from that early period can be seen in the nave, bellcote, and chancel, and there are even traces in the pulpit and altar rail. Some 4 miles south-south-east of Talkin the summit of Cold Fell is surmounted by a cairn measuring 4ft high and 50ft in diameter.

Leave Talkin, and in ¼ mile turn right SP 'Hallbankgate'. Ascend, with views which extend left over the tree-bordered waters of Talkin Tarn and the great expanse of the Cumberland Plain. Reach Hallbankgate and turn right on to the A689 SP 'Alston'. Continue through Halton Lea Gate, then in just over 1 mile turn left on to an unclassified road SP 'Coanwood'. Descend to the steep wooded banks of the River South Tyne, cross the river, and ascend past Coanwood to meet crossroads. Turn left on to the 'Haltwhistle' road, in ¾ mile enter the hamlet of Rowfoot, and turn left SP 'Featherstone Park'. After ½ mile descend steeply to reach Featherstone Castle.

The River South Tyne chatters over its stony bed through the grounds of secluded Featherstone Castle.

FEATHERSTONE CASTLE, Northumb

Beautifully situated in large grounds beside the River South Tyne, this fine house dates from the 13th century and is now a children's activity holiday centre.

Leave Featherstone Castle on a secluded, picturesque road along the east bank of the River South Tyne. Meet a bridge and keep forward SP 'Haltwhistle', then in ½ mile ascend to a T-junction and turn left. In 1¾ miles reach Bellister Castle on the right.

BELLISTER CASTLE, Northumb

In the 16th century the ruined tower attached to this 3-storey building was known as a bastell house, which perhaps gives a clue to the origin of the name. The house itself dates from 1669 and displays a number of good architectural features, Peel tower open by appointment.

Leave Bellister Castle and after a short distance turn left to cross a river bridge and reach the outskirts of Haltwhistle. Turn right on to the A69 to reach the town centre.

HALTWHISTLE, Northumb

William the Lion founded this old mining town's church in 1178, and as it stands today the building is considered a particularly fine example of early-English architecture. There is no tower, and the sanctuary preserves three carved coffin lids which are thought to date from the 14th century.

Return along the A69 'Carlisle' and follow the railway for 2¾ miles. Turn right on to the B630 to reach Greenhead.

GREENHEAD, Northumb

This little village lies south of Hadrian's Wall, close to a series of attractive ravines known as the Nine Nicks of Thirlwall. The route of a Roman track known as the Maiden Way extends from here to Penrith.

Leave Greenhead on the B6318 SP 'Gilsland'. In ½ mile pass a section of Hadrian's Wall on the left.

A section of Hadrian's Wall at Gilsland

HADRIAN'S WALL, Cumbria

Between AD 122 and 139 the Roman Emperor Hadrian ordered that a defensive wall should be built to discourage the independent Scottish tribes from marauding into the largely pacified territory to the south. Today this major engineering achievement still stands as a remarkable monument to the Roman occupation of Britain, stretching 73 miles from Wallsend-on-Tyne to Bowness. Its course was plotted from one natural advantage to the next, and it was built of the materials most readily to hand – stone in the east and turf in the west. Along its length were 20 or so major forts, interspersed with milecastles and signal towers close enough together to allow the quick transference of a warning by fire beacon. Much of the surviving structure is protected under the Ancient Monuments scheme.

Continue along the B6318 to Gilsland, and on the nearside of a railway bridge reach a left turn leading to the Roman wall's Poltross Burn Milecastle.

GILSLAND, Northumb

Gilsland has natural sulphur and chalybeate springs that once made it a popular spa resort, though it never developed to the rarefied fashionable heights achieved by its southern contemporaries. Part of the Poltross Burn Milecastle (AM) is incorporated in a railway embankment near by, and a section of the Roman wall (AM) stands east of the school.

Meet a T-junction in Gilsland and turn right. A detour from the main tour can be made to Upper Denton by turning left at the T-junction.

UPPER DENTON, Cumbria

It is thought that the Saxon builders of this fascinating little church may have used stone from Hadrian's Wall in its construction. Of particular note is the reconstructed Roman arch in the chancel.

Leave Gilsland by crossing the River Irthing. In ¼ mile turn left, and ascend with views of the Roman wall to the left. After 1 mile turn left on to an unclassified road SP 'Birdoswald, Lanercost', and in a further ¼ mile pass Harrow's Scar Milecastle (AM) to reach Birdoswald.

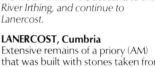

The excavated milecastle at Haltwhistle was one of several built at intervals along the length of Hadrian's Wall

BIRDOSWALD, Cumbria

The Roman fort of *Camboglanna* (AM) occupies a 5-acre ridge-top site overlooking the gorge of the River Irthing near Birdoswald. Access to the remains, which include a particularly well-preserved angle tower and postern gate, is controlled by the farmer.

Leave Birdoswald and drive forward along the line of the Roman wall, passing two Roman turrets (AM) to reach Banks.

BANKS, Cumbria

Notable Roman sites in the area around Banks include Coombe Crag, Pike Hill (AM) and Boothby Castle Hill, and there is a milecastle (AM) with a section of the Roman wall here. One mile south-west lies the partly-ruined Augustinian, Lanercost Priory, founded in 1166. The nave is still in use. In the rebuilt Abbey mill is a craft workshop for the handicapped.

Raiding parties from the Scottish side of the border inflicted heavy damage on Lanercost Priory during the 14th century

From Banks bear left, descend to the River Irthing, and continue to Lanercost.

LANERCOST, Cumbria

Extensive remains of a priory (AM) that was built with stones taken from the Roman wall can be seen here, including parts of a gatehouse showing 16th-century adaptations. The 12th-century nave serves as the parish church.

Pass the entrance to Lanercost Priory, cross the river, then immediately beyond the bridge turn left and ascend. After a short distance cross Naworth Park to reach Naworth Castle.

NAWORTH CASTLE, Cumbria

Pleasantly designed round a central courtyard, this 14th-century castle shows later additions and features a great hall, oratory, and rich tapestries. The building is open by arrangement.

At the castle entrance bear right and in ½ mile meet crossroads. Turn right on to the A69 SP 'Carlisle' to reach Brampton.

BRAMPTON, Cumbria

An unusual 8-sided moot hall stands in the cobble-flanked main street of Brampton, and the local church is the only ecclesiastical building known to have been designed by the inventive 19th-century architect, Philip Webb. The interior of the building is lit by a superb stained-glass window by the Victorian artist Burne-Jones.

Follow the A69 through Brampton, then keep forward on to the B6264 SP 'Carlisle Airport'. Proceed to Crosby-on-Eden.

CROSBY-ON-EDEN, Cumbria

The windows of the local church show the striking and original use of cut clear glass instead of stained glass. Other notable buildings here include Crosby House and High Crosby Farmhouse.

In 3½ miles turn left on to the A7 for the return to Carlisle.

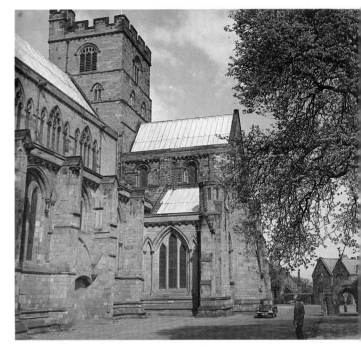

BESIDE THE SOLWAY FIRTH

A coastal tour through small towns and hamlets not widely known, tracing the footsteps of Charles Dickens and his companion Wilkie Collins. Roman forts, Norman buildings and ecclesiastical art abound, a pleasing but complementary contrast to the dramatic coastline and marshlands along the Solway Firth.

CARLISLE, Cumbria

Since early times Carlisle has been a strategically important city because of its position on the Anglo-Scottish border. The Romans occupied the town, calling it *Lugavulium*, and finding themselves repeatedly attacked by the Picts, they built Hadrian's Wall, parts of which can still be seen east of the city. Carlisle Castle (AM) was built by the Normans for the same reasons. It was founded in 1092 by William Rufus, strengthened by David I, and was for centuries the kingpin of conflicts between the Scottish and English, each often gaining the city, but never for long. Eventually, in 1745, the Scottish were finally ousted when Bonnie Prince Charlie's troops were driven from the town. Maintaining its military tradition, the castle's keep houses the former Border regiments' museum. Today Carlisle, known locally as 'Carel', is the chief administrative and agricultural centre of Cumbria and although the suburbs are industrialised, the centre has retained its ancient character. The red sandstone cathedral, where Sir Walter Scott was married in 1797, is England's 2nd smallest cathedral. Begun in the 12th century and rebuilt in the 13th century, it preserves one of the finest east windows in the country, superb carved choir stalls and a painted barrel-vault ceiling. Tullie House, the city's museum and art gallery, occupies a magnificent Jacobean mansion and contains Roman relics excavated from forts along Hadrian's Wall. The 15th-century Guildhall (OACT), a charming town house which became the meeting place for Carlisle's 8 Trade Guilds, is now a museum of Guild, Civic and local history. Exhibits include the great bell, pillory and stocks from the medieval castle.

Leave Carlisle on the A595 Workington road and ½ mile beyond the castle turn right on to the B5307. In 1 mile branch right into Burgh Road, SP 'Kirkandrews'. Pass through Kirkandrews-on-Eden and Monkhill to reach Burgh-by-Sands.

BURGH-BY-SANDS, Cumbria

Burgh-by-Sands boasts the strongly-fortified church of St Michael, built almost entirely from Roman stone. A monument to Edward I, who died in 1307 on his way to attack the Scots and lay in state here, may be found north of the village.

At the village end bear right, SP 'Port Carlisle'. NB: between here and Cardunock the road is liable to tidal flooding. Cross unfenced marshland, with views across the Solway Firth to reach Port Carlisle.

Carlisle's priory church became a cathedral in 1133

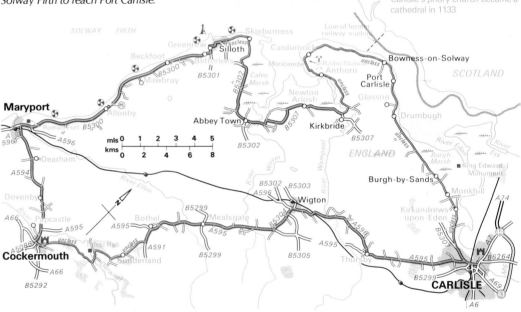

PORT CARLISLE, Cumbria

This was the brainchild of the Earl of Lonsdale, who built the harbour in 1819, and the canal to Carlisle in 1823. Unfortunately for him the harbour did not flourish and never grew beyond the row of terraced cottages and single detached house there is today. Over 140 acres of the Solway Firth lands here make up the Glasson Moss National Nature Reserve.

Continue to Bowness-on-Solway.

BOWNESS-ON-SOLWAY, Cumbria

The village of Bowness-on-Solway is situated on a low promontory overlooking the Solway Firth. At one time an iron trestle viaduct spanned the Firth here and carried a railway linking the iron manufacturing industries of west Cumbria with Annan and southern Scotland. The village is built on the site of a Roman settlement at the western end of Hadrian's Wall. The church, dedicated to St Michael, has 2 late-Norman doorways and in the porch rest 2 church bells, one of which is dated 1612. These were stolen from Scotland in the days of the Border raids by an English raiding party as reprisal for 2 bells removed from Bowness Church.

Continue forward, passing the embankment of the dismantled railway viaduct. Continue round the headland and through Cardurnock. 2 miles beyond Anthorn turn right SP 'Kirkbride', and cross the river. At the edge of Kirkbride turn right on the B5307 for the village centre.

KIRKBRIDE, Cumbria

Kirkbride is a pretty village, set amid trees on the tidal creek of the Wampol. Its ancient church, dedicated to St Bridget, is of Norman construction built with material from a Roman fort which stood in the area. There are wide areas of moss land in the parish which provide peat for many local hearths. On the marshes of Kirkbride and Whitrigg there grows a turf of remarkably fine quality which is cut and marketed to provide top-class bowling-greens.

Continue to Abbey Town.

ABBEY TOWN, Cumbria

The village of Abbey Town retains vestiges of a great ecclesiastical past. In approximately 1150, the Cistercian order founded Holme Cultram Abbey here, which soon prospered through the farming skills of its monks. However, over the years the abbey suffered considerably at the hands of Scottish raiders, and now all that remains is the 12th-century nave which forms the basis of today's parish church of St Mary. Abbot Robert Chambers built the west porch in the 16th century, and the church itself was restored many times during the 16th and 17th centuries.

At the crossroads go forward on to the B5302, SP 'Silloth' and 'Skinburness'. In 3¼ miles turn right, SP 'Skinburness', and shortly cross Skinburness Marsh. At Skinburness keep left and follow the coastal road to Silloth, joining the B5302 on entering the town.

SILLOTH, Cumbria

In the middle of the last century Silloth was transformed from a drowsy hamlet in to a busy port by the construction of the docks here, and today its pleasant lawns, putting green, children's amusements and sea-wall promenade (2 miles long), fill the town with holidaymakers during the summer months. West Beach, backed by sand dunes, is a fine expanse of sand where bathing and fishing are popular pastimes. The name 'Silloth' comes from a tithe barn built here by the monks of the great Cistercian abbey of Holme Cultram known as the 'sea lath'. From Silloth there are magnificent views of the Scottish hills across the Solway Firth.

At the crossroads turn left on to the B5300, SP 'Maryport', and shortly bear right. Continue through Greenrow and Blitterless to reach a pleasant coastal stretch with sand dunes, parking and picnic areas. Pass through Beckfoot and Mawbray to reach Allonby. Continue along the B5300 and in 4½ miles turn right on to the A596 for Maryport.

MARYPORT, Cumbria

Maryport was developed during the Industrial Revolution, and rose to prominence through coal mining, coal export and the great iron-making boom. The lord of the manor, Colonel H. Senhouse, was chiefly responsible for this development in 1748-9, and he named the port after his wife, Mary. The sea is Maryport's greatest attraction; miles of beach stretch north and south of the town and there is ample opportunity for sailing, fishing and safe bathing. On high ground to the north of the town are the remains of a Roman fort. This was defended by a double ditch which encloses 4½ acres. Outside the fort boundary there have been found the remnants of a considerable civilian settlement, with shops, workshops and taverns.

At the road junction by the church turn left on to the A594, SP 'Cockermouth'. In 6 miles, at a roundabout, take the 2nd exit and descend to cross the River Derwent into Cockermouth.

COCKERMOUTH, Cumbria

Cockermouth, famous as the birthplace of William Wordsworth, is a pleasant rural town that makes an ideal centre for touring the Lake District. See page 26.

Turn left into the main street and then keep forward. At the end bear left passing the castle (left) then turn left, SP 'Isel'. After 3¼ miles turn left again, SP 'Blindcrake, Isel'. Descend to cross the river then turn left. In ½ mile turn right, SP 'Bothel Sunderland'. Isel Hall,

Elizabethan, with a pele tower, is seen to the left at this point. In 1 mile turn left, continuing through Sunderland and in 1½ miles turn left on to the A591. At the roundabout, on the edge of Bothel, take the A595, SP 'Carlisle'. Later pass through Mealgate and in 3¾ miles turn left on to the B5304, SP 'Wigton'.

WIGTON, Cumbria

The town of Wigton, known locally as the 'Throstle Nest', is the market town of a wide area and has been for many centuries. In 1262 permission to hold the market was granted by King Henry III to Walter de Wigton. Popular for its market held on Tuesday; there are also cattle and sheep auctions. The red sandstone parish church of St Mary's was erected in 1788 on the site of an earlier church. The monument chest inside the church is thought to be pre-Reformation, and the church Registers date back to 1604. In the centre of the town is the memorial fountain erected in 1872 by George Moore, a merchant and philanthropist, in memory of his wife. The old parish pump and tall gas lamp which are to be found in West Road were immortalised by Charles Dickens in his book The Lazy Tour of Two Idle Apprentices. Dickens visited Wigton and the surrounding area with his friend Wilkie Collins, and as the many interesting nooks and crannies to be found in the town remain unchanged, it is easy to picture Wigton as he must have seen it.

In the town centre turn right on to the A596, SP 'Carlisle', and in 5¼ miles go forward on to the A595. In 5 miles re-enter the suburbs of Carlisle and keep forward for the castle and city centre.

TO THE VALLEY OF SONG

Walled Chester stands on the edge of England like the medieval guardian it once was. Across the border in Wales a natural wall of mountains encloses Llangollen, in a valley that rings with song during the International Eisteddfod.

Victorian architect W H Kelly designed this building, which stands in Park Street, Chester, in a convincing half-timbered style.

CHESTER, Cheshire

Founded nearly 2,000 years ago by the Romans, Chester boasts some of the richest archaeological and architectural treasures in Britain. It is the only city in England to have preserved its Roman and medieval walls in their entirety, and today they provide a 2-mile circular walk which affords excellent views of both the city and its surrounding countryside. At one point the walls overlook the Roodee, a racecourse where the Chester Cup has been run every May since 1824. Chester, or *Deva* as it was once known, remained a principal military station and trading town until the Romans withdrew from Britain, then was probably re-occupied by the Saxons to prevent the Danes from using it as a stronghold. It gradually regained its position as a place of importance, and after it had fallen to the Normans in 1070 became the capital of a county Palatine whose earls were almost as powerful as the king. The medieval town flourished as a port until silting of the Dee during the 15th century brought a decline in trade prosperity. The city continued as a commercial centre, however, and its fortunes largely revived during the rich 18th and 19th centuries. Much survives from all periods of Chester's history, but the source of its distinctive character is undoubtedly the galleried tiers of shops known as The Rows. The beautifully restored sandstone cathedral dates mainly from the 14th century. It incorporates extensive Benedictine monastic

remains, and is especially noted for its richly carved woodwork, the Lady Chapel, the refectory, and the cloisters. Partly ruined St John's Church retains excellent Norman workmanship. Most of Chester Castle now dates from the 19th century, but its 13th-century Agricola Tower is largely original. The castle contains the Cheshire Military Museum encompassing four separate regiments. Black-and-white buildings abound in Chester — God's Providence House, Bishop Lloyd's House and Old Leche House being outstanding — and there are also many timbered inns. The city's history is illustrated in the Heritage and Visitor Centres and the Grosvenor and Guildhall museums. Other museums located on the city walls are at the Water Tower and the King Charles Tower. There is also a Toy Museum in The Rows. Chester Zoo offers a variety of exhibits second only to London.

Leave Chester on the A483 SP 'North Wales' and cross the River Dee via Grosvenor Bridge. Reach a roundabout and take the 4th exit on to the A549 SP 'Saltney'. Reach Saltney and cross into Wales. In 2½ miles at Broughton roundabout take 2nd exit A5104 SP 'Corwen'. After ¾ mile turn left and 1¼ miles further left again. In 1 mile turn left into Penyffordd. In ¼ mile turn right and after 2 miles cross the River Alyn to pass through Portblyddyn.

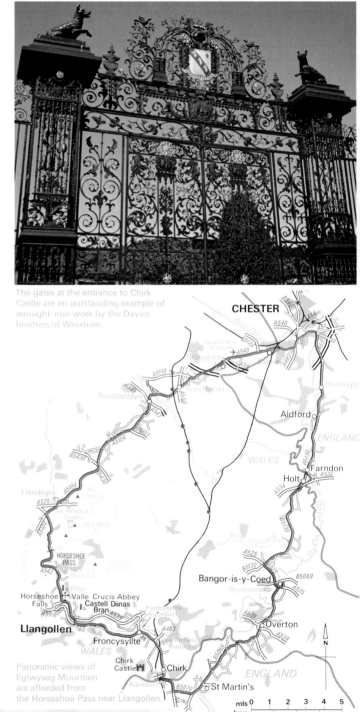

The gates at the entrance to Chirk Castle are an outstanding example of wrought-iron work by the Davies brothers of Wrexham.

Panoramic views of Eglwyseg Mountain are afforded from the Horseshoe Pass near Llangollen.

At the Bridge Inn turn left then immediately right and ascend. Proceed, with mountain views, through the village of Llandegla.

Turn right then immediately left, then after ¾ mile reach a roundabout and take the 1st exit on to the A542 'Llangollen' road. Ascend to the Horseshoe Pass.

HORSESHOE PASS, Clwyd

Fine views of the surrounding mountain scenery can be enjoyed from this 1,367ft pass. North-east is 1,844ft Cyrn-y-Brain, topped by Sir Watkin's Tower, and west are the slopes of Llantysilio Mountain.

Descend along the Eglwyseg Valley to Valle Crucis Abbey.

VALLE CRUCIS ABBEY, Clwyd

Pleasantly wooded hills frame the view from the picturesque ruins of this ancient abbey, which was founded in 1201 and has left extensive remains (AM). 'Valle Crucis' means 'Vale of the Cross' and derives from nearby Eliseg's Pillar (AM), which was erected to commemorate a nobleman of ancient times.

After a short distance reach the Horseshoe Falls.

HORSESHOE FALLS, Clwyd

Not a natural cascade but a beautifully curving weir with a fall of 18 inches, this lovely River Dee feature was built to feed water into the Llangollen Canal.

Continue with Castell Dinas Bran to the left.

CASTELL DINAS BRAN, Clywd

Ramparts of an Iron-Age fort partly surround this ruined 13th-century stronghold, which occupies a hilltop site overlooking Llangollen.

Turn right to cross the Dee and enter Llangollen.

LLANGOLLEN, Clwyd

This small town's world-wide reputation as a centre of Welsh culture and music comes from the International Eisteddfod held here for one week in July. During this time the small streets are transformed by a riot of colourful national costumes and chatter of foreign tongues, while the surrounding hillsides echo to the sound of great international choirs and poets performing in a huge 1,000-seat marquee. Plas Newydd (open) is a black-and-white house on the edge of the town which was, for many years, the home of the 'Ladies

Valle Crucis Abbey was founded by Madog ap Gruffyd, a prince of Powys, during the 13th century.

of Llangollen' who arrived here in 1779, entertained a string of celebrities and generated endless gossip with their lifestyle. Transport enthusiasts are covered by the Canal Museum and Passenger Boat Trip Centre with horsedrawn trips along the Shropshire Union Canal, and by the Llangollen Railway.

Poets, artists, and writers have praised Llangollen's hospitality since the early 19th century.

Follow the A5 'Shrewsbury' road through the winding valley of the Dee to Froncysyllte.

FRONCYSYLLTE, Clwyd

Thomas Telford's amazing 120ft high Pontcysyllte Aqueduct and the longest in the United Kingdom, was built to carry the Shropshire Union Canal over the deep ravine of the River Dee. It can be seen by turning left. Downstream is a railway viaduct whose impressive design is almost as remarkable.

Continue to Chirk.

CHIRK, Clwyd

An interesting section of the Shropshire Union Canal in this well kept village includes a long, damp tunnel which opens into a wide basin before the canal is carried high across the Ceiriog Valley.

CHIRK CASTLE, Clwyd

Outside Chirk behind superb 18th-century wrought-iron gates (AM) is Chirk Castle, a 13th-century border fortress in a commanding position above the Ceiriog Valley. Unlike many of its contemporaries this stronghold has been continuously inhabited since it was built, and considerable structural changes have been made to suit the tastes of successive owners.

Cross the River Ceiriog into England, and after 1¼ miles turn left on to the B5070 SP 'Overton'. In 1 mile reach St Martin's.

ST MARTIN'S, Salop

The interior of the beautiful 13th-century local church preserves Georgian furnishings which include boxpews and a double-decker pulpit. Attractive almshouses stand near by.

Join the B5069 and cross undulating countryside to re-enter Wales. Reach the A528 and turn left to enter Overton.

OVERTON, Clwyd

Very old churchyard yews in this pleasant small town are traditionally held to be among the 7 greatest wonders of Wales.

Keep forward on the B5059, SP 'Bangor' then turn right. Continue with views of the Dee and Bangor racecourse, to Bangor-is-y-Coed.

BANGOR-IS-Y-COED, Clwyd

An ancient stone bridge is the dominating feature of this picturesque village. At one time a monastery stood near by, but the buildings were destroyed and its monks slaughtered by order of King Aethelfrith of Northumbria in AD 615. Little survives today.

Turn right SP 'Wrexham' and shortly right again then in ¼ mile turn right on to the bypass A525. After 1¾ miles turn right on to the B5130 SP 'Wrexham Industrial Estate' then keep forward, no SP. In 5½ miles turn left then right across the bypass to enter Holt. Bear right then keep forward.

HOLT, Clwyd

Slight remains of a Norman castle can be seen near the 8-arched 15th-century bridge that spans the Dee here. The local church is a fine building which dates originally from the 13th century but was rebuilt in the 15th. Inside is an elaborately decorated font.

Cross the Dee on to the B5434 to Farndon and re-enter England.

FARNDON, Cheshire

In Farndon attractive houses group round a large church that was rebuilt after Civil War damage. An unusual feature of the church is a stained-glass window depicting a troop of Royalist soldiers.

Turn left on to the B5130 SP 'Chester' and continue through wooded scenery to Aldford.

ALDFORD, Cheshire

Earthworks of a Norman motte-and-bailey castle may be seen north of Aldford's Victorian church.

Return to Chester.

COCKERMOUTH, Cumbria

This attractive small town, situated at the point where the Rivers Cocker and Derwent meet, is rich in history and has the distinction of being one of 51 towns in Britain recommended by the British Council for preservation. The ruined Norman castle (OACT), which overlooks the River Derwent, was built of stone taken from a Roman fort at Papcastle. During the 16th century Cockermouth was a busy market town, and became the country's commercial centre in the 17th century. Today it is a rural town with a broad main street and a number of Georgian houses and squares and is a popular base for touring the Lake District. The most famous people in Cockermouth's history are, of course, the Wordsworths, and Wordsworth House (OACT) is internationally known as one of the 2 principal residences in the Lake District of Dorothy and her famous poet brother, William. The other is Dove Cottage at Grasmere. Their home in Cockermouth is a handsome house (NT) on Main Street which was built in 1745 and became the home of Wordsworth's father in 1766 when he was made steward to Sir James Lowther. William was born here in 1770 and his sister in 1771. Much of the house remains unchanged since Wordsworth's day, and he made reference to the garden in *The Prelude*. A stained-glass memorial window to him can be seen in the 19th-century Church of All Saints situated south of the market place.

From Cockermouth follow SP 'Workington', then in 1¼ miles turn right on to the A66 and follow the valley of the River Derwent to Workington.

NORTHERN LAKES AND THE SOLWAY FIRTH

This is Wordsworth's country, where the romance of majestic mountain scenery, flawless lakes and lush green valleys give way gently to flat pastoral farmland sprinkled with handsome Georgian farmhouses and tiny hamlets: a delicately-proportioned tapestry fringed with glittering stretches of golden sands and unspoilt resorts.

Above: the Norman doorway of the church at St Bees

WORKINGTON, Cumbria

A onetime Roman fort and town called *Gabrosentum*, Workington has an interesting history. It was from this port, where the River Derwent enters the Solway Firth, that the Lindisfarne monks fled from the Danes in the 9th century. In 1568 Mary, Queen of Scots, was received at the fine old mansion of Workington Hall (not open). An important industrial town in the area, Workington's main industries are iron and steel. An interesting museum known as the Helena Thompson Museum was bequethed to the town by the late Miss Thompson MBE, a native of Workington. Opened in 1948, it contains a fascinating collection of costumes, glass, ceramics and local history exhibits.

Leave on the A596, SP 'Barrow'. In 2¾ miles, at the T-junction, turn right on to the A595. Pass the edge of Distington, then in 3½ miles branch right on to the A5094 for Whitehaven town centre.

Left: Whitehaven's harbour and lighthouse date from the 18th century

WHITEHAVEN, Cumbria

Sir John Lowther was responsible for bringing industry to Whitehaven in 1690, transforming it from a cosy hamlet into the bustling seaport and coal-mining town it is today. During the 18th century, his son, Sir James Lowther, built Whitehaven Castle (now a hospital), and St James's Church was also built at this time. In 1701 George Washington's grandmother was buried in St Nicholas's Church, where she is commemorated by an inscribed tablet. The Washingtons were a Lancastrian family who later emigrated to America. The colourful American sailor John Paul Jones fired on Whitehaven in 1788.

Leave the one-way system on the B5345 for St Bees.

ST BEES, Cumbria

St Bees is a small coastal resort with fine cliffs and bathing sands. The 12th-century Benedictine priory church of SS Mary and Bega is reputed to be one of the most outstanding in Cumbria. It is thought that a princess, St Bega, came from Ireland in about AD650 to found a nunnery that preceded the priory. St Bees' church has an impressive Norman doorway, and a fine carved stone in the churchyard wall depicts St Michael fighting a dragon. A local man, who became Archbishop of Canterbury in 1576, founded St Bees Grammer School, which is now a public school.

Go over the level-crossing and at the end of the town keep left, SP 'Egremont'. After 2¾ miles go forward on to an unclassified road and continue to Egremont.

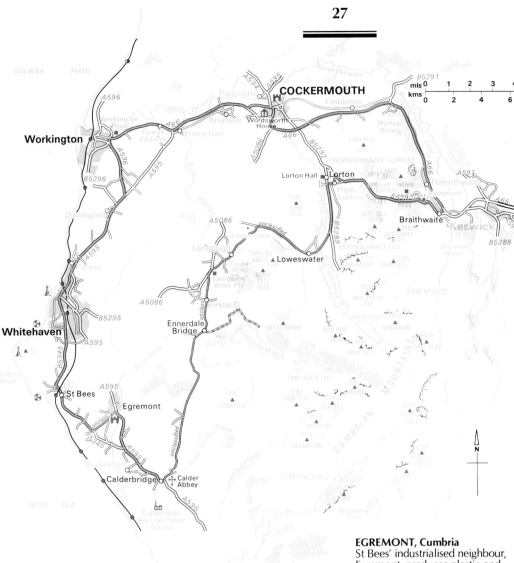

The most westerly of all Cumbria's lakes, Ennerdale Water, can only be approached by road from the west side

EGREMONT, Cumbria

St Bees' industrialised neighbour, Egremont, produces plastic and leather goods and it has a rather grimy air, due to the reddish iron ore with which the town has been particularly associated. However, Wordsworth found sufficient inspiration here to write, in 1806, *The Horn of Egremont Castle* — which none could sound 'save he who came as rightful heir'. The castle he refers to was built in the 12th century to bolster Norman rule but was destroyed at the Reformation in the 16th century, leaving the ruins of today.

Follow the A595 Barrow road to Calderbridge.

CALDERBRIDGE, Cumbria

Here is the site of Britain's first nuclear power station which was opened in the autumn of 1956 by Queen Elizabeth II. Contrasting with this are the ruins of the 12th-century Calder Abbey (OACT) which was originally built by Savignac monks from Furness Abbey. Remains include the nave, the church aisles and parts of the cloister.

At Calderbridge turn left, SP 'Ennerdale'. In ¾ mile turn left then right, and ascend along a narrow moorland road. After 3¼ miles skirt Ennerdale Forest and later descend to a T-junction. Here turn right to reach Ennerdale Bridge.

ENNERDALE BRIDGE, Cumbria

This tiny hamlet on the banks of the River Ehen is situated just a mile or so west of Ennerdale Water, amid breathtaking scenery. Its churchyard was the setting for Wordsworth's poem *The Brothers*.

The main tour turns left, SP 'Cockermouth', and proceeds to Kirkland. In 1 mile turn right on to the A5086, then in ½ mile right again, SP 'Loweswater'. Pass through the hamlet of Lamplugh and turn right. Follow this narrow road for 1¾ miles, then turn right and descend to pass Loweswater, and continue to the outskirts of Loweswater village.

LOWESWATER, Cumbria

A narrow road leads to this attractively-positioned village which lies halfway across the plains towards Crummock Water. Carling Knott rises to 1,781ft behind Loweswater lake and the great peak of Grasmoor (2,791ft) lies to the east. Opposite Grasmoor, the impressive screes of Mellbreak rise on the west side of Crummock Water.

Continue on the unclassified road then in ½ mile cross the River Cocker. Later join the B5289, SP 'Cockermouth', and continue to the edge of Lorton.

LORTON, Cumbria

Enjoying a pastoral situation beside the River Cocker in the Vale of Lorton, this village includes a church displaying a fine stained-glass window. The 17th-century Lorton Hall (not open) retains the ancient pele tower in which Malcolm III of Scotland and Queen Margaret stayed in 1089. Charles II visited Lorton Hall in 1650.

By the nearside of the village turn right, SP 'Keswick'. At High Lorton turn left into the village and at the end turn right, then at the T-junction turn right again on to the B5292. Continue across the Whinlatter Pass and at the bottom of the descent keep left to enter Braithwaite.

BRAITHWAITE, Cumbria

At the north-eastern end of the Coledale valley and the start of the Whinlatter Pass, this picturesque village is conveniently situated for the tourist. It enjoys great popularity among climbers as the starting point for an attack on Grisedale Pike, one of the northern peaks in the Grasmoor mountain group.

In Braithwaite turn left, SP 'Cockermouth (A66)', then turn left again to join the A66 and continue alongside the shore of Bassenthwaite Lake. At the north end the road veers away from the lake and continues through a wide valley. In 5½ miles turn right on to the A5086 for the return to Cockermouth.

AMONG THE HIGH PEAKS

Climbers and walkers come to this part of the national park for the stark ridges of weathered grit, towering rock outcrops, and refreshingly empty moorland. Villages of timbered cottages shelter in the valleys, making a contrast with the huge reflectors of Jodrell Bank's radio telescopes.

THE PEAK DISTRICT NATIONAL PARK
This tour starts west of the Peak District boundary and explores the brownstone towns and villages in the mid western part of the national park. In places massive limestone extraction has taken its toll of the landscape, but the sheep-cropped grass of high gritstone edges still rolls away to close horizons in areas of outstanding natural beauty that have been saved by the Peak Planning Board. Visitors should remember that although the region is protected it is not automatically accessible to the public. Some 40,000 people live and work in the park, and permission should always be sought from farmers and landowners before enclosed land is entered. Information centres are located in Buxton, Castleton, and Edale.

Leave Congleton via West Street and West Road to join the A34 'Newcastle' road. Proceed to Astbury.

ASTBURY, Cheshire
Notable Jacobean and earlier woodwork can be seen in Astbury's 14th- and 15th-century church, and the fine village Rectory dates from the 18th century.

Continue along the A34 to pass Little Moreton Hall.

Little Moreton Hall is one of the finest medieval houses in Britain

An attractive aqueduct carries the Macclesfield Canal over the road near Congleton.

CONGLETON, Cheshire
This market town stands on a bend on the River Dane and is a dormitory settlement for the vast industrial conurbations of Manchester and the Potteries. Its own industries include the manufacture of artificial yarn for the textile trade. Notable buildings in the town include three half-timbered inns and an 18th-century church with heavy woodwork that seems appropriate to Congleton's solid personality.

THE CLOUD, Cheshire
Some 3 miles east of Congleton a lofty hill known as The Cloud (NT) rises from farmed slopes to a 1,050ft summit offering magnificent all-round views. East are the Staffordshire hills, west the rolling Cheshire Plain, and south the towns and distinctively shaped chimneys of the Potteries.

LITTLE MORETON HALL, Cheshire
Beautiful carved gables and a distinctive black-and-white exterior of Elizabethan wood- and plasterwork have made this splendid 16th-century manor house (NT) one of the most famous examples in Britain. The dazzling effect of symmetrical timber patterns against brilliant white is increased by the reflection of the house in its own lovely moat. Inside are a long wainscoted gallery, a great hall, a chapel, and fine oak furniture.

Continue for ¾ mile to the edge of Scholar Green and turn left on to an unclassified road SP 'Mow Cop'. After ¼ mile turn left again, and after a further ¼ mile cross a canal bridge and drive beneath a railway before ascending Mow Cop.

MOW COP, Cheshire
Rough turf covers this stark limestone ridge for much of its 1,091ft height, but the rugged outcrop of rock known as the Old Man of Mow carries little but a sham ruin built in 1750. Known as Mow Cop Castle, this folly makes a picturesque addition to the distinctive outline of the Old Man.

Continue past a towered church and in 1 mile turn right (no SP) into Mow Lane. Descend through Gillow Heath to the main road and turn left, then in 300 yards turn right on to an unclassified road SP 'Biddulph Moor'. Climb to the village of Biddulph Moor and turn left SP 'Leek'. Take the next turning right, proceed for ¼ mile to reach a T-junction, and turn left. Continue for 1 mile and turn right. After 2¼ miles glimpse Rudyard Reservoir on the left and descend to Rudyard.

RUDYARD, Staffs
Rudyard Kipling's parents courted and became engaged in this lovely village, and when their talented son was born they named him after it. Attractive woodlands to the north border a 2-mile reservoir formed in 1793 to provide water for the Trent and Mersey Canal. Today the banks of this attractive lake are skirted by a 5-mile footpath dotted with secluded picnic spots near the water's edge. A section of the path follows the trackbed of an abandoned railway, and its route passes caverns, unusual rock formations, and the remains of Roman copper workings.

Continue on the B5331 'Leek' road, meet a T-junction, and turn right on to the A523. Take the next turning left on to an unclassified road SP 'Meerbrook', continue for ½ mile, then turn left again. Approach Meerbrook with Tittesworth Reservoir right.

MEERBROOK, Staffs
Wild upland country popular with climbers and fell walkers surrounds this tiny moorland village. A curious aspect of the area is its naturalized colony of red-necked wallabies. This numbers some 30 strong and began when several of the animals – natives of Australia – escaped from a private estate.

Turn right SP 'Blackshaw Moor, Leek', and after ½ mile meet a main road and turn left on to the A53 'Buxton' road. Climb on to open moors in the Peak District National Park, with a 2-mile stretch of rocky outcrops known as the Staffordshire Roaches to the left. The highest point of the Roaches is 1,658ft; Merryton Low rises to 1,603ft to the right. Pass the Royal Cottage Inn and reach an unclassified left turn leading to the village of Flash. A short detour can be made from the main route here.

FLASH, Staffs
Situated at 1,518ft, Flash is claimed to be the highest village in England and is itself dominated by 1,684ft Oliver Hill to the north.

Later enter Derbyshire and ascend to 1,631ft below the distinctive summit of Axe Edge.

AXE EDGE, Derbys
Rising from an area of fine walking country, this 1,810ft summit is the highest point in the moors from which the rivers Dove, Manifold, Wye, Dane, and Goyt spring.

Proceed to Buxton.

Extremely faint signals from outer space can be detected by the advanced Jodrell Bank radio telescopes

BUXTON, Derbys
Situated some 1,007ft above sea level, this natural touring centre is the highest town in England and has been known as a spa resort of one sort or another since Roman times. A superb legacy of 18th-century architecture has been left from its most popular period, and the tourists of today are catered for by a large range of entertainment facilities.

Leave Buxton with SP 'Congleton' to return along the A53 'Leek' road, and after 1½ miles turn right on to the A54. Make a winding ascent with 1,640ft Burbage Edge visible to the right, and after 1 mile enjoy views of 1,795ft Whetstone Edge on the same side. Below these ridges, in the deep Dane Valley, is a junction of Derbyshire, Cheshire, and Staffordshire boundaries in an area known as the Three Shire Heads. Descend from undulating moorland to Allgreave for distant views of a Post Office communications tower, and after passing close to the tower skirt Bosley Reservoir and turn right on to the A523 'Macclesfield' road. Continue for 2 miles to Oakgrove and turn left on to an unclassified road SP 'Gawsworth', immediately crossing the Macclesfield Canal. Proceed to Gawsworth.

GAWSWORTH, Cheshire
Spacious lawns and gardens watered by five lakes grace the grounds of Gawsworth Hall, a beautiful black-and-white timber-framed house (open) dating from Tudor times. Also in the park are rare traces of a tilting ground, where knights once displayed their prowess in jousts and mock battles. At one time the house was the seat of the Fytton family, whose daughter Mary was a favourite maid of Elizabeth I and may have been the 'Dark Lady' of Shakespeare's sonnets. Features of the village itself include the fine Old Rectory and an attractive church, both of the 15th century. The church carries quaint gargoyles and contains a notable range of monuments to the Fyttons. A nearby wood contains the tomb of 18th-century dramatist and eccentric Maggotty Johnson.

At Gawsworth turn left SP 'Gawsworth Church'. Continue to the end of the village and keep right, passing an attractive pond, with views of Gawsworth Hall. Continue along this unclassified road, pass the church, and at the Harrington Arms Inn turn right then right again on to the A536. After ½ mile meet crossroads and turn left on to an unclassified road for Marton.

MARTON, Cheshire
A famous oak tree in this village is said to be the largest in England. The local church is a quaint timbered structure dating from the 14th century.

Drive to a junction with the A34 and turn right SP 'Manchester'. Continue for 3¼ miles to reach the entrance to Capesthorne Hall.

Rudyard's extensive reservoir has been planned to cater for a wide variety of leisure pursuits

CAPESTHORNE HALL, Cheshire
A chapel which adjoins this lovely 18th-century house (open) may be the earliest surviving work of the architect John Wood of Bath. The house itself contains various relics, including pictures, ancient vases, old furniture, and Americana.

Continue along the A34 for 1 mile, meet traffic signals, and turn left on to the A537 'Chester' road. Continue to the Chelford roundabout and turn left on to the A535 SP 'Holmes Chapel' to reach Jodrell Bank.

Ramshaw Rocks are among the most striking gritstone crags in the Peak District

JODRELL BANK, Cheshire
Manchester University made the name Jodrell Bank internationally famous by building a giant steerable radio telescope here in 1957. Now known as Mark I, the instrument has a 250ft reflector and is still one of the largest of its type in the world. The Mark II was built in the early 1960s and has a 125ft reflector with an advanced form of digital control. Regular presentations of the stars and planets are given in the Planetarium (open), and there are fascinating working models of both the telescopes on view.

Keep forward on the A535. In 3¼ miles, near the outskirts of Holmes Chapel, turn left into unclassified Manor Lane (no SP). Continue to the A54 and turn left for the return to Congleton via Somerford.

GRANGE-OVER-SANDS, Cumbria

This quiet seaside resort is situated on Morecambe Bay. Its shingle and rock shore is scattered with fascinating rock pools at low tide, and is backed by lovely wooded fell scenery that sweeps right down to the sea. Bathing is dangerous. The mile-long promenade offers bracing walks, and the mild local climate has allowed the establishment of flourishing ornamental gardens throughout the town.

Leave Grange on the B5277 'Lindale, Kendal' road and drive through well-wooded countryside with views across Morecambe Bay to the right. Continue, with the Lakeland fells visible ahead, to Lindale.

LINDALE, Cumbria

John Wilkinson, the 18th-century iron master, is appropriately commemorated by a cast-iron obelisk in this pretty village.

In Lindale turn right SP 'Lancaster', and in 1¼ miles meet a roundabout. Take the 2nd exit on to the A590, later pass the craggy cliffs of Whitbarrow Scar on the left, and continue for 1¼ miles. Immediately before a river bridge turn left on to the A5074 SP 'Bowness' and follow the lovely Lyth Valley. Continue, with views of the Lakeland fells ahead, and ascend a winding road through picturesque countryside. Drive through Winster, continue for 2 miles to reach crossroads, and turn left on to the B5284. In ¼ mile turn right on to the A592 to reach the town of Bowness-on-Windermere.

LAKE WINDERMERE, Cumbria

The largest and one of the most beautiful lakes in England, Windermere measures 10½ miles long and is only 1 mile wide. Its surface is studded with charming little islands, and its steep banks are cloaked with dense masses of attractive woodland. Water-sports enthusiasts find it suitable for most of their requirements, and at one time it was the regular venue for world water-speed record attempts.

BOWNESS-ON-WINDERMERE, Cumbria

In summer the quaint narrow streets of this pleasant little Lakeland town are busy with anglers, sailors, walkers, and tourists who have come here just for the beauty of the surroundings. Its fine 15th- to 19th-century church has superb examples of medieval stained glass in the east window, and the picturesque quality of local stone can be seen everywhere. Motor launches operate from Bowness Pier to Belle Isle, an enchanting 38-acre island in the middle of Lake Windermere. The house (open) on this unusual estate was the first completely round building of its type erected in England and contains interesting collections of furniture, portraits, and miscellanea.

SOUTHERN LAKELAND

Characterized by narrow switchback lanes and tranquil lakes that recede far into the distance, this part of the Lake District was a favourite haunt of famous poets and artists. Relics of them remain, as does the timeless and indefinable quality of peace that first attracted them.

Return along the A592 SP 'Barrow' and in ¾ mile pass a right turn leading to Lake Windermere Ferry. An alternative route that shortens the tour by 15 miles can be followed by taking the ferry and rejoining the main route at Far Sawrey, on the other bank. On the main route, drive through thick woodland along the east shore of Lake Windermere to reach Fell Foot Park.

FELL FOOT PARK, Cumbria

Attractively situated on the shores of Lake Windermere, this 18-acre park (NT) offer facilities for bathing, boating, picnicking, and many other outdoor pursuits.

Meet a T-junction and turn right on to the A590 to reach Newby Bridge.

NEWBY BRIDGE, Cumbria

This unusual stone bridge dates from the 17th century and spans the River Leven at the southern extremity of Lake Windermere. It is an attractive ingredient of the beautiful local scenery.

Turn right on to an unclassified road SP 'Lakeside, Hawkshead' and follow a winding road along the west shore of Lake Windermere to Lakeside.

LAKESIDE, Cumbria

Steam locomotives run south from here to Haverthwaite on the Lakeside and Haverthwaite Railway, which connects with passenger ferries operating from Ambleside and Bowness-on-Windermere.

Leave Lakeside and after ¾ mile bear right. In 2½ miles reach Graythwaite Hall Gardens.

GRAYTHWAITE HALL GARDENS, Cumbria

In spring and summer the 7 acres of this landscape garden are glorious with the blooms and foliage of many different plants. The Elizabethan hall round which they were created was sympathetically re-modelled in the 19th century.

Leave Graythwaite Hall and branch right SP 'Sawrey'. In ¾ mile descend steeply, then in 1¾ miles bear left and ascend to Far Sawrey. If the alternative route via the ferry has been taken, resume the main tour here.

FAR SAWREY, Cumbria

This beautiful Lakeland village is situated between Lake Windermere and tranquil Esthwaite Water.

Keep left in Far Sawrey, then turn left on to the B5285 SP 'Hawkshead'. Continue to Near Sawrey.

NEAR SAWREY, Cumbria

In 1943 Beatrix Potter, creator of Peter Rabbit and a host of other engaging animals in her children's books, bequeathed Hill Top Farm (open) and about half the village to the National Trust. The 17th-century farmhouse was her home up until her death, and the lovely surroundings of the village must have influenced her enchanting and essentially rural tales.

Continue along the B5285 and follow the north shore of Esthwaite Water.

ESTHWAITE WATER, Cumbria

Rowing boats can be hired by those wishing to explore this picturesque small lake by water, and its shores offer mountain views in which the 2,631ft peak of the Old Man of Coniston is prominent.

Continue to the edge of Hawkshead. A detour can be made from the main tour route to the Grizedale Wildlife Centre by driving forward, turning left on to an unclassified road SP 'Newby Bridge', then continuing for ¼ mile and turning right SP 'Grizedale'; proceed across Hawkshead Moor to reach Grizedale.

GRIZEDALE, Cumbria

The variety of wildlife to be seen in this region is superbly illustrated in the Forestry Commission's Visitor and Wildlife Centre at Grizedale. The deer exhibit is of particular note, and among the best of several planned walks in the area is the 1-mile Millwood forest trail. Take care against fire in dry weather.

On the main tour, turn right to skirt the village of Hawkshead.

HAWKSHEAD, Cumbria

Hawkshead's distinctive charm comes from its unspoilt stone cottages, courtyards, and narrow winding alleys. The 16th-century grammar school numbers Wordsworth among its past pupils. The poet lodged in Ann Tyson's cottage while he studied there. The cottage still stands and is noted for its unusual outside staircase. The picturesque Courthouse (NT) houses the Folk Museum of Rural Crafts.

Keep forward on to the B5286 SP 'Ambleside' and follow a winding road that affords fine views of the local countryside. Drive through Out Gate, and in 2 miles reach an unclassified right turn offering a detour to impressive Wray Castle.

WRAY CASTLE, Cumbria

Lovely grounds (open) surround the 19th-century extravagance of Wray Castle (not open) on the banks of Lake Windermere, sweeping right down to the water's edge. The castle, estate, and much of the attractive local countryside are protected by the National Trust.

On the main route, continue to the village of Clappersgate.

CLAPPERSGATE, Cumbria

Magnificently situated at the northern end of Lake Windermere, Clappersgate is best known for the beautiful floral displays that can be enjoyed in the White Craggs Garden (limited opening) during spring and summer.

Leave Clappersgate and turn right on to the A593. Continue, with fine views of Wansfell and 1,581ft Wansfell Pike ahead, and cross a river bridge. Turn left to enter Ambleside.

Lake Windermere is a popular centre for boating and sailing as well as being a magnetic scenic attraction.

AMBLESIDE, Cumbria

Features of this very popular Lakeland tourist centre include a National Trust information office in tiny Bridge House. Excellent walking and climbing areas are nearby.

The area around Skelwith Bridge is graced by several lovely waterfalls.

Return along the A593 SP 'Coniston' and pass through Clappersgate. Cross Skelwith Bridge and continue along an undulating road with all-round mountain views. Tilberthwaite High Fells rise to the right, dominated by the strangely-shaped peak of 2,502ft Wetherlam. Continue, later driving below the steep slopes of the Coniston Fells with the Old Man of Coniston towering in the background, to Coniston.

CONISTON, Cumbria

This cluster of whitewashed cottages at the tip of lovely Coniston Water is a bright spot in a landscape dominated in the west by the 2,631ft Old Man of Coniston. A little farther west is the 2,555ft peak of Dow Crag, whose testing faces are popular with climbers. Features of the village itself include Coniston Old Hall, with its typical round Lakeland chimneys, and the Ruskin Museum. John Ruskin, the 19th-century writer and artist, loved this area and is buried in the local churchyard. Although the museum is devoted mostly to him, parts of it recall the death of the famous Donald Campbell.

Leave Coniston and turn left on to the B5285 SP 'Hawkshead' to skirt the northern end of Coniston Water.

CONISTON WATER, Cumbria

One shore of this tranquil 5½-mile-long lake is cloaked in the woodlands of Grizedale Forest, and the lake itself is famous as the place where Sir Donald Campbell died while trying to better the world water-speed record in 1965. Conditions were not ideal during the attempt, but its failure may not have been entirely due to the choppy surface and is still a matter for conjecture.

Keep left and climb through woodland, then in 1¼ miles turn left on to an unclassified road SP 'Tarn Hows'. In ½ mile turn left again and ascend steeply to reach Tarn Hows.

Evening gives a dramatic aspect to Morecambe Bay.

Marvellous views of the Langdale Pikes and other famous Lakeland features can be enjoyed from the peaceful shores of picturesque Tarn Hows.

TARN HOWS, Cumbria

Arguably the most outstanding of many beautiful areas in the Lakeland region, Tarn Hows (NT) is a group of lakes and woodland in an area ringed by the peaks of mountains. Visitors are catered for with carparks and picnicking facilities.

Descend steeply along a narrow road SP 'Coniston', meet a T-junction, and turn right on to the B5285. Take the next turning left on to an unclassified road SP 'East of Lake' and follow the eastern shore of Coniston Water. In 1¾ miles reach Brantwood.

BRANTWOOD, Cumbria

This house (open), once the home of writer and artist John Ruskin, is now a museum containing examples of his work and a variety of personal possessions. The grounds feature fine gardens, a deer trail, and one of the best nature trails in the Lake District.

Continue along a winding road that hugs the shore of the lake, with views of several waterfalls to the right. Above the road to the left are the steep wooded slopes of Grizedale Forest. On the far side of the lake descend into the Crake Valley, passing the wooded Furness Fells on the left, and meet a T-junction. Turn left to reach Spark Bridge, then turn left again and in ½ mile drive forward over crossroads SP 'Newby Bridge', then bear right and at T-junction turn left on to the A590 SP 'Bowness', then in 1¼ miles meet crossroads and turn right on to the B5278 SP 'Cark'. A detour from the main route to Rusland can be made by turning left at the crossroads instead of right.

RUSLAND, Cumbria

Rusland Hall (open) was built in 1720 and nowadays houses a museum of mechanical musical instruments and early photographic equipment. Its elegant landscaped grounds are the home of white peacocks.

On the main tour, continue along the B5278 to reach Haverthwaite.

HAVERTHWAITE, Cumbria

Steam-hauled trains on the standard-gauge Lakeside and Haverthwaite Railway connect with passenger steamers on Lake Windermere, at the other end of the line, and run 3½ miles through some of Lakeland's finest scenery.

Drive beyond Haverthwaite and bear right, then continue along the B5278 through thickly wooded countryside to reach Holker Hall.

HOLKER HALL, Cumbria

Originally built in the 16th century, this house (open) contains fine furniture and exquisite woodcarvings by local craftsmen. A motor museum exhibits over 100 cars and motorcycles, and the grounds include a deer park featuring a number of different species. During the summer Holker Hall is the scene of many local shows and events.

Proceed to Cark.

CARK, Cumbria

One of the main features in this pleasant little village is its 16th-century hall, which has mullioned windows and a grand 17th-century doorway.

Drive to the Rose and Crown Hotel and branch left on to an unclassified road. Continue to Cartmel.

CARTMEL, Cumbria

Little remains of the great priory (NT) that made this pleasant old town one of the most important religious centres for miles around, but the exceptionally beautiful priory church has survived. This large building was extended at various times up until the dissolution of the monasteries, after which it was left to decay until its restoration in 1618.

Keep forward, pass a school, and turn right SP 'Grange'. In 1 mile turn left into Grangefell Road and descend, with fine views over Morecambe Bay, for the return to Grange-over-Sands.

HELMSLEY, N Yorks

Helmsley is an old stone market town with venerable houses gathered about the borders of its spacious market square, which has an old market cross as its focal point. Among the buildings is the modest town hall and several old inns; the Black Swan has 2 Georgian houses and a 16th-century timber-framed house incorporated in it. All Saints Church, just off the square, was rebuilt in the 1860s, but retained some Norman characteristics. Walter L'espec, founder of Rievaulx Abbey, built Helmsley Castle (AM) in the 12th century. Although the stronghold rarely saw action, perhaps because of the strength still evident in the ruins of the great keep, tower and curtain walls, it did suffer a 3-month seige during the Civil War before being taken by Parliamentary forces. In 1689 Sir Charles Duncombe, a banker, bought the town of Helmsley and built Duncombe Park (now a school) and the picturesque ruins of the old castle lie in the grounds of the park.

Leave Helmsley on the B1257, SP 'Stokesley'. In 1½ miles turn left, SP 'Sawton'. Later descend through woodland before turning right for Rievaulx Abbey.

RIEVAULX ABBEY, N Yorks

Rievaulx Abbey (AM), magnificent even in ruin, lies in the richly-wooded valley of the River Rye and is a favourite subject of artists. Walter L'espec gave the site to the Cistercians in 1131, and this was the first church they built in the north of England. The ruins consist of the choir and transepts of the church, the lower walls of the nave and its attendant chapels, and the chapter house. Other remains include the shrine of the first abbot and the refectory. One of the best views of the abbey can be obtained from Rievaulx Terrace (AM), high up to the south, where 18th-century garden temples were built to take advantage of the delightful landscape. It belonged to Duncombe Park and the gentry used to drive out and enjoy the magnificent views.

Continue on the unclassified road and ascend to the junction with the B1257. To the right is the entrance to Rievaulx Terrace. Here, turn left, SP 'Stokesley', and climb to over 800ft before the descent into Blisdale.

BLISDALE, N Yorks

It was said that a Blisdale man left his dale so rarely that when he did he was regarded as a foreigner in his own county. It is only in comparatively recent times that a proper road was laid along the valley floor, giving the outside world access to one of the wildest and most picturesque dales in this part of Yorkshire. Between

THE LESSER-KNOWN DALES

Solid little market towns of grey stone dot the dales, above which rise the heather-clad slopes of the Cleveland Hills. Medieval monks found the peace and solitude they sought in the secluded river valleys of the North Riding, and here still stand the ruins of their beautiful abbeys.

Helmsley and Chop Gate the bubbling River Selph flows through a dale luxuriously wooded with birch and aromatic pine, but northwards, through Great Broughton to Stokesley, a moorland landscape emerges. Up on the high moors above the road are old coal-workings and lime pits — all that remains of the iron-smelting activities of the monks from Rievaulx Abbey.

Continue on the B1257 and beyond the hamlet of Chop Gate reach the summit of Clay Bank — a fine viewpoint. Descend from the Cleveland Hills to Great Broughton. In 2 miles, at the roundabout, take the 2nd exit to enter Stokesley.

STOKESLEY, N Yorks

This old market town of narrow, cobbled streets lies at the foot of the Cleveland Hills. At each end of the long market place is a green, and standing on an island in the middle is the 19th-century town hall. The River Leven runs along one side of the town and is spanned at frequent intervals by footbridges. Stokesley's many trees were planted in memory of Miss Jane Page, who, in 1836, emigrated to become the first white woman to settle in Victoria, Australia. Every September this normally quiet town explodes into activity when its fair and major agricultural show takes place.

Follow SP 'Thirsk (A172)'. In ¾ mile turn right on to the A172 and continue along the foot of the Cleveland Hills.

CLEVELAND HILLS, N Yorks/Cleveland

This great mass of sandstone hills runs in high ridges separated by secluded valleys and patches of open moorland; one of these is Urra Moor, at 1,500ft the highest point in the hills. The moorlands are famous for the bilberries which grow here, possibly an important part of the diet of the lost civilisation which left their burial chambers, tumuli, scattered all over the region. In winter snow covers the hills in a blanket, in summer they are carpeted in the glowing colours of flowering heather.

Remain on the A172 for 8 miles then branch left to join the A19. In ½ mile a track (left) may be taken to visit Mount Grace Priory.

MOUNT GRACE PRIORY, N Yorks

The old Carthusian monastery (AM, NT) was built towards the end of the 14th century by an order which vowed to austerity, isolation and silence. Within the inner cloister the remains of 15 cells survive, one of which has been restored. Hermit-monks lived in these self-contained apartments, working each day in their own private gardens and only meeting for services in the church and for a Saturday meal. On other days of the week their food was passed to them through a right-angled hatch so that the monks could not see or touch the server. It is a peaceful place, and pleasant to wander in, but the architecture, though softened by time, still reflects the grim austerity of its former inhabitants.

In another ½ mile branch left on to the A684 for Northallerton.

Top: the Fauconberg Arms in Coxwold dates from the 17th century. It still has the right to graze 4 cows on village land

Above: the striking ruins of Byland Abbey still show something of the great rose window that was 26ft in diameter

NORTHALLERTON, N Yorks

This old posting station retains many of its old inns in which travellers stayed while waiting for the stage coaches, which were given romantic names like the *High Flyer* and the *Wellington*. The town is built along a curving street, which broadens in the middle to form a market square, and narrows again at its north end near the church. There is a lot of Georgian housing, and a town hall, built in 1873, stands in the square.

Leave on the A168, SP 'Thirsk'. In 7 miles turn right on to the B1448 to enter Thirsk.

Sutton Bank, a dramatic escarpment of the Hambleton Hills, is a famous viewpoint. The white horse was cut in 1857

THIRSK, N Yorks
As an important coaching station, Thirsk once boasted 35 pubs and 4 breweries; determined, it would seem, to send travellers merrily on their way. Many of these establishments still ply their trade, perhaps foremost among them is the Georgian Golden Fleece Inn, formerly the most important coaching inn, and now the hub of the town on market days and race days. The vast square is still cobbled as it was when bull-baiting was held here in the 18th century. The church is probably the finest Perpendicular church in the county. Begun in 1430, it was founded on a chantry built by Robert Thirsk, who died in 1419. He was a member of the ancient family which gave the town its name.

From the one-way system leave on the A170, SP 'Scarborough'. Beyond Sutton-under-Whitestonecliffe climb on to the Hambleton Hills by means of Sutton Bank (1 in 4). Continue for 3¾ miles before turning right, then immediately right again, SP 'Wass' and 'Coxwold'. To the south-west of Wass short detours can be made to visit Byland Abbey, Coxwold and Newburgh Priory.

BYLAND ABBEY, N Yorks
Here stood the largest Cistercian church in the county. The great west front, incorporating the broken circle of what must have been a magnificent rose window, stands starkly with a single turret as a reminder of its past glory. The monks of Furness who founded it searched for 43 years for a suitable site, and after several false starts settled in the village of Old Byland, only to discover this was too close to the existing abbey at Rievaulx for comfort, so they moved to this pleasant broad valley, drained the marshes, and began to build. Until the Dissolution they led an uneventful life, apart from a visit by Edward II. He stayed briefly while fleeing the Scots whose country he had tried to conquer. Unfortunately, after he left the Scots followed, sacked the abbey and ousted the indignant monks as further punishment.

COXWOLD, N Yorks
Coxwold, with a wide sloping street lined with cottages of golden stone set back beyond broad green verges and spreading trees could be called the 'perfect' village. At one end the 15th-century church, with an unusual octagonal tower, serenely stands as guardian. Its fame as a beauty spot has brought many tourists, but the inhabitants have resolutely kept the village community, which has evolved over the centuries, intact. Fame also came to Coxwold in the form of Thomas Sterne, author of *The Life and Opinions of Tristram Shandy.* Sterne was a rector here for 7 years, and although he died and was buried in London, the Sterne Trust brought his remains back to the village churchyard. The Trust also owns the house in which he lived, Shandy Hall (OACT). It is an old brick farmhouse with medieval timber-framing and a warren of rooms.

NEWBURGH PRIORY, N Yorks
This is essentially an 18th-century hall (OACT) built on a site where Augustinian canons settled in 1150. It is set amid pleasant gardens featuring a pond and striking ornamental hedges. At the Dissolution Henry VIII gave the property to Anthony Belayse, who rebuilt the house. In time it passed to Lord Fauconberg, who, it is said, married a daughter of Oliver Cromwell's who brought her father's heart to Newburgh and had it bricked-up in an attic room of the house to save it from desecration. The vault has never been opened so the story has never been proved.

At Wass the main tour turns left, SP 'Ampleforth', and follows the foot of the Hambleton Hills to Ampleforth.

AMPLEFORTH, N Yorks
Perched upon a shelf of the Hambleton Hills, this village was chosen in 1802 as the site of a Roman Catholic school by English Benedictine monks who had fled from France to escape the French Revolution. The college and abbey of St Lawrence stands at the eastern end of the street along which most of the stone-built houses of the village are ranked, overlooking magnificent views towards Gilling Castle 2 miles to the south. Within the college library are some of Robert Thompson's earliest pieces of furniture. His much sought-after work is easily recognisable by the handcarved mouse he always hid somewhere on his furniture as his signature.

At the end of the village bear right, SP 'Oswaldkirk', and pass Ampleforth College. At Oswaldkirk keep forward and join the B1363, SP 'Helmsley', then in ¼ mile turn left on to the B1257. Continue to Sproxton and turn right on to the A170, SP 'Scarborough', for the return to Helmsley.

Map

mls 0 1 2 3 4 5
kms 0 2 4 6 8

N

Stokesley
Great Broughton
River Leven
Carlton in Cleveland
CLAY BANK
Faceby
1327
Swainby
Urra 1490
H I L L S
Chop Gate 1410
1326
NT Mount Grace Priory (ruins)
1379
Osmotherley
Ellerbeck
Brompton
B I L S D A L E
Northallerton
Thornton-le-Beans
1228
NEWGATE BANK
River Rye
Thornton le-Moor
H A M B L E T O N
Rievaulx Terrace
Rievaulx Abbey
HELMSLEY
Thirsk
Castle (ruins)
Gormire Lake
Sproxton
Sutton under Whitestonecliffe
Byland Abbey
Wass Moor
Ampleforth
Coxwold
College
Oswaldkirk
Shandy Hall NT
Newburgh Priory
C L E V E L A N D
B1365
A172
A173
A19
A172
A167
A684
A167
A168
A19
A19
A61
A168
A170
B1257
B1257
B1363

HADRIAN'S WALL

Along the length of the great wall the Emperor Hadrian built to protect England from the fierce Picts is a wealth of Roman remains; temples to the god Mithras, great forts and little townships, all set in a magnificent countryside of sweeping views and desolate quiet.

HEXHAM, Northumb

Hexham grew up around the entrance to the abbey which St Wilfred founded in 674, and the buildings nearest the abbey are therefore some of Hexham's oldest. Opposite the abbey church is the Moot Hall, originally the gatehouse to a 12th-century castle. In its time this has served as a Bishop's Palace, and up until 1838 was the town court: now it is the borough library. The archway beneath the Moot Hall leads to the Manor Office. This former medieval prison dealt with all the business of the Manor of Hexham from Elizabeth I's reign up until about the 1870's. Close by, overlooking the Tyne valley, is an attractive whitewashed building which was the old grammer school. The plight of its predecessor was an unhappy one, for in 1296 200 scholars were burnt alive by Scottish raiders, who also destroyed the abbey. St. Wilfred's Church was built from Roman stones taken from *Corstopitum*, near Corbridge, and of this original church the foundations of the apse, piers of the nave and the crypt remain. An Augustinian priory took over the church from the Saxon bishops in 1116, and they built the beautiful choir and transept, including the survival of the almost unique canon's Night Stair to the dormitory. The nave, destroyed by the Scottish raid, was not rebuilt until 1908. Treasurers of the past within the church include the Frith Stool, thought to be the throne upon which Northumbrian kings were crowned, later also used as a sanctuary stool. In the south transept is a remarkable Roman memorial to Flavinius, a standard-bearer, depicted mounted upon a horse astride a cowering Briton with a drawn dagger.

Leave Hexham on the A6079, SP 'Carlisle', and cross the Tyne. At the roundabout take the A69 then in ¾ mile turn right on to the A6079, SP 'Rothbury', and pass the edge of Acomb to Wall. In 1 mile, at the crossroads, turn left on to the B6318, then recross the Tyne for Chollerford.

CHOLLERFORD, Northumb

Chollerford's fine bridge dating from 1771 lies with the rest of the village near the site of *Cilurnum*, an important Roman station on the banks of the North Tyne. It

stands in Chesters Park (not open), a stately mansion which was once the home of John Clayton, archaeologist and antiquary, who pioneered the excavation of *Cilurnum*. Today most of the plan of the camp has been unearthed, and at the entrance to the site is a fascinating museum. Artefacts which have been recovered from this site are displayed within, as well as relics found along Hadrian's Wall, ranging from coins to mill-stones and including jewellery and everyday objects of Roman life.

At the roundabout take the 1st exit, SP 'Carlisle', and pass Chesters Park (left). Follow the line of Hadrian's Wall to Carrawbrough.

HADRIAN'S WALL, Northumb

Stretching across the width of Britain between Solway and Tyne, Hadrian's Wall was begun in AD122 by Emperor Hadrian to keep the barbarians from the north at bay. It took 7 years to build and required some 15,000 men to defend it. On the north side of the wall a steep ditch was constructed and to the south a flat-bottomed ditch and a road. The southern defence was found necessary to prevent the conquered tribes pilfering from the well-fed Roman soldiers. Further fortification was provided by small forts, called milecastles, at 1 mile intervals, and watch-turrets at every ⅓ mile. In addition, 17 auxiliary forts were placed on or near the wall. The skill of the Roman engineers in taking advantage of the lie of the land resulted in the wall crossing some splendid countryside, with magnificent views from the many walks which can be taken along its length.

CARRAWBROUGH, Northumb

Although this fort was a later addition to the fortifications of Hadrian's Wall, there is little left to see apart from the grassy ramparts. However, what has been uncovered is a Mithraeum temple. For some reason the deity of Mithras was especially popular among soldiers, but although it was a wide-spread religion, the groups of its followers were small, and so the temple buildings were small. Carrawbrough is no exception, the whole building measuring no more than 35ft by 15ft. The central passage is guarded by statues of lesser gods,

Above: the precipitous crags beneath Hadrian's Wall near Housesteads meant there was no need to build ditch barriers

Right: Blanchland was named after the white canons who founded the abbey here

leading up to the 3 main carved alters. Angry Christians destroyed the temple, not so much disturbed by the morality of the religion as by its close parallels with Christian rites, such as its similar baptism and communion.

Continue on the B6318 and in 5 miles reach the car park for Housesteads.

HOUSESTEADS, Northumb

This was the ancient Roman fort of *Vercovicium*, set astride a ridge in wild frontier country with magnificent views to the north and south. What has been excavated within the fort walls show that here were granaries, a commandant's house, military headquarters, a hospital, latrines, baths and barracks — a miniature town in fact. Outside the walls a civilian settlement grew up, and here are the remains of long narrow shops and inns, which had sliding shutters to the street fronts. In one of these the bodies of a man and a woman of the 4th century were found. A dagger was

embedded in the man's ribs, which prompted the excavators to name the house Murder House. The site museum contains many finds from the excavation.

Continue on the B6138 and after 3 miles pass a Northumberland National Park Information Centre, next to the Twice Brewed Inn. In another 2½ miles, at a crossroads, turn left, SP 'Haltwhistle'. A mile farther descend into the South Tyne valley then turn right into Haltwhistle.

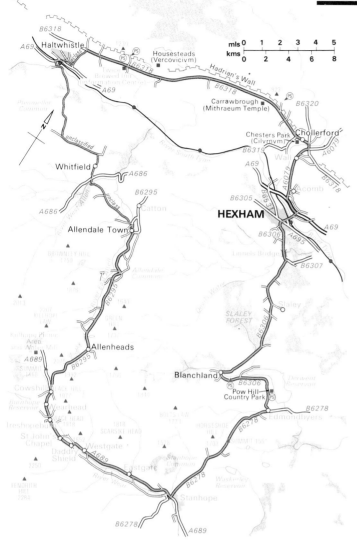

HALTWHISTLE, Northumb

This small industrial town lies between the junction of Haltwhistle Burn and the South Tyne, and is an excellent touring centre for Hadrian's Wall, which lies a little to the north. The towerless Holy Cross Church, hidden by trees and surrounded by houses, is considered a superb example of early English architecture.

Continue through the town and turn left, SP 'Carlisle', then turn right on to the A69. In ½ mile turn left on to the Plenmeller/Whitfield road. Cross the River Tyne and turn left. After 4 miles turn left and 2¼ miles farther turn right, then descend into West Allen Dale for Whitfield.

WHITFIELD, Northumb

In all Allendale there is no prettier village than Whitfield, set amid trees by the banks of the West Allen River. Whitfield has 2 churches, known as the 'Old' and the 'New'. The 'Old' is St John's, a Georgian building with Victorian alterations, which lies hidden off the main road; the 'New' is all Victorian, rather out of character in the dales, looking as though it has been transplanted from the gentler landscape of southern England.

Turn right on to the A686, SP 'Alston', then in ¼ mile turn left, SP 'Allendale'. Cross the West Allen River and in 3½ miles go forward to join the B6295. In ½ mile cross the East Allen River and ascend to Allendale Town.

ALLENDALE TOWN, Northumb

A sundial, set in a wall near the 14th-century church high up on the wooded banks of the River East Allen, records longditude and latitude, for Allendale claims to be the centre of Britain. The solid little town has a stone-built market place, and an attractive main street enhanced by trees and greens. The many boarding houses and hotels attract the same visitors every year, for this pleasant village is set in fine hill and dale country, and is superbly situated as a touring centre. New Year's Eve is a big occasion here. It is celebrated with a huge bonfire at midnight, and by a procession of costumed men parading the streets carrying tubs of blazing tar on their heads — a curious custom thought to have originated from a form of fire worship introduced by the Norsemen.

Turn right on to the the Allenheads/Cowshill road and follow East Allen Dale over the lofty and bleak Allendale Common to reach Allenheads.

ALLENHEADS, Northumb

At one time a seventh of all lead mined in the Kingdom once came from near Allenheads, although now the workings are all long grown over, in some areas producing a strange irregular landscape. The hamlet of Allenheads lies snugly in a pine-covered enclave surrounded by bare moorland criss-crossed by stone walls at the head of wide East Allendale.

Continue on the B6295 and in 1½ miles, at the summit (1,860ft), enter the county of Durham. Descend and in 1¾ miles join the A689 Durham/Stanhope road. Continue through Cowshill, Wearhead and St Johns Chapel then Daddry Shield, Westgate and Eastgate. At the Grey Bull PH at the edge of Stanhope turn left on to the B6278, SP 'Edmondbyers'. In ½ mile a steep climb leads to Stanhope Common and 2 miles farther bear right. Later turn left on to the B6306, SP 'Blanchland', and after 1 mile a side road (right) leads to Pow Hill Country Park.

POW HILL COUNTRY PARK, Durham

This delightful park is set in beautiful countryside in a sheltered valley above Derwent Reservoir. Waders and waterfowl can be seen here, which are best observed from a specially constructed hide beside the reservoir. Car parks, a picnic area and other amenities have been provided for the convenience of visitors and the protection of the wildlife.

Continue on the B6306 and in 3½ miles cross the River Derwent to re-enter Northumberland and continue to Blanchland.

BLANCHLAND, Northumb

Blanchland has a neat, orderly appearance, its grey-stone cottages arranged around an L-shaped, gravelled 'square'. The village occupies the site of a 12th-century abbey; the square was previously the abbey courtyard and the Lord Crewe Arms was part of the abbey's guesthouse; the monastery gateway is still one of the entrances to the village. Hidden deep in wild moorland, a story tells of how in 1327 Scottish raiders bent on sacking the abbey got lost in a mist, and decided to return home. The monks, hearing of this, were so joyous they rang the abbey bells in celebration. Unfortunately the Scots heard the bells too and, guided by their sound, returned.

Turn right, SP 'Hexham', then ascend. There are more views of the Derwent Reservoir to the right. After 2 miles keep left and continue past the edge of Shaley and cross the Devil's Water at the narrow Linnels Bridge (care needed) before the return to Hexham.

Remains of the bath house at the Roman fort of *Cilurnum*. It was a complex of rooms consisting of changing rooms and a series of hot and cold baths

THE NORTHERN LAKE DISTRICT

This is a district of beautiful mountains and lakes,
heathery slopes dotted with sheep and boulders between
valley woodland and the misty blueness of windswept crags.
Much of the countryside is owned or protected by the
National Trust, whose codes of conduct should be respected.

KESWICK, Cumbria

This touring centre is close to some
of Lakeland's finest scenery and
attracts thousands of visitors every
year. In Victorian times it was
beloved of poets and artists,
including such notables as
Wordsworth, Coleridge, Southey,
Ruskin, and Walpole. Many of their
works and personal possessions are
preserved in the fascinating Park
Museum, which also features an
impressive scale model of the Lake
District and a variety of exhibits
relating to the local area. Both
Coleridge and Southey lived in Greta
Park at different times, and there is a
memorial to John Ruskin close to the
town on the spectacular viewpoint
of Friar's Crag (NT). Moot Hall is a
handsome building that was
reconstructed in the early 19th
century. The superb 529ft viewpoint
of Castle Head (NT) is within easy
reach of Keswick.

*Before starting the main route it is
possible to take two rewarding
detours to interesting areas close to
the boundaries of Keswick. The first of
these can be taken to Crosthwaite by
driving through Keswick on the
A5271 'Cockermouth' road before
keeping forward on to the B5289 to
reach the village.*

CROSTHWAITE, Cumbria

Keswick's lovely 11th-century and
later parish church is sited here, and
is well worth a visit. Among its many
treasures are several fine
monuments, 21 consecration
crosses, and the churchyard grave of
poet and writer Robert Southey.

*For the second detour, continue
along the B5289 from Crosthwaite
for ¼ mile, bear left, then turn left to
join the A66. Again a further ¼ mile
turn left again on to an unclassified
road SP 'Portinscale' to enter
Portinscale village. Here turn right to
reach Lingholm Gardens.*

LINGHOLM GARDENS, Cumbria

The superb landscaped gardens of
Lingholm (open), the home of Lord
Rochdale, are laid out in a charming
situation on the wooded western
shores of Derwent Water. In spring
the ground is golden with the
famous Lakeland daffodils, and later
in the year the banks of
rhododendron bushes and azaleas
blaze with colour.

DERWENT WATER, Cumbria

Typical of everything that is beautiful
in the Lake District, this broad lake is
ringed by mountain peaks and
dotted with mysterious little tree-
clad islands. It measures 3 miles long
by 1¼ miles wide at its widest point,
and is best appreciated from the
lofty Friar's Crag Viewpoint (NT),
back along the route. At the foot of
the crag is the start of a nature trail
that runs for about 2 miles along the
shoreline of the lake.

*To start the main tour, leave Keswick
on the B5289 'Borrowdale' road and
pass the Friar's Crag Viewpoint (NT)
on the right. Drive beneath Castle
Head (NT) on the left and reach the
eastern shores of Derwent Water.
Steep wooded slopes rise to the left,
and farther on the road runs beneath
the cliffs of the Falcon Crag
Viewpoint. A detour can be taken
from the main route to Ashness
Bridge and Watendlath by reaching
Falcon Crag and then turning left on
to a winding unclassified road.*

ASHNESS BRIDGE, Cumbria

Thousands of visitors come here
every year to admire the unique and
enchanting combination of a single-
arched packhorse bridge with
beautiful falls on the little mountain
stream which it spans.

*Continue this detour by following the
unclassified road to Watendlath.*

Derwent Water is known as the
queen of the lakes, deriving
much of its beauty from the
many islands.

WATENDLATH, Cumbria

A small beck which rises close to this
delightful little hamlet (NT) threads its
way through a pretty valley and joins
Watendlath Tarn, which lies in the
shadow of 1,588ft Armboth Fell.

*On the main tour, drive forward on
the B5289. Continue, with excellent
views of the lake, and in 1 mile reach
the Lodore Swiss Hotel and the
impressive Lodore Cascade.*

LODORE CASCADE, Cumbria

Views of this spectacular waterfall,
which is situated at the southern
extremity of Derwent Water, can be
enjoyed from the carpark of the
Lodore Swiss Hotel.

*Drive through the short, green valley
of Borrowdale, keeping to the left
bank of the River Derwent, and in
1¼ miles pass Grange village on the
righthand side of the road.*

GRANGE, Cumbria

A double-arched bridge spans the
River Derwent in this lovely little
Borrowdale village. Superb views of
the dale can be enjoyed from the
summit of Grange Fell, which is
known as King's How (NT).

*Leave Grange and in ¼ mile pass a
track leading left to the Bowder Stone.*

BOWDER STONE, Cumbria

Although this remarkable 2,000-ton
boulder (NT) seems about to fall from
its precarious perch at any moment,
it is quite firm and makes a good
vantage point from which to survey
the surrounding countryside.

*Continue through Borrowdale to
Rosthwaite.*

The lush country
around Seatoller
suffers higher
than average rainfall.

ROSTHWAITE, Cumbria

As Borrowdale opens out on the
approach to this tiny village the
views widen into a spectacular
panorama of the mountains ahead.
Massive Castle Crag (NT) dominates
a narrow pass known as the Jaws of
Borrowdale, rising high above the
valley floor to a 900ft summit.

BORROWDALE, Cumbria

Much of Borrowdale, the beautiful
valley through which the last section
of tour has just passed, is owned or
protected by the National Trust. Its
impressive crags and fells offer a
challenge which draws climbers and
walkers from many parts of the
country, and its tiny unspoilt villages
are an essential part of the
tranquillity that underlies its scenic
grandeur. The southern end of the
dale is dominated by the summits of
2,560ft Glaramara and 2,984ft Great
End, and the north by high fells.

*Continue along the B5289 to reach
the village of Seatoller.*

SEATOLLER, Cumbria
During the 17th and 18th century this village was the centre of a busy mining industry. Seatoller is now known as a base from which walkers can ascend to the Sky Head Pass, in the south. Also south of the village is Seathwaite Farm (NT), one of England's wettest inhabited places.

A detour from the main route to Seathwaite Farm can be made by turning left in Seatoller on to an unclassified road and following a deep, steep-sided valley to the farm. On the main tour, continue along the B5289 and ascend Honister Pass.

HONISTER PASS, Cumbria
This part of the tour follows a steep, difficult road but offers some of the most spectacular scenery in the whole region. The summit of the pass is 1,176ft above sea level and affords distant eastern views of the craggy Helvellyn group, beyond the picturesque foreground of Borrowdale. Left towards Buttermere are the outstanding peaks of 2,479ft Red Pike and 2,644ft High Stile.

Descend between scree-covered slopes to the village of Buttermere.

BUTTERMERE, Cumbria
Well-situated between Crummock Water and the lake (NT) from which it derives its name, this pretty village stands in the heart of a spectacular landscape and is a popular base for walkers and climbers. Opposite the village curiously-named Sour Milk Ghyll tumbles down the flanks of lofty Red Pike. Scale Force, among the highest waterfalls in the Lake District, is nearby.

A detour from the main route to Newlands Hause and Moss Force can be made by driving to the outskirts of the village, turning right on to an unclassified road SP 'Keswick', and climbing steeply.

NEWLANDS HAUSE AND MOSS FORCE, Cumbria
Here the road climbs through the spectacular pass of Newlands Hause to a summit of 1,096ft, with an almost sheer drop plunging away into a deep valley on the left.

On the main tour, leave Buttermere village with the B5289 and follow the

Set amid mountains in one of Lakeland's most beautiful areas, Buttermere Lake is famous for the reflections that crowd its surface on calm days.

east shore of Crummock Water with views of the Loweswater Fell peaks on the far side of the lake. Leave the lakeside and after 2 miles meet a T-junction. Turn right SP 'Lorton, Cockermouth' and enter the broad expanse of Lorton Vale. Continue to the edge of Lorton and turn right on to an unclassified road SP 'Keswick'. Continue to High Lorton, turn left into the village, and at the end of the village turn right. Meet a T-junction and turn right again on to the B5292 and begin to ascend Whinlatter Pass.

WHINLATTER PASS, Cumbria
Drivers will find this one of the less taxing Lake District passes. Its gradients are reasonable and its bends are not quite as sharp as the others, but its 1,043ft summit affords views that are every bit as enjoyable as elsewhere.

THORNTHWAITE FOREST, Cumbria
Woodland walks planned by the Forestry Commission help the visitor to get the most out of this lovely area, the longest established national forest in the Lake District. Detailed information about all aspects of the forest is available from the Interpretative Centre near the summit of Whinlatter Pass.

Descend from the forest with fine views over Bassenthwaite Lake to the left. At the foot of the descent keep left into Braithwaite.

BRAITHWAITE, Cumbria
Climbers heading for the slopes and faces of 2,593ft Grisedale Pike generally start from this attractive village, which lies at the head of Coledale Valley.

Leave Braithwaite and take the 2nd turning left SP 'Cockermouth'. In ¼ mile turn left again on to the A66 and drive to the western shore of Bassenthwaite Lake.

BASSENTHWAITE LAKE, Cumbria
Opposite this wooded shore, towering above the peaceful waters of lovely Bassenthwaite Lake, are the stern slopes of 3,053ft Skiddaw.

After 2½ miles turn right on to the B5291 SP 'Castle Inn', then turn right again to follow the northern end of Bassenthwaite Lake. In 1 mile turn right SP 'Bothel', cross Ouse Bridge, and continue to Castle Inn. Meet a T-junction and turn right on to the A591. Take the 2nd turning left on to an unclassified road SP 'Bassenthwaite' and approach that village.

BASSENTHWAITE, Cumbria
Close to the lake in charming surroundings is the village church, which was restored in Victorian times and has a Norman chancel arch.

Do not enter the village on the main tour, but on its approach keep left (no SP) on to a narrow road and drive through pretty woodland. In 1½ miles meet a T-junction and turn left SP 'Caldbeck', then ascend a winding road to pass Over Water and smaller Chapelhouse Reservoir on the left. After 2½ miles cross open moors and meet a T-junction. Turn right, and in ¾ mile keep forward on to the B5299. In 1¼ miles cross a cattle grid, and in ¼ mile keep left to reach Caldbeck.

CALDBECK, Cumbria
In 1854 the local folk hero of nursery song fame, John Peel, was buried in Caldbeck churchyard. According to tradition he was ruined by his obsessive love of fox hunting.

Drive forward on to an unclassified road and proceed to Hesket Newmarket.

HESKET NEWMARKET, Cumbria
At one time this charming village on the northern flanks of Skiddaw was an important market town. Nowadays it rests in quiet retirement as yet another of the Lake District's picturesque communities.

Drive to the end of the village and bear right SP 'Mungrisdale'. Continue through agricultural country and in ½ mile bear right. In 1 mile turn left on to a winding road and continue to the Horse and Farrier (PH). Just beyond the PH bear right on to moorland and drive below the sheer rock face of 2,174ft Carrock Fell. Continue through Mungrisdale, pass below Souther Fell, then meet a T-junction with the A66 and turn right SP 'Keswick'; 2,847ft Saddleback rises to the right. Continue to the outskirts of Threlkeld; the main village lies just off the main road to the right.

THRELKELD, Cumbria
No less than 35 local huntsmen are commemorated by a monument in the local churchyard, and it seems likely that the fanatical John Peel would have made many friends here. The village itself stands at the head of St John's Vale, on the banks of a stream that threads its way along the valley floor. North is the unusually shaped peak of Saddleback.

Continue along the A66 and pass the junction with the B5322. In ½ mile turn left on to an unclassified road SP 'St John's in the Vale Church', and in 1 mile turn left again SP 'Stone Circle'. In ¼ mile turn left and ascend to the Castlerigg Stone Circle.

CASTLERIGG STONE CIRCLE, Cumbria
Situated in a superb mountain setting some 700ft above sea level, this prehistoric circle (AM, NT) measures over 100ft in diameter and is made up of 38 stones. An oblong space on the site contains another 10 stones.

Continue past the stone circle and descend to meet the A5271. Turn left and re-enter Keswick.

Castlerigg Stone Circle probably dates back to the bronze age.

MORECAMBE BAY AND THE LANCASHIRE MOORS

Between Morecambe Bay and the western edge of the Yorkshire Dales stretch the wild, remote moors of the Forest of Bowland, the haunt of grouse and hardy moorland sheep. North and west the steep fells drop down to one of the loveliest valleys in Lancashire, that of the River Lune, painted by Turner and extolled by Ruskin.

MORECAMBE, Lancs
Second in popularity only to Blackpool as a holiday resort for the north-west, Morecambe has excellent sands and a wealth of seaside entertainments, culminating in the famous 'illuminations' which take place every autumn. Its Marineland complex, billed as the first oceanarium ever built in Europe, boasts a vast swimming pool as well as a dolphinarium and fascinating aquaria displaying all types of marine life. The name Morecambe, as it applies to the town, is of very recent date. Until the railway era in the last century there was only a fishing village, Poulton-le-Sands, here. When the railway line was built, the new resort sprang up, engulfing not only Poulton but also the neighbouring villages of Bare and Torrisholme, and came to be known as Morecambe, which had formerly been simply the name of the bay.

Leave Morecambe on the A5105, SP 'The North and Hest Bank', and follow the seafront to Hest Bank.

HEST BANK, Lancs
From Hest Bank, there is a magnificent view of the bay to the hills of the Lake District. Morecambe Bay was, until the last century, the regular route to and from the Lake District. It was always a perilous journey, as there are shifting sands and 3 treacherous river estuaries to negotiate. Many people lost their lives, and the guides were even known to abandon travellers to their fate if they had not sufficient money to pay the charges. The 3-hour walk at low tide along the beach to Grange-over-Sands is still popular, but it must not be undertaken without an official guide, as the estuaries and shifting sands are a definite hazard.

Continue on the A5105 and in 1 mile turn left on to the A6, SP 'Kendal'. Pass through Bolton-le-Sands to reach Carnforth.

CARNFORTH, Lancs
To railway enthusiasts a visit to Steamtown, the railway museum that now occupies Carnforth's old locomotive sheds and marshalling yards, is a must. The *Flying Scotsman* is the most famous of the 30 steam engines from Great Britain, France and Germany that are maintained here. In the summer season, engines are in steam on Sundays (daily in July and August) and rides in vintage coaches are an added attraction.

On entering the town turn left (one-way), SP 'Warton', and shortly turn left again. Pass the railway museum (left) and continue to Warton.

WARTON, Lancs
The arms of the Washington family, ancestors of George Washington, once decorated the church tower and are now preserved inside the 15th-century church of this pleasant village. Although age has made it difficult to distinguish the symbols, it is said that this coat of arms was the inspiration of the stars and stripes motif of the United States flag. The last member of the English Washington family, Thomas, was the vicar of Warton until 1823.

Remain on the unclassified road for Yealand Conyers.

YEALAND CONYERS, Lancs
Tucked away in the far north of the county, Yealand Conyers is an outstandingly attractive village whose stone-built houses are fine examples of traditional architecture. An early Friends' Meeting House reminds the visitor that this is what the Quakers call '1652 country' because in that year the founder of the movement, George Fox (1624-91), first came into North Lancashire to preach.

From here a turning on the left leads to Leighton Hall.

LEIGHTON HALL, Lancs
Sheltering under Warton Crag, Leighton Hall (OACT) stands in extensive grounds. The Hall, built on the site of an earlier medieval one, dates from 1760-63, a Classical stone mansion with a charming Gothic façade that was added in the early 19th century. The home of the Gillow family for generations, their descendants still live here. In 1826 the estate was bought by Richard Gillow, a distinguished Lancaster furniture maker, and the house is a showplace for his artistry. There is a large collection of Birds of Prey with regular flying displays.

This lonely pass across the Forest of Bowland is called the Trough of Bowland

The main tour continues to Yealand Redmayne. Near the end of the village turn right, SP 'Kendal' on to a narrow byroad. In ¾ mile cross the M6 (no SP), then pass over the railway line, canal and M6 to reach the edge of Burton. Here turn left, then take the next turning right on to the Kirkby Lonsdale road. In 4¼ miles bear right and descend into Whittington. In the village turn left on to the B6254 and continue to Kirkby Lonsdale.

KIRKBY LONSDALE, Cumbria
Devil's Bridge (AM), 3-arched and possibly as old as the 13th century, spans the River Lune outside Kirkby. One of the finest ancient bridges in the country, it is now closed to traffic. Kirkby is a delightful small market town and it is an excellent centre for exploring the Lune valley. John Ruskin, the 19th-century writer and painter, was captivated by this, describing his favourite view as 'one of the loveliest scenes in England and therefore in the world'. Ruskin walks are signposted north of the churchyard.

Leave on the A65, SP 'Skipton', and re-enter Lancashire before reaching Cowan Bridge.

COWAN BRIDGE, Lancs
A few cottages mark the site of the Clergy Daughters' School to which Charlotte and Emily Brontë were sent as boarders from 1824-5. Later Charlotte was to describe the harsh treatment they suffered in her novel *Jane Eyre*, where the school appears under the name of Lowood.

In 1¾ miles enter North Yorkshire. In 2 miles a turning to the left may be taken to visit Ingleton.

INGLETON, N Yorks
Ingleton thrives as a centre for climbers, potholers and visitors to the Yorkshire Dales. The limestone hills of this region are honeycombed with caves, most of which are accessible only to experienced potholers, but the White Scar caves, with their stalactites, stalagmites, underground river and lake, are a noted tourist attraction. Above Ingleton loom the heights of Whernside (2,419ft) and Ingleborough (2,373ft). With Penyghent, these peaks are the most formidable in the Dales, and a walk taking in all 3 is a favourite feat of endurance for fell walkers. Even more gruelling are the 3-peaks races, one for runners and one for cyclists.

Continue on the A65 and after 4 miles pass the turning for Clapham.

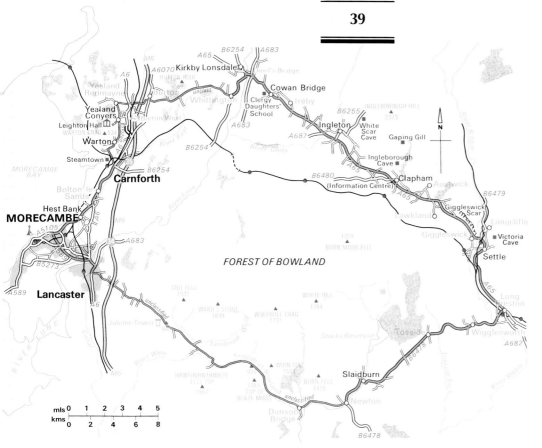

FOREST OF BOWLAND, Lancs

This wild region of grouse moor and high fells, dissected by deep, narrow valleys, was one of the ancient royal forests of Saxon England. There are no towns and few villages in the Forest, and no roads cross it, except for the lonely moorland road from Newton through the pass known as the Trough of Bowland to Lancaster. Parts of the Forest have now been designated an Area of Outstanding Natural Beauty and are therefore accessible, but much of the area remains a wilderness.

Continue on the unclassified road towards Lancaster. On entering the suburbs follow SP for city centre.

LANCASTER, Lancs

Lancaster, county town of the shire, was throughout the 18th century England's chief port for trade with America. St George's Quay, the elegant Customs House designed by Robert Gillow, whose family were famous furniture makers, and the many Georgian houses around the centre, are eloquent reminders of this prosperous era. The massive keep of the castle, 78ft high with walls 10ft thick, dates from the Norman era, when virtually the whole of Lancashire was given to Roger de Poitou by William the Conqueror. The castle was enlarged by King John and its magnificent gateway was built by John of Gaunt, 1st Duke of Lancaster, in the 14th century. The castle also served, and still does, as the county gaol. Among many distinguished prisoners was the Quaker leader George Fox, who was incarcerated in appalling conditions in the 17th century. Earlier in the same century, in 1612, the famous trial of the Lancashire Witches was held in Lancaster, and the iron rings by which they were chained can still be seen in the Well Tower. The City Museum in the Market Square is also the Museum of the Royal Lancashire Regiment.

Leave on the A589 for the return to Morecambe.

Leighton Hall's façade, built of a white local limestone, was added in 1810

CLAPHAM, N Yorks

Stone-built cottages in trim little gardens straggling along the banks of a stream characterise this delightful Yorkshire village where a National Information Centre for the Yorkshire Dales is situated, and where the monthly *Dalesman* magazine is published. Like Ingleton, this is a noted potholing centre. To the north of the village is Ingleborough Cave (access by foot only). The famous Gaping Gill pothole, 378ft deep with a central chamber vast enough to hold a small cathedral, lies not far away.

Remain on the A65 for Settle.

SETTLE, N Yorks

Just outside Settle rises one of the most impressive natural features of the region, the massive rock wall of Giggleswick Scar. Settle itself is one of the most delightful towns in Ribblesdale, with picturesque narrow streets and Georgian houses, sometimes grouped around small courtyards. Castleberg Crag, 300ft high, dominates the town centre, and from the summit the visitor can enjoy panoramic views of the town and the surrounding dales. In 1838 a chance discovery of the feature now known as Victoria Cave led to the retrieval of many fascinating prehistoric remains, including the bones of animals long extinct in the British Isles.

Leave on the A65 Skipton road and follow Ribblesdale to Long Preston. Here turn right on to the B6478, SP 'Slaidburn'. Beyond Wigglesworth gradually climb through moorland countryside to Tosside. Re-enter Lancashire and later descend to reach Slaidburn.

SLAIDBURN, Lancs

Although only a village, Slaidburn was for centuries the administrative 'capital' of the Forest of Bowland, and boasted the only grammar school for miles around. The Forest 'court' next to the inn was in use until the outbreak of World War I. The inn itself bears the unique name of Hark to Bounty. The story goes that Bounty was a foxhound belonging to a local vicar and that whenever his master and other hunting friends were in the inn, Bounty's barking was easily distinguishable above the hullabaloo of the whole pack.

At the war memorial keep left, then turn left, SP 'Trough of Bowland'. At Newton continue forward to reach Dunsop Bridge. After crossing the river bridge turn right and later ascend the Trough of Bowland.

Displays of heraldic shields and coats of arms of all sovereigns since Richard 1 adorn the Shire Hall in Lancaster Castle

MORPETH, Northumb

Quiet prosperity came to Morpeth in the early 18th century as it was the last market in Northumberland on the cattle route down to the south. Although the railway age subsequently made such markets largely redundant, Morpeth has remained a busy country town. In the old market place there stands a 17th-century tower whose curfew bell is rung at 8 o'clock every evening. The town hall, an elegant structure dating from 1718, was designed by the architect Vanbrugh. The imposing bridge was built at a later date, 1831, across the River Wansbeck which intersects the town. It leads to the parish church, set well away from the town centre on high ground. The church has a refreshingly plain 14th-century interior and in the churchyard is a little watch tower, built in 1831 to help restrict the practice of body-snatching. Behind the church lie impressive earthworks of the castle which was built after the Conquest but little masonry is left of the noble fortress which looked over the river and town. Around Morpeth the banks of the river are pleasantly wooded, and in the town itself a park runs along part of it. Every year Northumberland miners mix pleasure and politics at the gala held in the park.

Leave on the A192, SP 'Alnwick'. In 1½ miles, at the roundabout, join the A1, then in ¼ mile branch left on to the A697, SP 'Coldstream'. Pass through Longhorsley and in 2¾ miles turn left on to the B6344, SP 'Rothbury', to enter the Coquet valley. In 1½ miles a short detour to the left leads to Brinkburn Priory.

BRINKBURN PRIORY, Northumb

Within a loop of the River Coquet in charmingly wooded parkland stands a possible rival in grandeur to the abbeys of Fountains and Tintern. Although Brinkburn (AM) is a 12th-century church, it has all the hallmarks of a great cathedral. It was a roofless ruin by 1858, but the architect Thomas Dobson restored it superbly in that year.

Continue along the B6344 and in 3½ miles pass the fine hillside grounds of the Cragside Estate on the right.

CRAGSIDE ESTATE, Northumb

The 1st Lord Armstrong commissioned architect Norman Shaw in 1863 to design this delightfully romantic house. However, the real attraction to Cragside (NT) is the gardens. The house is built high above the River Coquet on a plateau where rock gardens, artificial lakes and masses of rhododendrons and azaleas create an enchanting landscape. The house itself claims its place in history as being one of the first houses in the world to be powered by electricity.

NORTHUMBERLAND'S QUIET LOWLANDS

'Northumberland may claim to the least spoiled, least known, county of England' and this proves true as the tour travels through the remote countryside between the Cheviots and Hadrian's Wall, by way of peaceful valleys and stone-built villages.

Shortly join the B6341 to enter Rothbury.

ROTHBURY, Northumb

Hill and river country surrounds the little town of Rothbury, whose name means a clearing in the forest. It is typical of the Border towns; solid, stone-built houses lining, in this case, a steep wide street where the verges are planted with trees. This was a lawless town, and at the time of the Reformation thieving by the inhabitants of Rothbury was such an art that 'they could twist a cow's horn or mark a horse so that its owner would not know it'.

Keep forward through the town on the B6341, SP 'Otterburn', to Thropton.

THROPTON, Northumb

Built on either side of the River Coquet, Thropton lies in the stunning countryside of Simonside. This pretty but straggling village is dominated by Simonside itself, the 1409ft-high peak giving its name to the whole range of sandstone hills, which, it is said, can be seen from every corner of Northumberland. Here the heather-clad hills contrast strongly with the gentle arable land of the lower reaches of Coquetdale, especially in August when the hills are purple with the flowering heather and the lower fields are a carpet of golden corn.

Continue on the B6341 for 2¼ miles then turn right, SP 'Harbottle'. In 3 miles descend and cross the River Coquet, then turn left for Holystone.

7 million trees were planted on the Cragside Estate in the 19th century, which helped transform it from a barren hillside into a magnificent garden

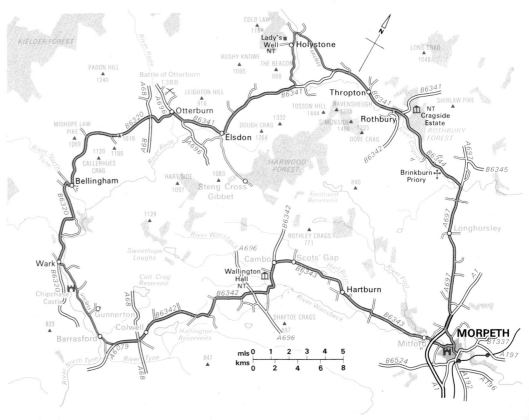

HOLYSTONE, Northumb

In the upper reaches of Coquetdale is the pleasing village of Holystone. Set within a circular enclosure surrounded by trees is the Lady's Well (NT), closely connected with St Ninian and St Paulinus. Paulinus is said to have come here to baptise the heathen Northumbrians and legend has it that on one Easter Day he baptised 3,000 souls. His statue stands in the centre of the well. Today the village has the holy water on tap, for the well supplies Holystone with its drinking water. Little remains of the priory that was built here for Augustinian canonesses, but the village, with its inn, church, and good stone houses, is one of the most attractive in Coquetdale.

Turn left at the edge of Holystone and continue along the valley, and in 2½ miles turn right to rejoin the B6341. Proceed through open and wilder countryside to reach Elsdon.

ELSDON, Northumb

Set among the rolling hills of Redesdale, Elsdon has a large triangular green with a few 18th-century houses gathered about it. By the church is a rare 14th-century fortified rectory, a reminder of more violent days, as is the Norman castle, c1080, nearby. When the chuch was restored 100 skeletons were found, and they are thought to be those of men who died at the Battle of Otterburn in 1388. Up above the village, on Steng Cross, are the remains of a gibbet. Here the body of one William Winter was hung after his execution in Newcastle for the murder of an old woman of Elsdon in 1791. In the hills hereabouts are many remnants and remains of prehistoric peoples — cairns, earthworks and hut circles.

Bear right through the village and in 2½ miles turn right on to the A696 for Otterburn.

OTTERBURN, Northumb

At the east end of Otterburn is Otterburn Tower — a largely Victorian building incorporating the remains of an old pele tower which withstood an assault by the Scottish army on its way to the Battle of Otterburn. This was fought 1½ miles north-west of the village in 1388 and was one of the many encounters between Scottish and English armies over this disputed territory. Today Otterburn is known for the textile mill by the bridge, where the famous Otterburn tweeds are made.

Turn left on to the B6320, SP 'Bellingham', and shortly cross River Rede. In 1½ miles cross the main road and ascend on to the moors, reaching 1,019ft before the long descent into the North Tyne valley and Bellingham.

BELLINGHAM, Northumb

Bellingham is a small market town, important in its own way as the capital of the North Tyne countryside and Redesdale. Its position also makes it an excellent base from which to explore this beautiful countryside. The church here has an unusual early stone roof. The story goes that the Scots, raiding from over the border, burnt the place so often it was decided a permanent, fireproof roof would be more economical in the long run. The inhabitants of this border country appear to have spent most of their time raiding the herds of their enemies over the border. Today, the farmers, many of them descendants of these lawless men, meet at Bellingham in autumn in a far more friendly fashion for the lamb sales, and again in September for the agricultural show.

Continue on the B6320, SP 'Hexham', and in ¼ mile turn left to cross the North Tyne River. In 5¼ miles enter Wark.

The kitchen at Wallington Hall is kept as if in daily use as it would have been at the turn of the century

WARK, Northumb

Now a few pleasant streets and a quadrangle of houses around a green, Wark was in medieval times the capital of North Tynedale; at the time this was a part of Scotland. It stands on a lovely stretch of the North Tyne River, near both Wark Forest and the Border Forest Park.

Turn left, SP 'Barrasford', recross the North Tyne and turn right. In 1½ miles pass (right) the 14th-century Chipchase Castle. Pass through Barrasford and in ½ mile turn left, SP 'Colwell'. In ¾ mile turn left again on to the A6079, SP 'Rothbury'. In 1½ miles bear left over the crossroads on to the B6342. Shortly pass the edge of Colwell. In 7½ miles turn right then immediately left across the A696. In 2 miles cross the River Wansbeck and pass through the grounds of Wallington Hall.

Tweed, being woven here at Otterburn Mill, is traditionally made with 2 or more colours of the same quality yarn

WALLINGTON HALL, Northumb

The exterior of Wallington Hall (NT) has hardly altered since Sir William Blackett built it in 1688. The house, which he demolished to make way for his building belonged to Sir John Fenwick, who was executed for treason by William III. However, Fenwick's famous house, which the king kept, brought him revenge when it stumbled on a mole hill and threw the sovereign, who consequently died. The modest façade of the Hall hides a sumptuous interior remodelled in the mid-18th century, when, among other things, the wonderful plaster decoration was added by Italian craftsmen. A century later, the architect John Dobson was employed to roof over the central courtyard to create the magnificent central hall. The gardens can be divided into 3 areas: the peaceful lawns and flowerbeds around the house, woodland and lakes, and an L-shaped walled garden and conservatory.

In 1 mile at Cambo turn right on to the B6343, SP 'Morpeth', and continue past Scots' Cap to Hartburn.

HARTBURN, Northumb

Hartburn lies in a superb position with steep, dramatic waterfalls on either side that drop down to the Hart Burn. In the village is a curious building known as Dr Sharpe's Tower. It is a castellated tower that was built to house the village schoolmaster on an upper floor reached by an exterior staircase, with a schoolroom below and stables for the village hearse. Next to it is the schoolhouse of 1844. There is also an elegant Georgian vicarage which has a 13th-century pele tower incorporated in to it. The church has a squat tower dating from the late 12th-century, and carved on a doorpost are 2 daggers and a Maltese cross.

Continue along the B6343 following the Wansbeck valley for the return via Mitford to Morpeth.

NORTH YORKSHIRE'S MOORS AND DALES

Savage, desolate moorland, lush farmland and deep peaceful dales blend into an area of unique contrasts and beauty where picturesque grey-stone villages are centres for magnificent walks by streams and waterfalls.

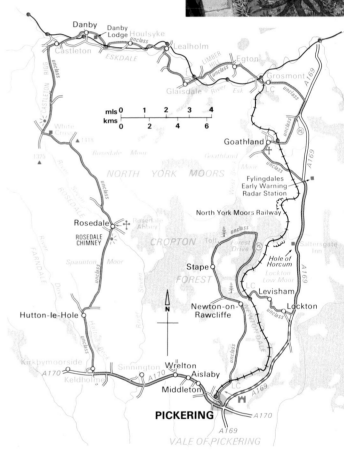

Part of the 15th-century wall paintings in Pickering's church

NB: The early part of this tour uses a Forestry Commission Forest Drive (toll). During periods of extremely dry weather the road may be closed owing to the high fire risk. If wishing to avoid this portion, leave Pickering on the A169, SP 'Whitby', and pick up the tour at the Saltersgate Inn (11 miles shorter).

PICKERING, N Yorks

This ancient market town, situated amidst beautiful countryside, is known as the Gateway to the Moors. The market place façades are mainly Georgian or Victorian, but older structures are often concealed behind them. The 12th century is evoked in the robust towers and ruined remains of Pickering Castle (AM), where Richard II was confined after his abdication. The Church of St Peter and St Paul, which stands above the main street, has retained fragments of a similar date. Its main attraction is the fine 15th-century wall paintings, depicting Bible stories with the figures in daily costumes of over 500 years ago. The Beck Isle Museum of Rural Life is housed in a fine Georgian house, formerly the home of William Marshall, a noted agriculturalist, and displays folk exhibits of local interest. Pickering is also the terminus of the North Yorkshire Moors Railway.

NORTH YORKSHIRE MOORS RAILWAY, N Yorks

The North Yorkshire Moors Railway operates over 18 miles of track between Pickering and Grosmont, taking in some superb panoramic views along the way. The private company which runs the railway was founded in 1967, and became a trust in 1972. Steam and diesel locomotives pull the trains, and at Grosmont there is a loco shed, viewing gallery, gift shop and catering facilities. At Pickering station there is an excellent bookshop and also a National Park information and audio-visual centre.

From the North Yorkshire Moors railway station at Pickering follow the Newton-on-Rawcliffe road to Newton-on-Rawcliffe.

NEWTON-ON-RAWCLIFFE, N Yorks

Newton-on-Rawcliffe stands close to the woodlands of Newton Dale on high ground overlooking a stupendous panorama of the Newton Dale canyon — a beautiful moorland glen bordered in places by crags and steep cliffs. The White Swan Inn in the village stands on one of the oldest hostelry sites in the district.

Continue to Stape.

STAPE, N Yorks

The hamlet of Stape was at one time the centre of besom-making; a besom being a kind of broom made of a bundle of supple twigs tied to a handle. This little community is also the home of the Stape Silver Band — many of these northern villages boast their own bands, which are the objects of much fierce competition and pride. Closeby a footpath, near Mauley Cross, leads to Needle Point, where well-dressing ceremonies — the garlanding of wells with flowers once connected with pagan worship — and rural fairs used to be held.

Continue on the Stape road and in 1 mile descend (1 in 6). In 1¾ miles keep left then in ½ mile bear right to enter Cropton Forest and join the Newton Dale Forest Drive (toll). In 3 miles pass a picnic area and turn right. After another 2¼ miles leave the Forest Drive and continue to Levisham.

LEVISHAM, N Yorks

Levisham, high on open moorland, has a green and a Hall and a church with a Saxon chancel arch. This church, St Mary's, stands forlorn at the bottom of a glen beside Levisham Beck, with an old watermill for company. Because the descent from the village to the church is so steep, a new church, St John the Baptist, was built in the village in 1884. Levisham has a typical North Riding main street, with a wide lawn to the left and right, although the view at one end is obscured by a cottage. At the head of Levisham Beck is a great natural amphitheatre called the Hole of Horcum.

Continue to Lockton.

The Hole of Horcum, a great natural hollow, is the curious product of erosion during the Ice Age

LOCKTON, N Yorks

Lockton, across the dale from Levisham, is another moorland village with a spectacular view. The 13th-century Church of St Andrew and St Giles has been greatly modified over the years and has a Jacobean pulpit, reading desk and communion table. There is no village public house, but over Lockton Low Moor to the north, past the gorge known as the Hole of Horcum, is the picturesque Saltersgate Inn. Smugglers, running silk and gin inland from Robin Hood's Bay, are said to have used the inn as a refuge.

At Lockton keep left, SP 'Whitby', then in ½ mile turn left on to the A169. Climb on to Lockton Low Moor and later pass the Hole of Horcum before descending to the Saltersgate Inn. After 2¾ miles (right) there are views of the Fylingdales Radar Station.

At Danby go over the staggered crossroads and continue to Castleton. Follow SP 'Rosedale' and in ½ mile bear left to climb along the 1,000ft-high Castleton Rigg. After 4 miles turn left (still SP 'Rosedale'). Cross the plateau of Rosedale Moor and after another 4 miles descend into Rosedale.

ROSEDALE, N Yorks
In the churchyard, near the attractive green of this main village in the dale of the same name, are a few stones which represent the remains of a 12th-century Cistercian abbey. South of the village, as the dale narrows, is the Rosedale Chimney, which is the remnant of an iron-ore working. What used to be the mineral railway at the head of the dale is now a walking trail with superb views of the countryside.

At the end of the village turn right and ascend Rosedale Chimney Bank (1 in 3). Beyond the summit cross Spaunton Moor and after 3 miles, at the T-junction, turn right for Hutton-le-Hole.

HUTTON-LE-HOLE, N Yorks
This attractive village was built randomly around wide greens dissected by 2 becks and various picturesque bridges, at the foot of a limestone escarpment. Grey-stone houses with red pantiled roofs complete the showplace-effect. Ryedale Folk Museum is housed here in an ancient cruck-type (timbered) building, once the home of prosperous Quakers. Craftsmen's tools, farm implements, an ancient dairy, Roman pottery and a reconstructed Elizabethan glass furnace are among the exhibits. The oldest building in the village, dating from 1695, belonged to John Richardson, who was a friend of William Penn the English Quaker who founded Pennsylvania. It is called, appropriately, Quaker Cottage.

Leave on the Kirkbymoorside road. In 2¾ miles, at the T-junction, turn left on to the A170, SP 'Scarborough', and continue to Wrelton.

WRELTON, N Yorks
The junction of the westward road from Pickering and the Roman Road is marked by the old village of Wrelton. The crossing is distinguished by a tiny green, set amidst sturdy Georgian farms and houses, and a substantial restored cruck building of 1665. An ancient alehouse, the Buck Inn, contains curios such as an old witness dock from Pickering magistrates' court. Back in 1779, the inn had its own brewhouse and served 'Old Tom' ale to passing stagecoach travellers.

Continue on the A170 to Aislaby.

AISLABY, N Yorks
One of the smallest villages on the main road, Aislaby was built by the Vikings. Among its most attractive buildings is the Georgian Hall (not open), with its lead statuettes and regal summer house which presides over a group of solid farmhouses.

Continue to Middleton.

MIDDLETON, N Yorks
A string of pleasant buildings lining the road make up the village of Middleton, with the early Georgian Middleton Hall (not open) just visible through the trees. Opposite the New Inn is the Church of St Andrew. The north aisle contains fragments of 3 fine Anglo-Danish crosses dating from the 10th century and the sculpted decorations include a dragon and an armed warrior.

Remain on the A170 for the return to Pickering.

FYLINGDALES EARLY WARNING RADAR STATION, N Yorks
A futuristic sight on the desolate Fylingdale Moor is the white domes of the Radar Station. This defence installation is a gaunt reminder of the consequences of technological development in an area which was previously uninhabited. The gruelling Lyke Wake Walk across the North Yorks Moors passes through Fylingdales Moor.

Turn left, SP 'Goathland', and cross Goathland Moor before descending to Goathland. Bear right to enter the village.

GOATHLAND, N Yorks
The grey-stone buildings of this delightful moorland village are set around a large village green where a group of sword dancers, the Plough Stotts, regularly perform traditional dances. Sheep graze between the houses scattered on the perimeter of the village. This is a marvellous centre for walking, and the local streams tumble over rocks forming spectacular waterfalls, some of which are named; for example: Mallyan Spout, Thomason Foss, Nelly Ayre Foss and Water Ark.

Follow SP 'Whitby' and cross the railway, then ascend. In 2 miles turn left on to the A169, then ¼ mile farther turn left again, SP 'Grosmont'. Cross Sleights Moor and later descend into Grosmont.

Continue over the level-crossing and the River Esk, then ascend to Egton. In the village bear right and at Wheatsheaf Inn turn left, SP 'Glaisdale'. In 1¾ miles descend (1 in 3), then cross the Esk and ascend through Glaisdale. Follow the Castleton road and in 1 mile bear right. In another ¾ mile turn right for Lealholm. Recross the Esk, then turn left, SP 'Danby'. Continue through Esk Dale and pass Danby Lodge before reaching Danby.

DANBY, N Yorks
Close to this village in the Esk valley is Danby Lodge, a former shooting lodge and now a visitor centre for the North Yorks Moors National Park. The village is also called Dale End, as it lies at the head of Danby Dale, which runs south into the moors. One mile south-east of the village is ruined 14th-century Danby Castle. The ruins have had a farmhouse added to them and are used as farm buildings. This was the home of the Latimers, and of their successors the Nevilles. Close to the castle is Duck Bridge, a packhorse bridge over the River Esk which dates from about 1386. All around are obscure circles and stones which are remnants of the Bronze and Iron Ages.

RICHMOND, N Yorks

Dramatically situated overlooking the River Swale, this attractive and historic town makes an excellent base from which to explore the lovely countryside of Swaledale. The dominant feature of the town is its massive Norman castle (AM), one of the earliest in Britain with 11th-century curtain walls round a splendid keep. In the shadow of its mighty presence are streets of lovely old buildings, all illustrative of important phases in Richmond's past. The cobbled Market Place is one of the largest in the country and is approached along little alleyways known as wynds. Greyfriars Tower is the remnant of an abbey that was founded here many centuries ago, and facing the Market Place is one of the strangest churches in England. Dedicated to the Holy Trinity, its main body and medieval tower are divided from each other by shops and offices actually built into its main structure. Other buildings in this area include several handsome Georgian and Victorian houses. The most outstanding Georgian building in the town is the Theatre Royal (open) of 1788, beautifully restored and the oldest theatre in the country to have survived in its original condition. A Green Howards' Museum displays the colourful and fascinating history of that regiment. Many fine walks can be enjoyed in and around Richmond, but one of the closest and best is along the banks of the Swale to spacious parklands at Lowenthwaite Bridge.

Leave Richmond on the A6108 SP 'Scotch Corner' at roundabout take 1st exit B6274 for Gilling West. Ascend to high ground, turn left on to the A66 'Brough' road, and continue along a pleasant road to Greta Bridge, on the Rivers Greta and Tees, with views across moors and valleys.

GRETA BRIDGE, Durham

Among the many artists and writers who have recognized and recorded the beauty of this charming little hamlet are Dickens, Scott, and Turner. Just to the north is the junction of the Greta with the Tees, and south-west of Greta Bridge the river runs through the lovely woodland of Brignall Banks. Features of the hamlet itself include a picturesque river bridge dating from the 18th century, and the Morrit Arms public house, whose site was once occupied by a Roman fort.

Continue along the A66 'Brough' road for ¼ mile and turn right on to an unclassified road SP 'Barnard Castle'. In 1¼ miles are views ahead of Egglestone Abbey.

EGGLESTONE ABBEY, Durham

The waters of the River Tees add an extra dimension to the picturesque quality of these lovely remains (AM).

Turn right and cross the River Tees to reach the Bowes Museum.

In the northern part of the Yorkshire Dales national park are the great ice-scoured valleys of Wharfedale and Swaledale, carved out to their present size by huge glaciers that flowed across the Pennines over a million years ago. On the moors above are greystone villages and steep, sheep-cropped slopes.

BOWES MUSEUM, Durham

Built in the style of a French château, the building that houses this museum is an architectural surprise to eyes that have come to expect the solid little stone houses of the area. Inside is one of the finest art collections in Britain, featuring fine European paintings, furniture, porcelain, tapestries, jewellery, and dolls.

Continue to Barnard Castle.

BARNARD CASTLE, Durham

Ancient houses and several inns line the main street of this enchanting town, which has grown up round the walls of its ruined medieval castle (AM) and is a busy market centre for its area.

Leave Barnard Castle with the A67 SP 'Brough, Bowes', re-cross the River Tees, and turn left on to the B6277 SP 'Scotch Corner'. Drive through woodland to meet the A66, turn right, and in ¼ mile turn left on to an unclassified road SP 'Reeth'. A short detour can be made from the main route to Bowes Castle by continuing along the A66.

Below the huge bulk of Richmond's 11th-century castle are picturesque streets displaying an attractive mixture of architectural styles. The abundance of Georgian design is particularly noticeable.

BOWES CASTLE, Durham

Close to the ruined keep of this Norman castle (AM) are the military remains of the Roman fort of *Lavatrae* (AM), which preceded it.

On the main tour, continue along an unclassified moorland road, with occasional steep hills (1 in 4), and drive through the pines of Stang Forest before climbing to a road summit of 1,677ft. Breathtaking views extend into lonely Arkengarthdale, in the vast and very beautiful Yorkshire Dales National Park.

YORKSHIRE DALES NATIONAL PARK

The boundaries of this national park encompass nearly 700 square miles of high dells scored by literally dozens of lovely river valleys that have collectively come to be known as the Yorkshire Dales. Many great dales exist in the region, but Wharfedale and Airedale are probably the most famous. The

desolate rocky scenery in the high part of the first mentioned gradually softens towards its lower reaches, and Airedale opens out into spectacular limestone scenery as it drops towards the village of Malham. In the south are the Three Peaks, well known for their dangerous potholes, while the length of the park is threaded by the Pennine Way long-distance footpath. Movement and sound is brought to the region by delightful waterfalls and lakes fed by rapid streams that rise in the rocky countryside of the high fells. This is one of the many interesting dales tours.

ARKENGARTHDALE, N Yorks

Lead mining was carried on in this lovely valley from the 13th to 19th centuries, and traces can be seen today. The dale itself is a lovely valley that follows the course of the Arkle Beck to impressive Swaledale in the south-east.

Cross Arkle Beck and drive along Arkengarthdale, passing through Langthwaite to reach Reeth.

REETH, N Yorks

During the 19th century this one-time market town became a busy centre of the lead-mining industry of nearby Arkengarthdale. Nowadays it is a peaceful village charmingly grouped round its large green, within easy reach of some of the wildest country in the national park.

In Reeth turn left on to the B6270 'Richmond' road. Continue through pleasant countryside to Grinton.

GRINTON, N Yorks

Grinton Church is a splendid building that has come to be known as the Cathedral of the Dales. It was founded in Norman times and contains an ancient font that is probably its original. Other features include beautiful screenwork and a Jacobean pulpit.

Gradually descend along Swaledale, between moorland heights that rise steeply to over 1,400ft from the river.

SWALEDALE, N Yorks

Among the many relics of 18th- and 19th-century lead mining that still litter this wild and deep valley are remains of some of the 20 smelt mills that were used to process the ore. The valley itself is a deep cleft that runs west from Richmond, and is connected to Wensleydale via the bleak Buttertubs Pass.

Enter woodland and meet the A6108: turn right and follow SP 'Leyburn' to reach Downholme.

DOWNHOLME, N Yorks

This tiny village stands high above the River Swale and has an attractive church that features Norman workmanship.

Proceed along a winding moorland road, passing through Bellerby to reach Leyburn.

Arkengarthdale is one of Yorkshire's more secluded dales

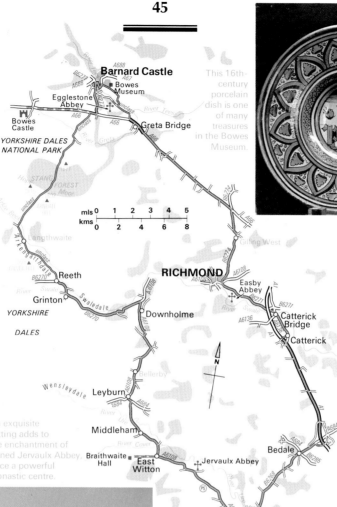

This 16th-century porcelain dish is one of many treasures in the Bowes Museum.

LEYBURN, N Yorks

The sloping market place in this old town is an appropriate example of the switchback landscape of the local countryside. Its Wensleydale position, above the River Ure, makes it an ideal touring base. Within easy walking distance of the town centre is a 2-mile limestone scar known as The Shawl, which affords excellent views into Wensleydale.

An exquisite setting adds to the enchantment of ruined Jervaulx Abbey, once a powerful monastic centre.

WENSLEYDALE, N Yorks

Dairy herds from the many farms scattered along the length of this fertile valley convert the freshness of its lush pastures into rich milk from which the distinctive Wensleydale cheese is made. The villages of the dale are generally small and without exception charming. Here and there its pastoral solitude is emphasized by the sound of falling water.

To leave Leyburn follow SP 'Middleham' to the end of the town and turn right on to the A6108. Descend and cross the River Ure via an unusual bridge to reach the village of Middleham.

MIDDLEHAM, N Yorks

Once the chief town of Wensleydale, this scenic village is now an important horse breeding and training centre and a good touring base. Its impressive ruined castle (AM) was the seat of the powerful Neville family, who controlled much of the area from the massive keep that still stands at its full height behind well-preserved 13th-century curtain walls. Close by is the curious Swine Cross.

Continue along the A6108 'Masham' road, with moorland to the right and gentle riverside pastures to the left. Continue to East Witton.

EAST WITTON, N Yorks

Most of the houses in this compact village are contained in two main rows facing two 19th-century churches and an attractive 17th-century bridge.

A detour can be made from the main route to Braithwaite Hall by turning right in East Witton and driving in partly-wooded country for 2 miles.

BRAITHWAITE HALL, N Yorks

Now in use as a farm, this fine 17th-century house (NT) stands in attractive pastoral countryside and is open by appointment. Near by a large hillfort occupies a 2½-acre site.

On the main tour, continue along the A6108 to reach Jervaulx Abbey.

JERVAULX ABBEY, N Yorks

Cistercian monks chose this beautiful riverside site as a fitting setting for their abbey in the 12th century. Although it was destroyed in the 15th century, enough remains to show today's visitors the exquisite proportions of their achievement. Particularly notable are the remains of the monks' dormitory, which features a hall and beautiful lancet windows of the period.

Continue along the A6108 and pass the Ellington Firth Picnic Site before entering Masham.

MASHAM, N Yorks

Masham's former importance as a market town can be judged from the huge square which is dominated by a Market Cross. In the churchyard of St Mary's are important remains of a Saxon cross, and the mainly-Norman church carries a beautiful 15th-century spire.

Leave Masham on the A6108 'Ripon' road. Cross the river, then immediately turn left on to the unclassified 'Bedale' road. Follow the river and in 1 mile turn right, then continue for ¾ mile and turn left on to the B6268. Continue to Bedale.

BEDALE, N Yorks

This mainly Georgian town features an old stepped market cross in the main street, and an unusual church whose first floor is reached by a stair guarded by a portcullis. These elaborate precautions were taken against the very real possibility of Scottish raids. Opposite the church is Georgian Bedale Hall (open), a fine house with a museum and a complete ballroom wing.

Continue along the A684 'Northallerton' road and later turn right, following SP 'Scotch Corner' to join the A1. Continue on a fast section of dual carriageway on the Great North Road. After 5 miles bear left, join the A6136 to reach Catterick.

CATTERICK, N Yorks

Known mainly for the military training area on its borders, this delightful little grey-stone village has a good church of c1500. Inside the church are two 15th-century brasses.

Drive through Catterick to Catterick Bridge, on the Swale.

CATTERICK BRIDGE, N Yorks

Most people come here to watch horse racing on the famous local course, but the lovely little local bridge that spans the Swale dates from 1422 and is worth attention. The local scenery is superb.

Turn right and cross the River Swale, then turn left SP 'Richmond' and meet the B6271. On the left are the river and Easby Abbey.

EASBY ABBEY, N Yorks

Picturesque ruins of an abbey founded in 1155 grace the beautiful surroundings of this Swaleside site. The remains (AM) are considerable.

Continue along the B6271 for the return to Richmond.

RIPON, N Yorks
Popularly known as the Gateway to the Dales, this attractive city stands at the meeting of the Rivers Ure, Skell, and Laver and boasts a small but impressive cathedral. The main features of this lovely 12th-century building include a Saxon crypt that may be the earliest Christian survival in England, a fine early-English west front, and a beautiful 15th-century screen. Excellent examples of local woodcarving are the finely worked misericords and curious Elephant and Castle bench. Every night Ripon's market square is the scene of a 1,000-year-old custom, when the town Hornblower or Wakeman strides out in his tricorn hat and sounds his ancient horn at each corner of a huge 18th-century obelisk. Years ago this sound indicated that the Wakeman had begun his night watch over the town, and that the townspeople could sleep secure in their beds. The half-timbered Wakeman's house, later used by the mayor, dates from the 13th century and now contains a museum. An interesting Prison and Police museum is housed in the old prison building dating from 1686.

Before Ripon is left on the main tour route, a short detour can be made to Newby Hall: follow SP 'Boroughbridge' to pass Ripon Racecourse and cross the River Ure, then turn right on to an unclassified road and in ¼ mile turn right again to reach Newby Hall.

NEWBY HALL, N Yorks
Some of Robert Adam's finest work can be seen in his additions to this splendid Queen Anne House (open), which contains superb Gobelin tapestries and an important collection of classical sculpture. The beautiful grounds run down to the River Ure and contain a miniature railway.

To leave Ripon on the main tour follow SP 'Pateley Bridge B6265'. In 2¼ miles reach Studley Royal and Studley Royal Park.

STUDLEY ROYAL, N Yorks
The fine house that once graced this lovely park burned down in 1945, and the present owner lives in a converted stable block that dates from the 18th century. Attractive estate cottages cluster round a 19th-century church that is considered the ecclesiastical masterpiece of architect William Burges and has a very rich interior. The park (open), landscaped in the 18th century, features many of the conceits of the period, including a temple folly and various statues. Its lakes and woodland combine in a sylvan beauty which is enhanced by grazing herds of deer and livestock, and at one point adjoins the magnificent ruins of Fountains Abbey.

Leave Studley Royal on the B6265 and after ¾ mile turn left on to an unclassified road to reach the impressive ruins of Fountains Abbey.

ALONG THE EDGE OF THE DALES
Between York and the deep Dales country is a gentler area of farmland. Here the landscape is dotted with curiously-weathered rocks rising from deep vegetation, peaceful reservoirs, and ancient ruins beside enchanting rivers. A foretaste of the Dales is given in How Stean Gorge.

Ripon's Town Hall reminds the citizens of the Wakeman's traditional role.

FOUNTAINS ABBEY, N Yorks
Generally considered to be the finest in England, the remarkably well-preserved ruins of this 12th- to 15th-century Cistercian abbey (NT) are part of the Studley Royal estate (open) and clearly demonstrate the layout of a Norman and medieval monastic foundation. Particularly notable are the nave, tower, and lay-brothers' quarters. Opposite the ruins is Fountains Hall, which was built with stone taken from the abbey in the 17th century.

Return to the B6265 and turn left, drive through wooded countryside, and emerge on to Pateley Moor for views over Nidderdale. A short detour from the main route to Brimham Rocks can be made by driving to the road summit on the moor and turning left.

Fountains Abbey was once the wealthiest Cistercian house in England.

BRIMHAM ROCKS, N Yorks
Thousands of years of wind and rain have sculpted the millstone grit of this group of rocks into a variety of weird and wonderful shapes. The surrounding moorland (NT) offers excellent views and is a popular site for picnics.

On the main tour, continue along the B6265 and later turn right to descend to Pateley Bridge.

PATELEY BRIDGE, N Yorks
Since ancient times this pleasant market town has been a focus for the everyday life of Nidderdale, but nowadays its steep main street is busy as much with tourists as with local traffic. The picturesque ruins of Old St Mary's Church occupy a lofty hillside site, and the Nidderdale Museum displays over 3,000 items relating to life in the Yorkshire Dales. Of particular note are the Victorian Room and a replica cobbler's shop. West of the town are the fascinating Stump Cross Caverns – more than ¼ mile of natural passages and caves featuring many strange rock formations (open).

Leave Pateley Bridge and cross the River Nidd, then take the next turning on the right SP 'Ramsgill' to join an unclassified road. Drive for 1 mile to reach Foster Beck Flax Mill.

FOSTER BECK FLAX MILL, N Yorks
Industrial archaeology enthusiasts will find this well-restored flax mill of considerable interest. Now a restaurant, it is built of local stone and features a huge 17th-century water wheel that is the second largest in the country.

Drive alongside Gouthwaite Reservoir and continue to Ramsgill and Lofthouse, at the head of Nidderdale.

NIDDERDALE, N Yorks

Part of the lovely valley of the River Nidd, Nidderdale is rich in mineral deposits and has been mined for lead and iron for many centuries. Its stone has also been in great demand for building, and the landscape is pitted with the overgrown remains of worked-out quarries. All along the river, from its high source in the rugged fell country of Great Whernside to the lush lower parts of its valley, the scenery offers plenty of incentives for the motorist to leave his car and explore on foot.

LOFTHOUSE AND HOW STEAN GORGE, N Yorks

The pretty Upper Nidderdale village of Lofthouse is a good centre from which to explore the beautiful How Stean Gorge, a 70ft-deep cleft accessible by footpaths that thread their way along its rocky sides and over little bridges. The largest of two interesting caves here is Elgin's Hole, which penetrates nearly a mile into the roots of Middlesmoor Hill.

Return alongside Gouthwaite Reservoir to reach the B6265 and turn left to re-enter Pateley Bridge. Leave the town on the B6165 SP 'Harrogate' to reach Summer Bridge, then turn right on to the B6451 'Otley' road. Follow a long climb past Menwith Hill Wireless Station and turn right on to the A59 'Skipton' road, then proceed to Blubberhouses, at the north-west end of Fewston Reservoir. Drive to the village church, turn left on to the unclassified 'Timble' road, then take the next turning left SP 'Fewston'. Continue through pine forests, cross a dam separating Fewston and Swinsty Reservoirs, and continue to Fewston.

FEWSTON, W Yorks

This charming village faces across Fewston Reservoir to the historic lines of a 16th-century hall (not open). The lovely village church dates from the 17th century.

Keep right through Fewston and cross part of Swinsty Reservoir, then meet the B6451 'Otley' road and turn right to cross Sandwith Moor. Follow a long descent to Lindley Wood Reservoir and enter Otley.

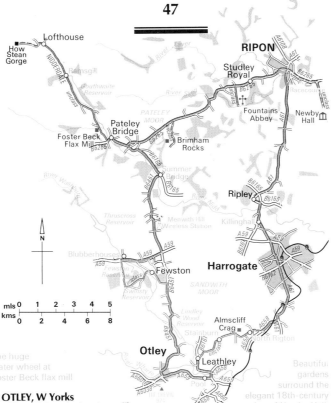

OTLEY, W Yorks

Although largely dominated by modern industry, this old market town on the River Wharfe retains several good buildings as reminders of its long history. Among these are old inns and a fine cruciform church containing fragments of Saxon crosses and a good Georgian pulpit. A curious memorial in the churchyard commemorates the men who lost their lives while working on the Bramhope railway tunnel between 1845 and 1849. Close to the town are the fine Elizabethan halls of Farnley, where the artist Turner was a visitor, and Western. Above the town is the 925ft summit of Otley Chevin, from which panoramic views over the lovely countryside of Lower Wharfedale can be enjoyed.

Leave Otley on the A659 'Tadcaster' road and follow the River Wharfe to reach Pool. Turn left on to the A658 SP 'Harrogate', then cross the river and turn left again on to the B6161 to reach Leathley.

LEATHLEY, N Yorks

Outside the Norman and later church in Leathley are the old village stocks and a mounting block. The local almshouses and hall date from the 18th century.

In Leathley turn right on to the unclassified 'Stainburn' road and follow SP 'Rigton' to reach lofty Almscliff Crag.

ALMSCLIFF CRAG, N Yorks

This high crag affords superb views and has been the training ground for some of Britain's best-known rock climbers. The climbing faces should not be attempted without proper experience and equipment.

Continue to North Rigton and turn left, then right, to meet a junction with the A658. Turn left SP 'Harrogate' and in 1¾ miles turn left again on to the A61 to reach Harrogate.

HARROGATE, N Yorks

One of the chief towns in Yorkshire's old West Riding, Harrogate achieved early fame as a spa resort and nowadays is an important conference centre. Its mineral springs were discovered in the 16th century, and the Royal Pump Room was built as the country's first public baths in 1842. From that time onwards the town's popularity steadily increased, resulting in a wealth of dignified stone buildings and beautiful gardens that have made it known as the Floral Resort of England. The Valley Gardens are particularly notable, and the Harlow Car Gardens contain 60 acres of ornamental and woodland gardens (open). Some 200 acres of commonland known as The Stray, a popular place for walking and picnics, borders the southern boundary of the town. An interesting museum of local history, Victoriana, and costumes is housed in the 19th-century Pump Room.

Leave Harrogate on the A61 SP 'Ripon' and drive to Killinghall. Continue for 1 mile beyond that village, cross the River Nidd, and meet a roundabout. Take the first exit on to an unclassified road and enter Ripley.

RIPLEY, N Yorks

Much of this attractive village was rebuilt during the 19th century, but it is largely unspoilt and retains an ancient market cross and stocks in its cobbled square. Ripley Castle (open), home of the Ingilby family since 1350, shows workmanship of mainly 16th- and 18th-century date and stands in beautiful grounds landscaped by Capability Brown. Its gatehouse is a fine building of c1450, and one of its floors was made from the timber of a British man-of-war. Oliver Cromwell stayed at the house on the eve of the Battle of Marston Moor in 1644, and armour from the opposing Royalist army is on view. Notable tombs and memorial brasses can be seen in the village church, and the churchyard features a curious weeping cross with eight niches in which sinners could kneel and repent.

Drive through Ripley, meet a roundabout, and take the 2nd exit to rejoin the A61. Return through undulating countryside to Ripon.

FROM THE COAST TO THE MOORS

Every summer thousands of visitors flock to Scarborough and Whitby, bustling resorts with much to entertain the holidaymaker. Inland are the forest and heather-clad hills of the North Yorks Moors, where the colours are green and brown and silence is broken only by small natural sounds.

Time and war have desecrated Whitby Abbey.

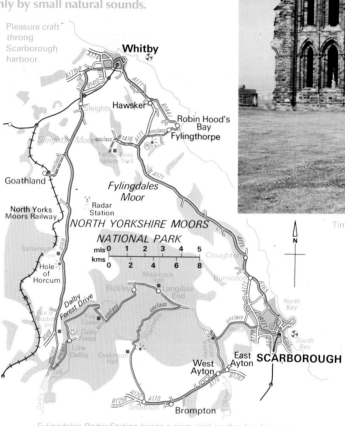

Fylingdales Radar Station keeps a grim vigil on the desolate moor.

SCARBOROUGH, N Yorks

An important conference centre and one of the most popular seaside resorts in Yorkshire, this charming old town overlooks two sandy bays divided by the massive bulk of a 300ft headland. In Roman times this excellent vantage point was the site of a signalling station, and the foundations of that ancient structure still exist amongst the magnificent 12th-century castle ruins (AM) that stand here today. Views from the 100-acre site, which is accessible through a 13th-century barbican, extend across the red roofs of the medieval old town to the harbour far below. Of particular note among the remains are the fine keep and three medieval chapels. During the 18th and 19th centuries the town became caught up in the fashion for seaside holidays and acquired several fine terraces of hotels and boarding houses, many of which still offer accommodation. The Natural History Museum, Art Gallery, and The Rotunda Museum are housed in notable Victorian buildings, and a museum of general interest can be visited in Woodend, the one-time holiday home of the Sitwell family. Typical resort facilities and amusements offered to the visitor include fine promenades and well-tended seafront gardens, plus a good zoo with a dolphinarium. Views can be enjoyed from pleasant clifftop walks and the 500ft eminence of nearby Oliver Hill.

Leave Scarborough with SP 'North Bay' and join the A165, then in 1 mile meet a roundabout and take the A165 to reach Burniston. Meet a junction with the A171 and turn right SP 'Whitby'. Continue to Cloughton, bear left with the A171, and drive through an afforested area to Fylingdales Moor.

FYLINGDALES MOOR AND RADAR STATION, N Yorks

The huge white domes of Fylingdales Early Warning Station seem a constant reminder of doom in the lonely desolation of the surrounding moor. At one time the area was inhabited, and the intrusive evidence of advanced technology contrasts strangely with prehistoric burial mounds and the Wade's Causeway, which is Roman.

Continue along the A171 for 8¾ miles. A detour from the main route can be made by turning left on to the B1416, driving 1¾ miles, then turning left again on to an unclassified road to reach Newton House and the start of the Falling Fosse Nature Trail. On the main route, continue along the A171 and in ¾ mile turn right on to an unclassified road SP 'Fylingthorpe' and 'Robin Hood's Bay'. Pass a viewpoint and picnic site on the right and

descend (1 in 4) through hairpin bends to reach Fylingthorpe.

FYLINGTHORPE, N Yorks

This residential area of Robin Hood's Bay boasts the fine 17th-century Old Hall, which was built by the Chomley family of Whitby Abbey.

Keep forward to Robin Hood's Bay.

ROBIN HOOD'S BAY, N Yorks

Considered one of the most picturesque villages in England, this charming collection of old houses, shops, and inns occupies a precarious cliff-top site and was once a favourite haunt of smugglers. Its steep flights of steps and narrow passages recall unlit boats at the bottom of the cliffs, and furtive movements between houses where well-disguised hiding places waited to be filled with contraband. It is difficult to establish any real connexion between the village and the folk hero after whom it is named, but it may be that the famous outlaw leader came here to escape by boat to Europe. During the last decade coastal erosion has destroyed two rows of houses, and the sea is so close that at high tide its waves lash the Bay Hotel. Superb sands are revealed at low tide.

Leave the village on the B1447 SP 'Whitby' and continue to Hawsker.

HAWSKER, N Yorks

It is thought that the well-preserved 10th-century cross shaft at Old Hall in Hawsker may mark the site of a medieval church. The intricate design of interlaced knot work and bird figures is typical of traditional Norse design.

Drive through the village, meet the A171, and turn right. Descend to Whitby.

WHITBY, N Yorks

Ruins (AM) of an abbey founded here by St Hilda in 657 can be seen above the town on the East Cliff. Close by is a huge carved cross that was erected in 1898 to commemorate Caedmon, the ancient poet whose *Song of Creation* is considered by some to mark the start of English literature. Below the abbey ruins the River Esk divides the old part of the settlement from the more recent West Cliff area, which is connected to the harbour via a rock-cut passage romantically named after the Khyber Pass. Whitby has always had a strong sea-going tradition and has been the home of many famous maritime figures, including Captain Cook. His house in Grape Street is identified by a plaque, and the stimulus that prompted his nautical career is still a persuasive element in the town's atmosphere – though the 18th-century colliers on which he worked have long since vanished. One of the finest buildings here is St Mary's Church, which stands at the top of a spectacular 199-step flight and contains superb 18th-century craftsmanship. The museum in Pannet Park illustrates fascinating episodes from the town's long history. Local craftsmen have been making ornaments and jewellery from jet, a particularly hard, shiny form of coal found in the area, for hundreds of years. One of the most unusual features of Whitby is a whalebone arch from Norway.

Leave Whitby on the A171 'Teesside' road and in 1½ miles turn left on to the A169 SP 'Pickering'. Drive through Sleights and climb on to Sleights Moor, in the North Yorks Moors National Park.

Several restored steam locomotives run on the North Yorks Moors Railway.

NORTH YORKS MOORS NATIONAL PARK

Heather-clad moors occasionally scored by fertile valleys are the main ingredients in the startlingly open landscape of this 553-square-mile national park. To the west are the rounded heights of the Cleveland and Hambledon Hills, east the rugged beauty of the Yorkshire coast, and south the lush woodlands of the Vale of Pickering.

Continue across Sleights Moor for 3 miles. A short detour from the main route to Goathland can be made by turning right on to an unclassified road and entering the village.

Old cottages line the hills on both sides of Whitby harbour.

GOATHLAND, N Yorks

All around this greystone moorland village are lovely walks leading past streams that suddenly plunge over rocky lips as spectacular waterfalls. Three superb examples in the immediate neighbourhood are Nelly Ayre Foss, Mallyan Spout, and Thomason Foss, and dozens of others in varying sizes can be visited by the rambler willing to venture a little farther. The village itself is well known for the Plough Stotts, a traditional group who perform sword dances in the area. A well-preserved stretch of Roman Road (AM) can be seen to the south, and the North Yorks Moors Railway is close by.

The Hole of Horcum is a vast bowl of rich grazing land.

NORTH YORKS MOORS RAILWAY

Steam railway enthusiasts have restored and re-opened the old British Rail link that connected Grosmont with Pickering, and in doing so have provided a superb mobile viewpoint from which 18 miles of beautiful national park countryside can be enjoyed in comfortable conditions.

On the main tour, follow the A169 over bleak moorland, with views of Fylingdales Early Warning Station, then pass the lovely Saltersgate Inn and ascend to the Hole of Horcum.

HOLE OF HORCUM, N Yorks

This vast natural hollow in the Yorkshire moorlands shelters the farms of High and Low Horcum, forming a lush oasis of pasture in the wilderness of Levisham Moor.

After 4 miles reach the Fox and Rabbit Inn, then turn left on to an unclassified road SP 'Thornton Dale'. After another 2 miles turn left SP 'Low Dalby (Forest Drive)' on to a Forestry Commission toll road. Proceed to the hamlet of Low Dalby and turn left on to the Forest Drive SP 'Bickley'.

DALBY FOREST DRIVE, N Yorks

Some 10 miles of well-surfaced roads offer the motorist a route through the beautiful woodlands of Dalby and Bickley Forests, where conifer plantations and stands of mature deciduous trees provide a vast haven for many species of wildlife. Red squirrels inhabit the conifers, the glades are full of wild flowers in spring and summer, and there is constant activity from such common woodland birds as jays, nuthatches, and the tiny goldcrest. A footpath which starts just beyond Staindale leads left to a curious formation of layered limestone known as the Bridestones. Amenities include numerous parking places, picnic sites, and forest trails, while many footpaths allow an uninhibited appreciation of the area. The Forest Drive is likely to be closed during periods of very dry weather, when the ever-present fire risk is abnormally high.

Continue along the Forest Drive to a fire tower and turn left, then drive for 2 miles to leave the Forestry Commission roads. Descend (1 in 8), and after ¾ mile meet a T-junction and turn right SP 'Scarborough'. Pass the Moorcock Inn at Langdale End and after 1 mile turn sharp right SP 'Troutsdale' and 'Snainton'. Continue along a winding road through Troutsdale; fine views can be enjoyed along the length of this valley, and there is a picnic site near a viewing spot at Cockmoor Hall (not open). Meet a T-junction in Snainton and turn left on to the A170 SP 'Scarborough'. Proceed to Brompton.

BROMPTON, N Yorks

Brompton's greystone Church of All Saints features fine stained glass.

Leave Brompton and continue along the A170 to West and East Ayton.

AYTON, WEST AND EAST, N Yorks

Situated on either side of the River Derwent, the twin villages of East and West Ayton are linked by an attractive 4-arched bridge which dates from 1775. The ruined pele tower of Ayton Castle makes a good counterpoint to the tower of East Ayton's church, on the other bank.

Immediately after crossing the Derwent to enter East Ayton turn left on to an unclassified road. In 2 miles turn right on to a road SP 'Private'. Keep forward at this junction to reach a picnic site and viewpoint. After 2 miles on the private road pass a pond on the right, then after another 1 mile meet a T-junction and turn right to re-enter Scarborough.

WAST WATER AND THE WESTERN DALES

The high fells sweep down almost to the sea and above Wast Water, deepest and wildest of the Cumbrian lakes, tower the formidable peaks of Scafell and Scafell Pike. In the shelter of the mountains lie 2 of the loveliest and quietest of the valleys, Eskdale and Dunnerdale, whose scenery inspired many of Wordsworth's poems.

Above: Eskdale, ideal for walking, is one of the few Lakeland valleys with no lake

Right: Scafell towers above the River Irt which flows through Wast Water

SEASCALE, Cumbria
Good sandy beaches and long rolling breakers, ideal for surfing, make Seascale a popular seaside resort. The village lies on a narrow coastal strip of flattish land, with the magnificent scenery of the distant fells of the Lake District as a backdrop. To the north loom the giant towers of Windscale and Calder Hall Nuclear Power Stations; the latter was the first atomic reactor in the world to generate electricity on a commercial scale. Recently, both plants were re-designated and are now known collectively as Sellafield. There is an information centre here open to the public.

Leave Seascale on the B5344 Gosforth road. In 2½ miles cross the main road on to an unclassified road and enter Gosforth.

GOSFORTH, Cumbria
In this remote Cumbrian village churchyard stands one of a very few survivals of the earliest Christian times in these islands, Gosforth Cross. This 1,000-year-old sacred monument is intricately carved with figures of men and beasts which may represent the pagan gods of Norse mythology, as well as orthodox Christian symbols, a sign that the 'new' religion had not yet completely supplanted the old beliefs of the Viking settlers.

Turn right, SP 'Wasdale Head', then in ¼ mile turn left. In ¾ mile bear right and continue to the shores of Wast Water.

WAST WATER, Cumbria
Bleak fells and cliffs of wild, grey scree sweep down to the shores of Wast Water. In places the water is more than 260ft deep, making this the deepest of the English lakes. To the east, dominating the surrounding hills, rise the towering jagged crags of Scafell and Scafell Pike, at 3,162ft and 3,206ft, the highest peaks in England. The mountain scenery of this remote stretch of water is incomparable.

From here a short detour to the left leads to Wasdale Head.

WASDALE HEAD, Cumbria
The only road through Wasdale ends abruptly at this small village, overshadowed by the massive bulk of Great Gable. From here the only way into the neighbouring valleys is on foot: over Black Sail Pass into Ennerdale, or by Sty Head into Borrowdale. The village is a famous centre for rock climbers: tracks lead up from Wasdale to climbs on Scafell, Napes ridges on Great Gable, and Pillar Rock. The first recorded ascent of Pillar was in 1826; Scafell Pinnacle and Lord's Rake were not climbed until the 1890s, and the Central Buttress not until 1914, but now climbers come from all over the country to tackle these ascents. In the graveyard of the tiny church at Wasdale Head several of the unsuccessful lie buried.

The main tour turns southwards alongside Wast Water, SP 'Santon Bridge'. In 1¾ miles turn left then left again and continue to Santon Bridge. Here turn left, SP 'Eskdale', and ascend through the Miterdale Forest, then continue to Eskdale Green.

ESKDALE GREEN, Cumbria
The easiest way to enjoy the scenery of this beautiful lakeland dale is to take the miniature railway, either at Irton Road, nestling in the shelter of Miterdale Forest, or at Eskdale Green station in the nearby village. The line runs from Ravenglass on the coast high up the valley to Dalegarth station at the foot of Hard Knott Pass, one of the highest and steepest motor roads in the Lake District. It was laid in 1875 to transport slate and minerals from the hills to the coast, but the steam locomotives, named after Lake District rivers, are not antique; they have been specially made by the railway company to carry passengers. The local name for the railway, 'Laal (little) Ratty', still sometimes used, comes from the name of the original contractor, Ratcliffe. From the top of the road leading from Eskdale Green into Ulpha can be seen one of the finest Lake District views, a panorama of the high fells, encompassing Harter Fell, Crinkle Crags, Bow Fell, Esk Pike, Scafell, Great Gable, Kirk Fell and Pillar.

Continue on the unclassified road and in ½ mile branch right, SP 'Ulpha'. Follow a narrow moorland road across Birker Fell then later descend and, at the T-junction, turn right into Ulpha.

HAYCOCK ▲ 2618   2760 STEEPLE   2630 KIRK FELL

2270 ▲ SEATALLON   Wasdale Head ○   2649 ▲ LINGMELL

3206 ▲ SCAFELL PIKE

Copeland Forest   BUCKBARROW ▲

Wast Water

SCA FELL 3162 ▲

THE SCREES

Sellafield Nuclear Power Station

A595

Gosforth   *unclass*   *unclass*

THE ILLGILL HEAD 1983 ▲

River Irt   WHINRIGG 1755 ▲   Beckfoot Station

Burnmoor Tarn

CUMBRIAN MOUNTAINS

River Esk

Santon Bridge   *Miterdale Forest*

B5344

SEASCALE

A595

The Ravenglass and Eskdale Railway

Eskdale Green   Dalegarth Station

King George IV Inn

HARTER FELL 2129 ▲

B5344   Holmrook

Irton Road Station

BIRKER FELL

Muncaster Castle

Ravenglass   Glannaventa Roman Fort   *unclass*

Devoke Water   ULPHA FELL

A595

1632 ▲   1566 ▲ HESK FELL

Lane End

STAINTON PIKE

1735 ▲ CAW

WHITFELL 1881 ▲   Ulpha

1799 ▲ BUCK BARROW

DUNNERDALE

unclass   A593

Duddon Bridge   Broughton-in-Furness

Bootle

1548 ▲

A595

1361 ▲   A595

BLACK COMBE   WHITE COMBE 1970 ▲

A5093

IRISH SEA

Whicham   Silecroft

Duddon Sands

A5093

Millom

N

mls 0   1   2   3   4
kms 0   2   4   6

Above: during medieval times the present entrance hall of Muncaster Castle was used as the great hall. It contains some intricate panelling and several family portraits of the Penningtons

ULPHA, Cumbria
Ulpha lies at the foot of the steep fell road out of Eskdale, looking across the River Duddon to the slopes of the Dunnerdale Fells. The poet Wordsworth wrote about the Chapel of St John, calling it the Kirk of Ulpha, in one of his sonnets. The chapel contains wall paintings dating from the 17th and 18th centuries.

In ¼ mile bear left across the river bridge, SP 'Broughton', and follow a winding road through Dunnerdale.

DUNNERDALE, Cumbria
Dunnerdale is the name given to the lower reaches of the lovely Duddon valley whose beautiful scenery inspired no less than 34 of Wordsworth's best-known sonnets. The poet had come to know the valley as a boy when staying with relations at Broughton. The River Duddon, which rises in the bleak moorland near Wrynose Pass, was until 1974 the old county boundary between Cumberland and Lancashire. It flows out to the sea beneath Duddon Bridge, into the deep estuary of Duddon Sands which washes the western shore of the Barrow-in-Furness peninsula.

After 3¼ miles turn right on to the A595, SP 'Workington,' cross Duddon Bridge, then continue to Whicham.

WHICHAM, Cumbria
A footpath from the village winds up the steep hillside to the summits of Black Crags and Black Combe with superb views on all sides. Black Combe, in the days before the postal service had established a reliable nationwide system of communications, was one of a chain of beacon hills stretching across the country, on which signal fires were lit to warn the people of danger or inform them of important events.

At the T-junction turn right and follow the foot of the fells to Bootle. Remain on the A595 and pass the edge of Waberthwaite, then in 1 mile descend into the River Esk valley. Cross the Esk and later pass the entrance to Muncaster Castle.

MUNCASTER CASTLE, Cumbria
The castle (OACT) stands on a superb site near Ravenglass, looking out westwards to the sea and eastwards to the high hills of Cumbria. The old medieval castle and pele tower still form part of the building which was enlarged and remodelled by Anthony Salvin in the 19th century. The Penningtons have lived here since the 13th century and there is a curious tradition associated with the family that dates back to 1461, when they gave shelter to King Henry VI after his defeat at the Battle of Towton. In gratitude, he gave them a bowl of greenish glass, enamelled and gilded, which has been known ever since as the 'Luck of Muncaster' because it is believed that while the bowl remains unbroken the Pennington succession at Muncaster will be assured. Among the other treasures of the castle is a fascinating collection of 17th-century miniature furniture. Muncaster is also famous for its bird gardens; small, brightly-coloured exotic species flit about the old courtyard and stately flamingoes, ibises and storks adorn the lakes.

½ mile beyond the castle keep forward on to an unclassified road for Ravenglass.

RAVENGLASS, Cumbria
Three rivers, the Irt, the Mite and the Esk, flow into the sea at Ravenglass, forming a sheltered, triple-pronged estuary, at the head of which lies the small resort. The town was granted a market charter in 1209, and flourished through the Middle Ages. In 1825 the beacon on the hill above the port was built as a lighthouse for the coastal traffic Ravenglass relied on, until alternative inland routes and the railway took this trade away. Today the sandy beaches, seafront and good bathing attract another trade — tourism. The village, as it now is, is the starting point of the Ravenglass and Eskdale Railway. On the north shore of the estuary, at Drigg Point, the Ravenglass Gullery and Nature Reserve (permit only) has the largest colony of black-headed gulls in Europe. Straight through the entrance of the harbour the Isle of Man can be seen 40 miles out to sea.

To the south of the village is Glannaventa.

GLANNAVENTA, Cumbria
Ruined walls, in places 13ft high, mark the site of a Roman fort, sometimes known as Walls Castle. The course of the old Roman road can still be traced along Eskdale to the site of another fort that once commanded the strategic heights of Hard Knott Pass, and thence by way of Wrynose Pass down to Ambleside.

Return to the A595 and turn left. At Holmrook turn left on to the B5344 for the return to Seascale.

AROUND THE THREE PEAKS

High fells and isolated dales sheltering the stone houses and outbuildings of hill farms surround Yorkshire's Three Peaks, rugged summits whose flanks are riddled with caves and pounded by the constant drop of lovely waterfalls. The roads are narrow and hilly, but the scenery is spectacular.

SEDBERGH, Cumbria

This market town lies below Howgill Fells, a range of rounded bracken-topped hills which links the Yorkshire Dales with the edge of the Lake District. A famous public school for boys was founded here in 1525, but the majority of the town's buildings are 19th-century and the general feel of the place is very Victorian. Permanent displays relating to the topography of the area can be seen in the National Park Centre.

Leave Sedbergh on the unclassified 'Dent' road and follow the River Dee through beautiful Dentdale. Continue through pleasant countryside to Dent

DENTDALE, Cumbria

Lower Dentdale is a broad and well-wooded valley that narrows to a gorge and mountain pass beyond Dent village. Dent marble, a particularly hard form of limestone prized as a building material, is found in small quarries along its length, and beautiful fell scenery rises from both banks of the Dee.

DENT, Cumbria

In the heart of Dentdale is the attractive old village of Dent, a picturesque collection of houses and cottages centred on the twisting course of a cobbled main street. The village drinking fountain commemorates Alan Sedgwick, a pioneer geologist born here in the 19th century.

Drive to the George and Dragon Inn in Dent, turn right, and after 1 mile turn right again SP 'Ingleton'. Follow a narrow winding road into Deepdale, with Whernside rising on the left.

WHERNSIDE, Cumbria & N Yorks

Whernside, the cave-riddled flanks of Pen-y-Ghent, and lofty Ingleborough are neighbouring summits of a massive millstone-grit formation known as the Three Peaks. The first-named rise to 2,419ft above sea level. The area's many potholes and tunnels should not be entered by any but the most experienced and well-equipped explorers.

Ascend steeply along a gated road to White Shaw Moss and a road summit of 1,553ft. Descend through Kingsdale, on either side of which runs a lofty limestone scar, and reach Thornton-in-Lonsdale. Turn left over a railway bridge, then left again. After a short distance turn left to enter the Dales centre of Ingleton.

INGLETON, N Yorks

This popular dales centre is a good rambling and touring base situated close to several beauty spots. Waterfalls in the area include 40ft Thornton Force and Pecca Falls, and lovely rock and river scenery can be enjoyed on a 2¼-hour round walk that follows the enchanting Doe Valley and returns alongside the River Twiss. The summit of Ingleborough is less than 4 miles from the village.

INGLEBOROUGH, N Yorks

Ingleborough is the second highest of the Three Peaks, and its 2,373ft summit forms a curious 15-acre plateau that was once guarded by an ancient stronghold. All that remains of the fortification today is a low rampart pierced by three openings. A well-known section of the massive cave systems that riddle the local limestone is known as the White Scar Caves (open). Potholers come from all parts of the country to explore its tunnels, where an underground river flows amongst strange rock formations into a sunless lake. Farther east is Gaping Gill, an awesome pothole whose 360ft shaft leads to a main chamber that extends a full 500ft below ground. It has the longest shaft in Britain and is a severe test of nerves and skill for the experienced climbers that attempt it.

Leave Ingleton and follow SP 'Settle' to join the A65. Drive through farming country and after 4 miles turn left on to the B6480 to enter Clapham.

CLAPHAM, N Yorks

A Yorkshire Dales National Park centre is based in this attractive little village, and the local caves attract potholing enthusiasts from all over Britain. About 1 mile north is the entrance to Ingleborough Cave (open), which runs for 900 yards and is noted for its splendid stalagmites and stalactites. The village is a charming collection of greystone houses and whitewashed cottages on the banks of Clapham Beck.

Great Shunner Fell towers over the village of Muker.

The windswept character of the Yorkshire Dales is particularly striking near Muker.

Leave Clapham on the 'Settle' road to join the A65, then in ¼ mile turn left on to an unclassified road for Austwick village. In ¾ mile reach Austwick.

AUSTWICK, N Yorks

Many of the Craven District's outstanding geological features lie close to this village. Of particular interest is a series of perched boulders, huge rocks left in precarious positions by the melting glaciers of the ice ages.

Leave Austwick by returning to the A65 and later pass beneath Giggleswick Scar to reach the edge of Giggleswick.

GIGGLESWICK, N Yorks

A well-known public school founded here in 1553 occupies impressive 19th-century buildings, but the early history of Giggleswick is best represented by its old market cross, stocks, and tithe barn. The local church features an ancient reading desk and a carved pulpit of 1680.

Leave Giggleswick and proceed to the town of Settle.

SETTLE, N Yorks
The charm of this small Ribblesdale market town is in its narrow streets of unpretentious buildings and secluded courtyards. Folly Hall, also known as Preston's Folly, is an unfinished 17th-century house with an elaborate front that contrasts severely with a very plain back. In many ways this sudden difference reflects the startling changes of the local countryside. In Victoria Street is an interesting museum of North Craven life.

Return through Settle along the A65 and turn right on to the B6479 SP 'Horton in Ribblesdale' to begin a drive through scenic Ribblesdale. After a short distance reach Langcliffe.

LANGCLIFFE, N Yorks
In 1838 a chance discovery of the feature now known as Victoria Cave led to the retrieval of many fascinating prehistoric remains, including the bones of animals long extinct in the British Isles.

Leave Langcliffe and proceed on the B6479 to reach Stainforth.

STAINFORTH, N Yorks
A 17th-century packhorse bridge that spans the River Ribble here is said to have replaced a similar structure built by monks in the 14th century. Some 300 yards downstream is the impressive waterfall of Stainforth Force. The lovely Ribblesdale Valley extends north and south along the river's rambling course.

From Stainforth, continue to Horton in Ribblesdale.

HORTON IN RIBBLESDALE, N Yorks
Alum Pot, one of the best-known potholes in the Craven district, lies 4 miles north-west of this picturesque moorland village.

Continue past Horton-in-Ribblesdale, with views of Pen-y-Ghent (right).

RIBBLESDALE, N Yorks
This long, wide valley of the Ribble cuts through a varied landscape and is popular with walkers, climbers, and potholers. The railway line from Settle to Carlisle runs through Ribblesdale and is considered one of the most scenic routes in the country.

PEN-Y-GHENT, N Yorks
One of the famous Three Peaks, this mountain rises to 2,273ft and is known for its potholes. In clear weather the views from its summit extend as far as Helvellyn, some 45 miles away.

Continue along the B6479 through desolate countryside beside the Leeds–Carlisle railway line to Ribblehead. A fine railway viaduct can be seen on the left, and 2,419ft Whernside rises straight ahead. Meet a T-junction and turn right on to the B6255 SP 'Hawes'. Ascend Redshaw Moss to a road summit of 1,434ft, then later descend through the steep fell country of Widdale. Meet the A684 and turn right to enter Hawes.

HAWES, N Yorks
This sheep-marketing centre is the focal point of Upper Wensleydale life and a major supplier of the distinctive Wensleydale cheese. Within the old station buildings are a National Park Centre and the Upper Dales Folk Museum, which depicts life and trades in the dales.

In Hawes turn left on to the unclassified 'Muker' road and cross the River Ure. Reach a T-junction and turn left, then take the next turning right. A short detour can be made from the main route to Hardrow Force waterfall by keeping forward with SP 'Hardrow Force'.

HARDROW SCAR & FORCE, N Yorks
Considered one of the most spectacular in England, this magnificent waterfall plunges 90ft over the limestone rim of Hardrow Scar into a glen that was once used for brass band contests because of its superb acoustics. Access to the falls is by foot only, through the grounds of the Green Dragon Inn.

On the main tour, climb through the fine scenery of Buttertubs Pass.

BUTTERTUBS PASS, N Yorks
This 1,726ft pass links the lovely valleys of Swaledale and Wensleydale, and is named after deep limestone shafts that pock the countryside a short distance from the road. It is thought that these may have been dug by farmers and used to cool and harden butter that had got too warm on the way to market.

Continue along Buttertubs Pass and meet the B6270. A detour from the main route to Muker can be made by turning right here and driving for 1¼ miles through fell country.

MUKER, N Yorks
Set among the high moors and fells of Upper Swaledale, this remote little cluster of greystone houses is attractively set below the 2,340ft summit of Great Shunner Fell.

On the main tour, turn left on to the B6270 to Thwaite and later skirt the village of Keld.

KELD, N Yorks
Lovely Kisdon Force is one of several attractive waterfalls to be seen near this village, and the desolate area of Birkdale Common lies to the west.

Beyond Keld drive along a narrow hilly road through Birkdale Common, climbing to a road summit of 1,698ft on the Cumbrian border. Descend steeply (1-in-5) with views over the Eden Valley to reach Nateby, and turn right on to the B6259. Later turn right on to the A685 to enter Kirkby Stephen.

KIRKBY STEPHEN, Cumbria
This picturesque little market town is attractively set amongst moorland in the Eden Valley, and features a fine parish church containing several ancient carved stones. To the south the River Eden rises from its remote source in the wild Mallerstang Valley.

Leave Kirkby Stephen on the A685 SP 'Kendal' and after 2 miles turn left on to the A683 'Sedbergh' road. Continue among high fells along the attractive Rawthey Valley to reach Cross Keys Inn.

CROSS KEYS INN, Cumbria
Originally built c1600, this inn (NT) was altered somewhat in the 18th and 19th centuries but is still a fine building. The impressive 600ft waterfall of Cautley Spout is accessible by footpath from here.

Leave the Cross Keys Inn and continue along the A683 to re-enter Sedbergh.

SHEFFIELD, S Yorks

Chaucer's *Canterbury Tales* refer to Sheffield cutlery as early as the 14th century, and when Flemish craftsmen settled here in the 16th century Sheffield began to specialise in cutlery in earnest. In about 1740 Benjamin Huntsman discovered how to produce steel, and Thomas Boulsover discovered how to roll silver plate; the 2 products for which Sheffield is world famous. Bomb damage in World War II necessitated the rebuilding of the city centre and there is little pre-Victorian building. The town hall, with a statue of Vulcan on the very top, was opened in 1897, and nearby the Cutlers Hall of 1832 contains a fine collection of silver from 1773 to the present. The City Museum in Weston Park, however, has the best collection, and the world's largest collection of Sheffield plate. There are 2 art galleries in Sheffield; the Graves, above the Central Library, which has an excellent collection of Chinese ivories and Mappin Art Gallery in Weston Park, specialising in English art.

Leave Sheffield on the A625, SP 'Chapel-en-le-Frith', and climb out of the suburbs on to Totley Moor (1,254 ft). To the left there are fine

THE PEAK DISTRICT

Great dams and small stone villages, bleak moorlands and narrow wooded valleys, fast-flowing rivers and placid lake waters; here is a mountain country in miniature, where ruined mills and tumbled stone walls testify to nature's supremacy. However, man has long inhabited the Peaks, and remnants of prehistoric cultures litter the hillsides.

views of the Derwent valley before entering Derbyshire and the well-known 'Surprise View', from where the entire Hope valley can be seen. Descend to Hathersage.

HATHERSAGE, Derbys

This small town in the Hope valley was well-known by the Brontë family, and nearby North Lees Hall and Moorseats Hall were depicted in Charlotte Brontë's novel *Jane Eyre*. Charlotte stayed with her friend Ellen Nussey in the vicarage, and her pearl inlaid writing desk is kept here. Over the church porch are the arms of the Eyre family, and within are fine brass portraits representing generations of Eyres. A grave in the churchyard is said to be that of Little John, Robin Hood's comrade.

Continue along the Hope valley and in 1¾ miles pass the junction with A6013, SP 'Glossop', which provides a short detour through Bamford to the Howden, Ladybower and Derwent reservoirs.

LADYBOWER, HOWDEN & DERWENT RESERVOIRS, Derbys

Howden, Derwent and Ladybower reservoirs lie in the valley of the Upper Derwent, forming a lovely landscape of tree-clad slopes and glittering lakes. Howden and Derwent, built in 1912 and 1916 with great castellated dams, were used for target practice during World War II by the famous Dambusters squadron. Ladybower was opened later, in 1945, at the cost of 10 farmhouses and 2 villages which lay in its path.

An unclassified road to the right immediately beyond the 2nd viaduct (A57) leads past an arm of the Ladybower reservoir up to the Derwent reservoir. The main tour continues for 2½ miles to Hope.

HOPE, Derbys

The village stands in the middle of a valley named after it, and was an important trading centre in medieval times. Today it is noted for the fishing and rough shooting to be had hereabouts. A weekly stock market is still held here and during late summer the Hope valley agricultural show with its popular sheepdog trials is a local highlight. Before this on Midsummer Day (25 June), a well-dressing ceremony takes place in which the village well is decked in flowers. The ceremony is pagan in origin and the flowers were offerings to the gods who supplied the spring water.

Continue on the A625 to Castleton.

The Mam Tor/Losehill ridge is a 3-mile barrier which separates Edale from the Hope valley

Inset: many Peak District villages ceremonially decorate their wells with clay panels inlaid with flower petals, such as this one at Hope

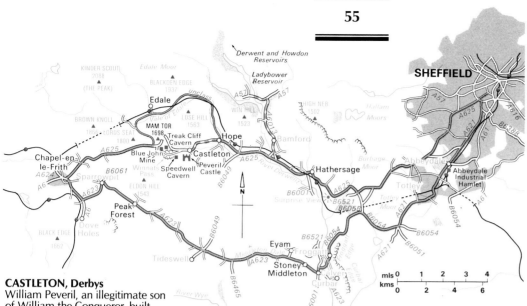

CASTLETON, Derbys

William Peveril, an illegitimate son of William the Conqueror, built the castle (AM) around which this popular Peak District village grew. The keep which remains today was erected by Henry II in 1176, and is the most impressive medieval landmark in the Peak National Park. However, the feature which attracts the visitor most to this pleasant village is its group of limestone caverns (OACT): Peak, Speedwell, Treak Cliff and Blue John, the last named after the rare, blue semi-precious stone found in these hills. Speedwell Cavern is the most spectacular as it consists of one huge chamber and has to be toured in a boat. The nearest cavern to the village is Peak Cavern which is the largest and stretches 2,000ft into the hillsides. Castleton Garlanding, held on 29 May, is a strange custom, believed to be a fertility rite praising some long-forgotten god. A bell-like garland covers the wearer who is usually led through the village on horseback.

To visit Speedwell Cavern and the Winnats Pass, continue on the A625 (now closed at Mam Tor) and at the end of the village branch left on to the unclassified road. The Blue John Cavern can be reached by turning right beyond the end of the gorge, and Treak Cliff is reached by staying on the old A625 at the end of Castleton village. The main tour returns along the A625 to Hope and at the church turns left on to the Edale road.

EDALE, Derbys

In the shadow of the Kinder massif — the highest point in the peak District — is broad, green Edale valley. Along its length are hamlets known as booths (Upper Booth, Barber Booth, Grindsbrook Booth and so on), the name refers to the shelters used by cattle herdsmen in Elizabethan times when the valleys were divided into great ranches. Today sheep rather than cattle roam the valley pastures. On the other side of the valley from Kinder is a massive 3-mile-long ridge, with Mam Tor

The cottage in Eyam where the plague, brought from London, broke out in 1665

(1,696ft) as the highest point. This is crowned by a great Iron-Age fort, which was once a sizeable town. Part of the earthworks have fallen away on the east side, giving rise to landslides which have given Mam Tor the nickname 'shivering mountain'. These slides have recently destroyed the main road running along its lower slopes. Mam Tor is a very old name, the 'Mam', referring to a pagan belief in a mother goddess.

Follow this unclassified road through the valley passing Edale village, and near the end bear left and later ascend to a 1,550ft pass, behind Mam Tor. Descend to the A625 and turn right and in 4¼ miles enter Chapel-en-le-Frith.

CHAPEL-EN-LE-FRITH, Derbys

The first church here was a chapel built in the 13th century by local foresters, and the site would then have been at the edge of the forest — hence, en-le-Frith. The present church dates from the early 14th century. The position of this small market town is high up in the Peak District and it is the gateway to the famous walking and climbing country for which the Peaks are renowned.

Follow SP 'Buxton' to join A6 and in 1½ miles turn left again on to the A623, SP 'Chesterfield'. At Sparrowpit turn sharp right, and in 2 miles pass through Peak Forest.

PEAK FOREST, Derbys

In high, exhilarating countryside this straggling village was once the 'Gretna Green' of the Peak District. The original church, dedicated to King Charles the Martyr in 1657, was extra-parochial, and therefore independent of episcopal jurisdiction, and so up until the early 19th century was able to hold marriage services outside usual church law.

In 2½ miles pass an unclassified road on the right for Tidswell. In 4 miles start the descent into Middleton Dale and in 1½ miles the B6521 to the left leads to Eyam.

EYAM, Derbys

One day in 1665 a clothes chest was delivered to a cottage in Eyam from plague-ridden London. The chest carried plague germs, and between 1665-1666 two-thirds of the population was wiped out. The villagers, led by their rector William Mompesson and his

predecessor Thomas Stanley, resolved to isolate themselves to prevent the plague spreading. Whether this heroic act saved or lost life is disputed by modern-day theorists, but either way it has earned Eyam an honoured place in history. The cottage which took delivery of the clothes chest still stands, and Cucklett Church, a nearby crag, where Mompesson held open-air services during the plague, is the scene of an annual commemorative service.

Shortly pass through Stoney Middleton.

STONEY MIDDLETON, Derbys

Stoney Middleton is as beautiful as Castleton, except for the white dust from the nearby limestone quarries, which covers trees for miles around and produces a most eerie landscape on a moonlit night. In the village is one of the few truly octagonal churches in the country. Two wells stand before the church, and are decorated every August with pictures from the Bible made from thousands of flower petals and bits of bark and moss which are pressed into soft clay.

Continue to Calver and turn left at the traffic signals on to the B6001, SP 'Grindleford', and in ¼ mile branch right on to the B6054, SP 'Sheffield'. Shortly turn left across the River Derwent and climb to Totley Moor. At the summit keep right. To the left is a ventilation shaft of the 3½ mile-long Totley railway tunnel which lies 650ft below the top of the moor. Further on join the A621 before reaching the Abbeydale Industrial Hamlet.

ABBEYDALE INDUSTRIAL HAMLET, S Yorks

Ranged round a large courtyard on a half-acre site on the banks of the River Sheaf, is a remarkable piece of industrial archaeology. This is the Abbeydale Industrial Hamlet, dating mainly from the 18th century, and consisting of workshops and workers' cottages. The main industry here was scything and there is a grinding shop, a tilt-hammer house, a steel melting shop and 6 hand forges. The hamlet has been restored to working order and opened to the public.

Continue on the A621 for the return to Sheffield.

THE PEAK NATIONAL PARK, Derbys

The National Park was the first to be designated as such in Britain, the green 'lung' of industrial England. Peak incidentally comes from Old English 'peac' for knoll or hill. The area comprises the White Peak central and southern limestone area, a gentle, rolling countryside of wooded slopes and rounded hills, and Dark Peak the northern gritstone region, hard, bleak and wild.

SKIPTON, N Yorks

Attractively situated on the Airedale moorlands at the eastern edge of the Craven district, Skipton is dominated by a medieval castle (open) that was restored by Lady Anne Clifford in 1658. Founded in Norman times, the building was subsequently extended and was strong enough to resist a 3-year siege before falling into the hands of Cromwell's parliamentarian army in the Civil War. The Lord Protector dismantled the castle to make sure that it could never again be manned against him, but thanks to Lady Anne its six massive towers still punctuate the skyline of the town that grew beneath its walls. Opposite the massive castle gateway is the Craven Museum, where exhibits and displays illustrate the geology and folk history of the district. An old four-storey corn mill, on a site where similar buildings have operated since the 12th century, houses the George Leatt Industrial and Folk Museum, where working waterwheels and a collection of carts and horse traps can be seen.

Leave Skipton on the A59 'Harrogate' road. A detour from the main route to the Yorkshire Dales Railway can be made by taking the B6265 from Skipton and turning left on to an unclassified road to Embsay.

YORKSHIRE DALES RAILWAY, N Yorks

This small preserved steam railway with its centre at Embsay, runs on 1¼ miles of track and has over 20 locomotives at various stages of restoration. Existing facilities for visiting enthusiasts include access to the current work, a signal box, and a personalized saloon car.

On the main tour, leave Skipton via the A59 and drive through a countryside of drystone walls and quarries to Bolton Bridge. Reach the Devonshire Arms Hotel and turn left on to the B6160 SP 'Bolton Abbey', then continue to Bolton Abbey.

THE YORKSHIRE DALES

Some of England's most impressive scenery can be seen in the rocky clefts of Airedale and Wharfedale, the superb natural amphitheatre of Malham Cove, and the breathtaking gorge of Gordale Scar. Underground are miles of water-worn tunnels, many resplendent with rock and ice formations.

BOLTON ABBEY, N Yorks

Woodlands and pastures in a bend of the River Wharfe make a fittingly peaceful setting for the remains of this once-powerful 12th-century priory (open). Most of the structure lies in ruins, but the nave has served as a parish church for hundreds of years and the old gatehouse was incorporated into a mansion during the 19th century. The little river can be crossed by stepping stones or a footbridge here, and attractive riverside walks extend from the ruins to The Strid.

Continue through a wooded stretch of Wharfedale to reach The Strid and later Barden Tower.

A man-made order is brought to parts of Wharfedale by a pattern of drystone walls.

Augustinian monks selected a magnificent site for their abbey at Bolton.

THE STRID & BARDEN TOWER, N Yorks

The modern translation of the old English word Strid is Turmoil, which is an apt description of the way in which the River Wharfe boils through a 12ft constriction of its gorge at this point. Farther north are the picturesque ruins of Barden Tower, a 12th-century structure that was restored by Lady Anne Clifford of Skipton Castle in 1659.

Reach Barden Tower and turn right on to an unclassified road SP 'Appletreewick'. Cross the river, and turn sharp right on an ascent with SP 'Hazlewood' and 'Storiths'. Continue along a gated road beneath Barden Fell, descend (1 in 5), and cross a ford. Ascend steeply (1 in 4) from the ford,

passing The Strid again, and meet the A59. Turn left and ascend a winding road on to Blubberhouses Moor. Enter a narrow rocky valley and climb to the edge of Blubberhouses, at the end of Fewston Reservoir. Cross a river bridge and turn sharp left on to an unclassified road SP 'Pateley Bridge'. Continue over high moorland, and turn left on to the B6265. Stump Cross Caverns lie to the left of the road.

STUMP CROSS CAVERNS, N Yorks

Dramatic subterranean formations of ice and eroded rock can be appreciated from a pathway that extends ¼ mile into these caverns.

Continue, with views into beautiful Upper Wharfedale, to Grassington.

GRASSINGTON, N Yorks

The lovely area in which this Upper Wharfedale village stands has been mineral deposits and has been settled since very early times. Many iron-age camps and barrows survive, and during the Roman occupation the area was extensively mined for lead ore. The village itself is a popular tourist centre with a cobbled market square reached via a picturesque medieval bridge. A National Park Interpretation Centre is based here.

Leave Grassington and follow an unclassified road SP 'Conistone' through wooded country, occasionally passing close to the River Wharfe. Reach Conistone and keep left to meet the B6160. Turn right and continue to Kilnsey Crag.

KILNSEY, N Yorks

This village is completely dwarfed by the great limestone scar of Kilnsey Crag, one of the best-known landmarks in Yorkshire.

A pleasant detour can be made from the main route by continuing along the B6160 to Kettlewell.

KETTLEWELL, N Yorks

At one time this attractive Wharfedale village was a small oasis of civilization in a great tract of forest, but nowadays the drystone-scattered expanses of the open moor extend right to its boundaries. Great Whernside rises to 2,310ft in the north-east.

On the main tour, leave Kilnsey on the B6160 and drive north. In ¾ mile branch left on to an unclassified road SP 'Arncliffe' and drive through Littondale to reach Arncliffe.

ARNCLIFFE, N Yorks

Typical greystone houses of the Dales area nestle amongst clumps of mature sycamores in this secluded Littondale community. Evidence of long occupation is apparent in a clearly-defined Celtic field system in the immediate district, and the village church stands on the site of a building dated c1100. South of Arncliffe is the dramatic mile-long cliff of Yew Cogar Scar.

In Arncliffe turn right SP 'Halton Gill' and continue through Littondale.

LITTONDALE, N Yorks

Once a medieval hunting forest, this lovely dale in the national park has avoided the depredations of the early lead miners. It retains extensive areas of wild woodland, and its farmlands show signs of having been cultivated since early times.

Reach Halton Gill and turn left on to a gated unclassified road. Continue, following SP 'Stainforth' and 'Settle', and ascend (1 in 5) to a road summit of over 1,400ft, with views of Pen-y-Ghent to the right.

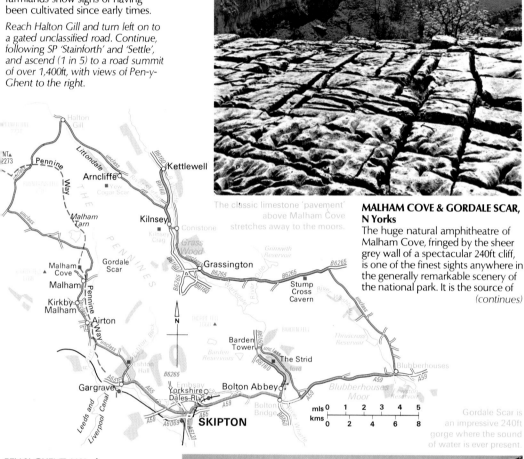

The classic limestone 'pavement' above Malham Cove stretches away to the moors.

MALHAM COVE & GORDALE SCAR, N Yorks

The huge natural amphitheatre of Malham Cove, fringed by the sheer grey wall of a spectacular 240ft cliff, is one of the finest sights anywhere in the generally remarkable scenery of the national park. It is the source of *(continues)*

the River Aire and forms part of a 22-mile fault that resulted from the intolerable stresses imposed by enormous glaciers during the ice ages. An energetic climb leads to the moorland above and Malham Tarn. Gordale Scar, a precipitous, winding gorge filled with the sound of waterfalls and dashing cascades, can be reached from the cove via a 1½-mile footpath.

MALHAM, N Yorks

In the height of the summer season this little stone village is inundated by visitors who flock to the area for its magnificent scenery. Information about the Malham district is available from the Yorkshire Dales National Park Interpretation Centre, which is based in the village.

THE PENNINE WAY

From its southern extremity in Derbyshire, this 250-mile footpath follows the mountainous spine of England and passes through Malham before crossing Pen-y-Ghent on its way to Kirk Yetholme in Scotland. Prospective walkers should realize that this is a fairly rugged route, particularly in its northern sections, and can be positively hazardous in bad weather.

Leave Malham with SP 'Skipton' and continue to Kirkby Malham.

KIRKBY MALHAM, N Yorks

Close to the local 17th-century vicarage is the charming village church, containing a 12th-century font and family box pews of the Georgian period.

Drive through the village to Airton.

AIRTON, N Yorks

Situated in Upper Airedale, this charming village is on the route of the Pennine Way and boasts several good 17th-century buildings. The most notable are the Manor House, the Friend's Meeting House, and the Post Office.

Leave Airton, continue for ¾ mile, and turn left. Drive through the grounds of Eshton Hall (not open) and turn right to reach Gargrave.

GARGRAVE, N Yorks

Although Gargrave's parish church is mostly Victorian, it retains a 16th-century tower and fragments of several Saxon crosses.

Meet the A65 in Gargrave and turn left to cross the Leeds and Liverpool Canal.

LEEDS & LIVERPOOL CANAL

Wonderful scenery that can only be guessed at by the road-bound tourist is revealed to anybody who takes the trouble to hire a boat on this 127-mile canal. It is one of the longest waterways in Britain, rising to 500ft above sea level as it crosses the high ridge of the Pennine Chain.

Continue along the A65 to re-enter Skipton.

PEN-Y-GHENT, N Yorks

Potholing enthusiasts come here to dare the uncertainties of aptly-named Hell Pot and Hunt Pot, two entrances to the cave system that riddles Pen-y-Ghent. Above ground, this 2,273ft summit, one of the famous Three Peaks, affords wide views that extend more than 40 miles to Helvellyn in clear weather.

Continue along the gated road and turn left on to the 'Malham' road. Ascend (1 in 5) to cross wild moorland, and in 3 miles bear right to meet crossroads. Drive forward on the gated 'Grassington' road to reach the Malham Tarn carpark.

MALHAM TARN, N Yorks

All around the isolated waters of Malham Tarn (NT) are heathery moorlands and unusual raised bogs. The tarn itself is the habitat of many species of aquatic wildlife, and the serious naturalist can familiarize himself with the area at the Field Centre in Malham Tarn House, on the northern shore. Above the field centre are the high white cliffs of Highfolds Scar and a natural limestone pavement.

Leave the Malham Tarn carpark and descend steeply to pass Malham Cove and Gordale Scar.

Gordale Scar is an impressive 240ft gorge where the sound of water is ever present.

SOUTHPORT, Merseyside

Particularly well known for its beautifully laid out gardens, this attractive and elegant resort is also noted for its wide range of sporting facilities. It is the home of the Royal Birkdale Golf Club, which has been the venue for Ryder Cup competitions, and is host to county cricket matches, horse jumping trials, and lawn tennis matches. The annual flower show is also a popular event. Amenities for holiday-makers include 6 miles of excellent sands, the largest pier in England, a model village, and boat hire on the 91-acre Marine Lake. The Victorian heyday of seaside holidays is recalled by old salt-water swimming baths and a room of the Botanic Gardens Museum. An interesting collection of fine buildings and shops can be found in Lord Street, which is considered one of the finest thoroughfares in the north of England. Churches in Southport include St Cuthbert's, which displays fine woodwork and a clock of 1739, and a curious red and yellow building in the suburb of Crossens. The latter building shares its churchyard with a very ornate neo-Norman mausoleum. The expanding Steam Transport Museum boasts a fine collection of locomotives, buses, traction engines, and various commercial vehicles. It is planned to become the largest centre of its type in the north west of England, and will be a valuable aid to the understanding of industrial archaeology in transport.

Leave Southport on the A565 SP 'Preston', passing through Crossens. After 3 miles turn right on to the B5246 SP 'Rufford'. Continue through Mere Brow, Holmeswood, and Rufford, and meet the A59 SP 'Preston'. Turn left, and after ¼ mile reach the entrance to Rufford Old Hall on the right.

TO THE WEST PENNINES

Between the elegant seaside resort of Southport and the wild western slopes of the Pennines is the Lancashire Plain, an area of farm and parkland where much of the county's folk history is preserved in picturesque villages, great houses in fine grounds, and fascinating small town museums.

The village cross guards a picturesque approach to St Michael's Church, Croston.

RUFFORD OLD HALL, Lancs

This superb timber-framed Tudor building (NT) stands in 14½ acres of beautiful grounds and is one of the finest examples surviving in England today. Built by the Hesketh family in the 15th century, it was slightly extended during Victorian times but has not been spoilt by 19th-century over restoration. The exterior is a startling combination of decorative black timbers infilled with brilliant white plaster, and the great hall carries an extremely ornate hammerbeam roof. Inside the house is a rare 15th-century screen, and one of the wings contains the Philip Ashcroft Museum of folk crafts and antiquities.

Leave Rufford Old Hall and continue along the A59 for 1 mile, then turn right on to the A581 'Chorley' road. Continue along the A581 to the Leeds and Liverpool Canal.

LEEDS AND LIVERPOOL CANAL, Lancs

As it crosses the rugged Pennine Chain this 127-mile waterway between two of northern England's major cities reaches an amazing 500ft above sea level. The canal took 40 years to build and has many features of interest to naturalists and industrial archaeologists.

Proceed along the A581, crossing the River Douglas, and later turn left over a bridge to reach Croston.

CROSTON, Lancs

Picturesque countryside following the twisting course of the River Yarrow makes a fine setting for this tiny village. Among its most notable buildings are 17th-century almshouses and a 15th-century church containing a curious memorial brass.

From Croston, turn right and in ¼ mile meet a war memorial. Turn left here and in 1 mile meet a T-junction. Turn right and continue along the A581 for 3¼ miles. Cross the M6, then meet the A49 and turn left. Turn right on to the A581. Drive for a short distance to reach Astley Hall on the left.

ASTLEY HALL, Lancs

Charmingly set in nearly 100 acres of wood and parkland, this fine 16th-century and later house (open) has a drawing room with lovely tapestries depicting scenes from the legend of the Golden Fleece. Throughout the house are fine collections of furnishings, pottery and paintings, and special exhibitions are frequently mounted in its rooms.

Leave Astley Hall and proceed along the A581 into Chorley.

CHORLEY, Lancs

Industry is this old textile centre's way of life. It was once known for cotton weaving and calico printing, but in recent years these traditional concerns have been largely replaced by a variety of modern enterprises. The town stands at the edge of farming country close to the foot of the Pennines. The area is dominated by the imposing height of 682ft Healey Nab which rises to the east.

Meet traffic signals in Chorley and turn left on to the A6 SP 'Preston'. In 1 mile cross a railway bridge, meet a roundabout, and take the 2nd exit on to the A674 SP 'M61' and 'Blackburn' Continue, with Healey Nab rising to the right, and drive through Higher Wheelton. In 2 miles meet a roundabout; a detour from the main route can be taken here by following the 1st exit on to the A675 to reach Hoghton Tower.

HOGHTON TOWER, Lancs

Ancestral home of what is claimed to be the oldest baronetcy in England, this fine 16th-century mansion occasionally opens its state rooms, ballroom, Tudor wellhouse, and dungeon to the public. The gardens can also be visited at certain times. In 1617 King James I stayed here, and is said to have been so taken with a loin of beef prepared by the house kitchen that he drew his sword and knighted it, ever since which that particular cut has been sirloin – a charming, if dubious, tale.

On the main tour, take the 2nd exit from the roundabout and continue for ½ mile to a T-junction. Turn right on to A6061 to Fensicowles, then meet the A6062 and turn right SP 'Darwen'. In ¼ mile drive under a railway bridge and immediately turn right on to an unclassified road, then turn left. Continue for 1 mile to the Black Bull (PH), meet crossroads, and drive forward. In 1 mile meet the A666 and drive forward on to the B6231 SP 'Accrington'. In ¼ mile pass a railway bridge and ascend to Guide, then meet crossroads by the King Edward VII (PH). Turn right on to the B6232 SP 'Bury', then keep left and after 2 miles reach the Grey Mare Inn; turn right on to an unclassified road SP 'Edgworth'. Drive to Edgworth, meet crossroads, and continue forward to reach Turton Bottoms. Meet a T-junction with the main road and turn sharp right on to the B6391 SP 'Darwen'. Turton Tower stands to the left.

Unusual 17th-century windows at Astley Hall dominate the exterior.

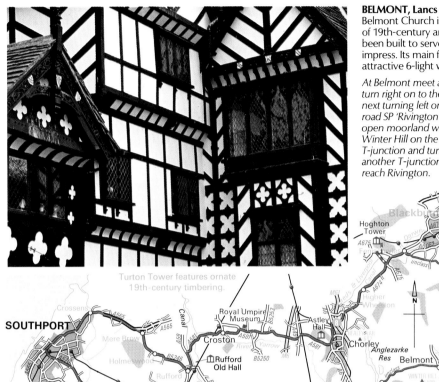

Turton Tower features ornate 19th-century timbering.

BELMONT, Lancs

Belmont Church is a good example of 19th-century architecture that has been built to serve rather than impress. Its main feature is an attractive 6-light window.

At Belmont meet a T-junction and turn right on to the A675. Take the next turning left on to an unclassified road SP 'Rivington', and drive through open moorland with views of 1,498ft Winter Hill on the left. Descend to a T-junction and turn right, then meet another T-junction and turn left to reach Rivington.

RIVINGTON, Lancs

Rivington Pike rises to a 1,190ft summit above this attractive little moorland village. It is crowned by an 18th-century stone tower and commands excellent views over miles of countryside. In the village itself is a good church housing a fine screen and a 16th-century pulpit. Rivington Hall, which stands in 400-acre Lever Park, was rebuilt in 1744 and contains a general interest museum. Close to the village are the Rivington and Anglezarke Reservoirs.

RIVINGTON AND ANGLEZARKE RESERVOIRS, Lancs

These broad sheets of water add an extra dimension of beauty to the somewhat severe moorland countryside around them. They were built in the 19th century to supply Liverpool with water, and have naturalized into perfect habitats for many types of wildlife.

Leave Rivington and drive forward SP 'Adlington', crossing the Rivington Reservoir. Meet a T-junction, turn left SP 'Horwich', and in ¾ mile meet a junction with the A673. Turn right on to the A673 and take the next turning left on to an unclassified road SP 'Blackrod'. In 1 mile meet the A6, drive forward, and in ½ mile turn right. Continue for 1 mile, meet a T-junction with the B5239, and drive forward SP 'Standish'. In 1½ miles meet a T-junction and turn right on to the A5106, then in 200 yards turn left on to the B5239 and continue to the town of Standish.

STANDISH, Gt Manchester

This colliery town stands on the line of a Roman road and features a good church that was rebuilt in the 16th century. Inside the building, particularly in the roof, are good examples of woodwork. The old village stocks are preserved on the steps of a modern town cross.

Meet traffic signals in Standish and drive forward on to the A5209. In 1¼ miles turn right to follow SP 'M6', then meet a roundabout and take the 2nd exit to cross the M6 motorway. Continue to Parbold.

PARBOLD, Lancs

Parbold Hall is a splendid stone-built Georgian house (not open) with a Venetian-style doorway. Excellent views of the surrounding countryside can be enjoyed from the summit of Parbold Hill, which is crowned by the impressive 19th-century building of Christ Church.

Leave Parbold and cross the Leeds and Liverpool Canal, then the River Douglas, to reach Newburgh. Continue to Burscough.

BURSCOUGH, Lancs

Slight remains of a priory lie to the south-west of Burscough, which has a Victorian church with four attractive pinnacled buttresses.

From Burscough, join the A59 SP 'Southport' and in ¾ mile turn right on to the B5242. Continue through Bescar, meet traffic signals, and turn right on to the A570 to reach Scarisbrick and its hall.

SCARISBRICK, Lancs

Designed by the architect Pugin in 1837, ornate Scarisbrick Hall (open on application) is an excellent example of the opulence favoured in the Victorian period. It is gothic in style and was the architect's first major work, taking 4 years to complete. The 150 rooms of the house are now occupied by a school.

Leave Scarisbrick and continue along the A570 for the return to Southport.

TURTON TOWER, Lancs

The core of this L-shaped building (open) is a 15th-century pele tower, a type of fortified dwelling that was once common in the north of England. Two wings were added in the 16th century, and the house now contains fine collections of paintings and furnishings, plus a fascinating local history museum.

Good views of Turton and Entwhistle Reservoirs can be enjoyed from the Turton to Belmont road.

Continue north along the B6391 with views of the Turton and Entwhistle Reservoirs on the right. In 1 mile meet a T-junction and turn left on to the A666 SP 'Bolton'. In ¼ mile turn right on to an unclassified road SP 'Belmont', then take the next turning right and descend with views of Delph Reservoir to the left and Belmont Reservoir to the right. After 1 mile drive over crossroads to reach Belmont.

LAKES AND FELLS

Magnificent lakes, fells and mountains border the winding roads in this area beloved by poets, writers and painters, and immortalised by William Wordsworth. Some of the most dramatic scenery in England is here, including Kirkstone Pass — the highest pass open to motorists in Cumbria.

WINDERMERE, Cumbria
The quaint, crowded town of Windermere lies on the eastern shore of Lake Windermere which has been a well-known centre for sailing and boating since the 19th century, and a number of clubs are based on its shores. Lake Windermere, at 10½ miles, is the longest lake in England. It has 14 islands, including the delightful privately-owned 38-acre Belle Island which can be visited by steamer and has a historic round house (OACT) full of curios. The Steamboat Museum has a collection of Victorian and Edwardian boats that were used on the lake in the days of steam. They are kept in working order in a covered dock and an exhibition recalls the development of navigation at Windermere. Casual visitors can travel up and down the lake by steamer and it is an ideal way to enjoy the scenery.

Leave Windermere on the A591, SP 'Kendal', and proceed to Staveley.

STAVELEY, Cumbria
This small village is set beside the second fastest-flowing river in England — the Kent. The Kentmere valley to the north of Staveley was once a lake, but it was drained a century ago for the mineral deposits on the bed. At the head of the valley, at Kentmere, is the 16th-century ruin of Kentmere Hall, birthplace in 1517 of the evangelist Bernard Gilpin. High fells dominate this lovely, lonely valley, with Ill Bell, to the north, the loftiest peak at 2,476ft.

In 3 miles, at the roundabout, take the A5284 for Kendal.

KENDAL, Cumbria
The largest of the south Lakeland towns, Kendal, known as the Auld Grey Town, is a blend of both ancient and modern architecture. Limestone buildings, their walls a dozen subtle shades of grey, dominate its narrow old streets and picturesque yards. The River Kent meanders through the town, its banks lined by well-tended gardens and high on the hill in the centre of the town are the imposing ruins of Kendal Castle. Built during the 14th century, the castle was the birthplace of Catherine Parr, last of Henry VIII's 6 wives. A famous son of the town is George Romney, the portrait painter, born in 1734, and a collection if his works hangs in the Mayor's Parlour. Other collections can be viewed at Abbot Hall Art Gallery, close to the 12th-century parish church, and in the Borough Museum, which specialises in natural history. The Castle Dairy in William Street is a well-preserved example of vernacular Tudor architecture. Kendal has long been a centre of commerce and in 1331 a woollen industry was established and became famous for 'Kendal Green', mentioned by Shakespeare.

Leave on the A6, SP 'The North' then 'Penrith'. Later climb across Shap Fell and continue to Shap.

Ullswater, second largest lake in the Lake District, is a popular centre for boating and water sports

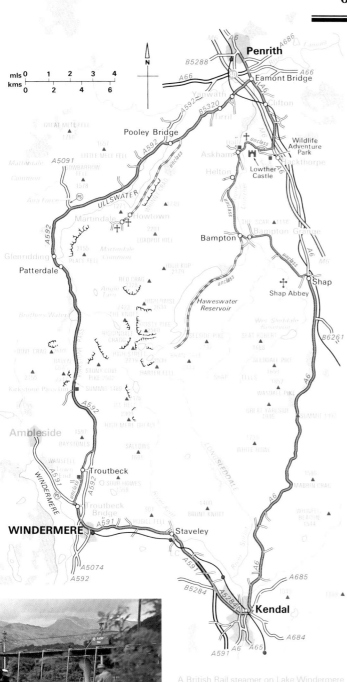

mls 0 1 2 3 4
kms 0 2 4 6

N

Penrith

A British Rail steamer on Lake Windermere

At the end of the village turn left, SP 'Bampton'. In ½ mile bear right (passing the track to Shap Abbey) and continue to Bampton Grange. Cross the river bridge and turn right for Bampton.

BAMPTON & HAWESWATER RESERVOIR, Cumbria.
The small village of Bampton lies about 2 miles north-east of the spectacular Haweswater Reservoir which can be reached via an unclassified road from Bampton. The reservoir was created to supply Manchester with water and although the road to the north of the lake was submerged in the waterworks scheme, a footpath along the valley remains.

At Bampton turn right, SP 'Penrith', and later skirt Helton to reach Askham. At the crossroads turn right, SP 'Lowther'. Cross the river then pass through Lowther Park.

SHAP, Cumbria
Shap village, nearly 1,000ft above sea level, lies north of the wild, desolate Shap Summit which reaches to 1,300ft. The A6 crosses the summit and is frequently blocked by snowdrifts in winter. Hidden in the valley west of Shap village are the ruins of Shap Abbey (AM). Founded around 1191 by Premonstratensian canons (a French order) most of the ruins date from the early 13th century. There are dramatic views of the High Street group of peaks here.

LOWTHER PARK, Cumbria
This 3,000-acre park is sculpted out of beautiful countryside that surrounds the ruins of Lowther Castle (not open). This was once a grand house, home of the Earls of Lonsdale and visited by Mary, Queen of Scots. Also in the park is the 12th-century church of St Michael. This was considerably rebuilt during 1686 and outside it stands the mausoleum of the Earls of Lonsdale.

After 1 mile, at the crossroads, turn left, SP 'Lowther Wildlife Park', and in ½ mile reach the A6. At Hackthorpe (right) is the entrance to the Wildlife Adventure Park.

WILDLIFE ADVENTURE PARK, Cumbria
About 100 acres of parkland provide a natural setting for deer, rare breeds of sheep and cattle, and cranes. There are also special enclosures for many European mammals, including otters, badgers and wild pigs.

The main tour turns left on to the A6, SP 'Penrith', and continues through Clifton to Eamont Bridge.

EAMONT BRIDGE, Cumbria
The village of Eamont Bridge is distinguished by a triple-arched medieval bridge which carries traffic over the River Eamont. Nearby is a prehistoric earthwork, 300ft in diameter, called King Arthur's Round Table. It is nearly circular and originally had 2 entrances, one of which survives, and is surrounded by a ditch and a 5ft-high bank. Mayburgh, ¼ mile to the west, is another prehistoric site. This originally occupied 1½ acres and still has 15ft ramparts.

Continue from Eamont Bridge on the A6 and at the roundabout take the 2nd exit to enter Penrith.

PENRITH, Cumbria
Capital town of the old Cumbria in the 9th century, Penrith was probably initially occupied by the Celts c 500BC. Penrith Castle (AM), built in the 14th century as a defence against the Scots, is now just a ruin. The castle was enlarged by the Duke of Gloucester, later Richard III, who is said to have resided in The Gloucester Arms; dating from 1477, it is one of the oldest inns in England. Penrith town hall, built in 1791, is constructed from 2 houses designed by Richard Adam. In the graveyard of the partly-Norman church are 2 strange stone monuments named 'Giant's Grave' and 'Giant's Thumb'. They are believed to commemorate Owen, King of Cumbria c 920.

Return along the A6, SP 'Shap', and at the roundabout take the 3rd exit to re-enter Eamont Bridge. Here, turn right on to the B5320, SP 'Ullswater', for Yanwath. Continue on the B5320 and pass through Tirril to reach Pooley Bridge.

POOLEY BRIDGE & ULLSWATER, Cumbria
Pooley Bridge, a small village beside the River Eamont, is an ideal centre from which to explore the majestic, spectacular Ullswater lake and its surrounding fells and mountains. Boats may be hired from Pooley Bridge and passenger vessels sail regularly in summer. A small, unclassified road to the south of the lake ends at Martindale where there is a forest with red deer and 2 lonely old churches. The lake is 7 miles long, and about 5 miles from the east end is Gowbarrow Park, seen in spring as a sea of golden daffodils and immortalised by Wordsworth in his famous poem. Close by is Aira Force, a splendid waterfall. High mountains dominating the south-western end of the lake include some of the High Street peaks to the east and the Helvellyn range to the west. Glenridding is a hamlet towards the south-westerly tip of the lake, dominated by a large hotel; boats from Pooley Bridge put in here.

At Pooley Bridge cross the river bridge and in nearly ½ mile turn left on to the A592, SP 'Windermere'. Continue along the shore of Ullswater to Patterdale.

PATTERDALE, Cumbria
This attractive village at the head of Ullswater is encircled by mountains — Place Fell to the east is over 2,000ft and Helvellyn and Lower Man to the south and west are over 3,000ft. The summit of Helvellyn, the third highest peak in the Lake District, is a 3-mile walk along the mile-long Striding Edge, approached by the Grisedale valley. On a clear day, almost every peak in the Lakes is visible from the summit, with the mountains of Scotland rising to the north and the Pennines to the east.

The tour continues southwards and later ascends the dramatic Kirkstone Pass. Beyond the summit (1,489ft) there is an easier descent for 3 miles before turning right, SP 'Ambleside', to enter Troutbeck.

TROUTBECK, Cumbria
Spread along the side of a wild and beautiful valley of the same name, Troutbeck is dominated by lofty pikes of the Kirkstone Pass to the north. At the south end of the village is Townend — a typical yeoman's house (NT) of the early 17th century, with whitewashed walls and mullioned windows: it still retains much of the original oak furniture. At the north end farms and houses cluster around a 17th-century inn called The Mortal Man. The east window in the church was designed by the artist, Edward Burne-Jones.

Follow the Windermere road and in 1¼ miles turn right on to the A591 for the return to Windermere.

IN THE VALE OF YORK

Away from the gothic completeness of York's superb minster are the rolling farmlands of the Vale of York and dry limestone ridges of the Howardian Hills. Everywhere are monuments to the skills of past generations, and close by are the untamed tracts of the Yorkshire Moors and Dales.

YORK, N Yorks

Capital of a British province under the Romans in AD 71, this ancient centre is still the chief city of northern England and preserves many fascinating reminders of its historic past. The earliest surviving building is the Roman Multangular Tower, though parts of the city walls derive from the same period – particularly in the section south of Monk Bar. The walls themselves complete a 3-mile circuit round the medieval boundaries of the city and are among the finest examples of their type in Europe. Micklegate Bar, one of four main gates giving access through the defences, is traditionally the only one used by royalty. York's chief glory is its magnificent Minster, which towers over the little streets and houses of the old town. It is the largest gothic cathedral north of the Alps, and its fine windows contain more than half of all the medieval glass surviving in England. One reason for the purity of the Minster's architectural style is the speed with which it was built – between 1220 and 1470 – and the consequent absence of modifications brought about by changing ideas in church design. Many people consider the octagonal Chapter House to be the loveliest part of the overall medieval design. In 1984 the South Transept was seriously damaged by fire; fortunately it is now undergoing extensive restoration. As far as fine old churches are concerned, York probably has more from anywhere else in the country except perhaps Norwich. Holy Trinity is of 13th-century date and contains good box pews, All Saints' North Street has medieval glass and carries a beautiful 15th-century tower, and St Mary's Castlegate has a rare Saxon dedication stone. Many of the city's buildings have been standing for 500 years and more, including the lovely Guildhall (AM), the Merchant Adventurers' Hall and Chapel (open), Taylors' Hall (open), and the lovely timbered front and picturesque courtyard of William's College. The latter shows work from later periods, and the 17th-century Treasurer's House (NT) preserves good collections of painting and furniture. Elizabethan King's Manor (open), once the home of the Abbot of St Mary's Abbey, is now owned by York University. It is not surprising that a city with as rich and well-documented history as this should have as many museums as York. York's newest museum is the Jorvik Centre, where time cars take you back in time to a reconstruction of Jorvik 'a viking city'. Relics from the Roman occupation can be seen in the Yorkshire Museum, in the grounds of ruined St Mary's Abbey, and close to the 13th-century fragments of York Castle (AM) is the Castle Museum of Yorkshire life. Close by in the old Debtors' Prison are collections of dolls and militaria,

(continues)

The glorious architecture of the Minster can be glimpsed at the end of many of York's old streets and alleyways.

(continued)
and the National Steam Museum preserves great old locomotives such as the *Mallard*. St Mary's Heritage Centre, in Castlegate, uses audio-visual displays and the work of contemporary artists to describe the city's architectural development. Over all is a sense of permanence fostered by the mellow stone of a city that is more medieval than modern.

Leave York on the A1036 SP 'East Coast' and 'Malton', then in 3 miles at a roundabout take 2nd exit then 1st exit at next roundabout on to the A64 SP 'Malton'. Passing agricultural country and in 7½ miles pass the Spittle Beck Inn. In 1½ miles it is possible to make a short detour from the main route by turning right on to an unclassified road SP 'Kirkham Priory', descending over a level crossing and the River Derwent, and driving to the hamlet of Kirkham.

KIRKHAM, N Yorks

Ruined Kirkham Priory (AM) includes a beautiful 13th-century gatehouse and a lavatorium, where the monks used to wash.

On the main route, continue along the A64 and in 1 mile turn left on to an unclassified road SP 'Welburn, Castle Howard'. Pass through Welburn, meet crossroads and turn right, then drive through an arch and wall gateway to reach Castle Howard.

CASTLE HOWARD, N Yorks

One of the most spectacular houses in Britain, Castle Howard (open) dates from the 17th and 18th centuries and is considered to be the greatest achievement of the architect Vanbrugh. A central dome forms the focal point of the house and is echoed in the 1,000-acre grounds by a circular mausoleum designed by Hawksmoor. Other garden follies include the lovely Temple of the Four Winds, and the huge gatehouse is crowned by a pyramid. Among many treasures inside the house is an extensive collection of period costumes.

The square wooden tower of Raskelf Church, a most unusual feature in this part of England, contrasts pleasantly with the masonry body.

Leave Castle Howard, cross the Howardian Hills, and descend to meet a T-junction at the edge of Slingsby. It is possible to make a detour from the main route to Slingsby by driving forward at the village crossroads.

SLINGSBY, N Yorks

Misnamed and never completed, the 17th-century house known as Slingsby Castle is a picturesque ruin that adds an air of gothic mystery to the countryside round the village. It was originally started for the soldier, philosopher, and mathematician, Sir Charles Cavendish. A feature of the village itself is its maypole, the scene of great celebrations every May 1.

On the main tour, meet the aforementioned crossroads and turn left on to the B1257 SP 'Helmsley'. Continue to Hovingham.

HOVINGHAM, N Yorks

The stone cottages of this lovely little village cluster round the green under the Saxon tower of All Saints' Church and the stately presence of Hovingham Hall. The latter is an unusual building in distinctive yellow limestone, with a gatehouse that was designed as a riding school where horses could be exercised out of the rain (open by appointment only).

In Hovingham turn left on to an unclassified road SP 'Coulton' and 'Easingwold'. Drive through Hovingham High Wood and meet crossroads. Turn right SP 'Gilling' and follow a narrow road for 1¼ miles. Meet a T-junction and turn right on to the B1363 to reach Gilling East.

GILLING EAST, N Yorks

It is thought that the architect Vanbrugh may have designed the west front of Gilling Castle (open), though most of the building is much too old for him to have had any hand in its construction. The keep dates from the 14th century, and a well-preserved ribbed plaster ceiling helps to make its dining room one of the finest in England. On either side of the village are the lovely Hambledon and Howardian Hills.
Return south along the B1363 to reach Brandsby.

BRANDSBY, N Yorks

Features of this harmonious hillside village include a woodcarver's shop, an 18th-century hall, and an unusual church with a stone cupola. Neat terraces of cottages complete the picture.
Continue to Stillington, in the Vale of York.

STILLINGTON, N Yorks

The 18th-century writer Laurence Sterne was vicar here for a time, and the lovely old church in which he served features a 12th-century priest's door.

VALE OF YORK, N Yorks

Numerous country lanes bordered by thick hedgerows criss-cross the fertile farmlands of the Vale of York, a large lowland expanse watered by the River Ouse and its many tributaries. Broad water meadows known as 'ings' border the rivers, providing an ideal habitat for marshland wildlife and water loving plants. Here and there large areas of heathland have survived uncultivated, providing ideal hunting grounds for nightjars and vipers.

The Devil's Arrows are a mysterious group of prehistoric standing stones near Boroughbridge.

Drive through Stillington village and pass the church. Keep forward on to an unclassified road SP 'Easingwold', then in 3½ miles meet the A19 and drive forward to enter Easingwold.

EASINGWOLD, N Yorks

An unusual bull ring can be seen in the market place of this pleasant town of red-brick houses and cobbled lanes. The local church contains an ancient parish coffin.

Meet crossroads in Easingwold and turn left on to an unclassified road to reach Raskelf.

RASKELF, N Yorks

The 15th-century tower of local St Mary's church is made of wood and is said to be unique in Yorkshire. Parts of the building's main body date back to Norman times.

In Raskelf bear left then right SP 'Boroughbridge', and drive to Brafferton.

Castle Howard is a superb example of Vanbrugh's architectural genius.

BRAFFERTON, N Yorks

Brafferton Church was extensively restored in Victorian times, but still displays good examples of 15th-century workmanship.

In Brafferton village turn right and after 1 mile cross the River Swale and turn left. In 2¾ miles turn left then immediately right, then in 1 mile meet a T-junction and turn left. Continue to a roundabout and take the 1st exit on to the B6265. Cross the River Ure and enter Boroughbridge.

BOROUGHBRIDGE, N Yorks

Three large monoliths known ominously as the Devil's Arrows stand a few hundred yards to the west of Boroughbridge. The largest rises to 22½ft, and it is thought that the group may be some 3,000 years old. On the town side of a fine bridge that spans the Ure is a market place with a 250ft-deep well.

Turn left then keep left through Boroughbridge with SP 'York', and at the far end of the town branch left on to an unclassified road to reach Aldborough.

ALDBOROUGH, N Yorks

This pretty village stands on the site of Isurium, the northernmost town to be built without any military motives during the Roman occupation. Remains (AM) revealed through excavation include sections of a boundary wall, two tessellated pavements, and a wide variety of coins, pottery, and artefacts on display in the small site museum. In the village itself are a striking maypole and a cross that probably commemorates the Battle of Boroughbridge, which was fought here in 1322.

Drive to the battle cross and bear right. Pass the church to reach the B6265, turn left to follow the old Ribchester Roman road, and continue to Green Hammerton. Join the A59, and in 1¾ miles cross the River Nidd. Drive through low-lying country for the return to York.

YORK, N Yorks

The many strands of York's proud history can be traced in its fascinating streets, its ancient buildings, superb museums and, above all, in the fabulous minster, the largest Gothic church in England. The Romans built *Eboracum* at this point on the River Ouse; the Anglo-Saxons made the city capital of their kingdom of Deira and, when the Vikings came, they named it Jorvic, from which we get the name of York. Sacked by the Normans, York rose again as a great medieval city, surrounded by massive walls within which a maze of narrow streets grew up around the towering minster. The medieval atmosphere is felt most vividly in the Shambles, the street of the butchers, where in places the overhanging storeys of the ancient houses almost touch across the narrow way. Old street scenes and exhibits of life in bygone times can be seen in the fascinating Castle Museum, and the power of the medieval guilds is displayed in the Merchant Adventurers' House, a restored 14th-century guild house in Fossgate. The minster reigns majestically over the city as it has done for more than 700 years, its beautiful interior lit by glowing stained-glass windows, created by medieval craftsmen at the height of their powers. The graceful design of the west window has earned it the title of the Heart of Yorkshire. The minster undercroft houses the cathedral treasury. In Jacobean and Georgian times York had 2 famous citizens, both of

THE VALE OF YORK

Yorkshire's mighty capital city looks out over the ancient kingdom of Elmet and the lowlands of the Vale of York where 3 great rivers, the Ouse, the Derwent and the Wharfe, meander through rich farmland sheltered by the rolling hills of the Yorkshire Wolds.

whom met a tragic fate: the first was Guy Fawkes, born at a house in Petergate and executed for treason in 1605; the second was Dick Turpin, a legendary hero of the ride from London, hanged as a highwayman in 1739 on the Knavemire, now York racecourse. At the Jorvik Viking Centre is one of Britain's newest and most exciting museums. Here visitors are transported — in 'time cars' — back to the sights, smells and sounds of 10th-century York. Providing a contrast is the National Railway Museum, which pays tribute to York's importance as a railway centre from the early days of steam. Here can be seen locomotives, rolling stock, models, films, and posters.

Leave York on the A1036, SP 'Leeds (A64)'. In 3¼ miles join the A64 and after 6 miles branch left on to the A659 for Tadcaster.

TADCASTER, N Yorks

Tadcaster is the home of traditional Yorkshire ales and the scent of the breweries pervades the old streets which are famous for the large number of public

houses. A restored 15th-century house called the Ark (OACT) has been converted into a museum of pubs and brewing, with a unique collection of fascinating relics of British drinking habits. The dignified stone church has an interesting past; it was completely dismantled in the last century and reconstructed on a site higher above the River Wharfe to save it from flooding. The limestone for the church was quarried locally, and much of this stone was used to build York minster.

In Tadcaster turn left on to the A162, SP 'Sherburn-in-Elmet', and continue to Towton.

TOWTON, N Yorks

One of the most savage battles in English history took place near this peaceful little village in wooded Wharfdale. A stone cross just outside Towton marks the place where more than 30,000 men were slaughtered on Palm Sunday, 1461, during the Wars of the Roses. The bodies were interred in a mass grave in a field nearby, and for centuries after ploughmen would often turn up bones.

At the end of the village turn right on to the B1217, SP 'Garforth'. After ½ mile pass (right) the War of the Roses memorial cross and continue for 2½ miles to reach the entrance to Lotherton Hall.

LOTHERTON HALL, N Yorks

Lotherton Hall (OACT), with its outstanding collection of European works of art, furniture and porcelain, was given to the city of Leeds by the Gascoigne family and is now a country house museum. In addition to the Gascoigne collection, there are superb Chinese ceramics, 20th-century pottery and a fascinating display of historical costumes, including examples of the best of the fashion designs of our own time.

Return along the B1217 for 200 yards and turn right on to an unclassified road, SP 'Sherburn-in-Elmet'. In 3¼ miles turn left on to the B1222 for Sherburn-in-Elmet.

SHERBURN-IN-ELMET, N Yorks

A white church stands like a beacon on the hill above Sherburn, once the eastern capital of the ancient Brigantine kingdom of Elmete. The church, built of local limestone, was the secret meeting place for loyal Catholics during the Reformation, when they are said to have made their way by night through underground passages, to worship according to their faith. The medieval Janus cross in the church, so called after the double-headed Roman deity because the carved figures face opposite directions, was buried for safety during the 16th-century Reformation; when it was later exhumed, a quarrel over its ownership caused it to be sawn in half vertically, but the 2 sections have finally been brought together. The old gabled grammar school dates from the 17th century.

At the crossroads turn right on to the A162, SP 'Ferrybridge', and proceed to South Milford. From here an unclassified road on the right may be taken to Steeton Hall Gatehouse.

STEETON HALL GATEHOUSE, N Yorks

Across the woods and meadows from the village of South Milford, stands the 14th-century gatehouse (AM) of a medieval castle, once owned by the Fairfax family. A forbear of the famous Cromwellian general is said to have ridden out from here to escape with his sweetheart, a wealthy heiress, who was incarcerated in Nun Appleton Priory.

York minster, one of England's best examples of Gothic architecture, has the largest lantern tower in Britain and contains more stained glass than any other cathedral in the country

Water lilies are the speciality of Burnby Hall's lovely gardens

Continue on the A162 and in 1¼ miles, at the roundabout, turn left on to the A63, SP 'Selby', for Monk Fryston.

MONK FRYSTON, N Yorks
This delightful little village with a Tudor Hall (not open) and old cottages around a small square was given to the monks of Selby Abbey in Norman times, hence the first part of its name. The village church predates the Norman Conquest and has preserved intact its Anglo-Saxon tower.

Remain on the A63 to Selby.

SELBY, N Yorks
Famous for its beautiful abbey church, Selby is an ancient town and port on the River Ouse, where small ships still put in and out of the small dock. When boats were built here they had to be launched sideways because the river was too narrow for the usual method. The abbey was founded in 1069 by a monk of Auxerre in France who, following a vision, came to England and sailed up the River Ouse, stopping at a place where 3 swans settled on the water. Here he built a hermitage and received permission from the king to found an abbey. Unfortunately he fell out with the authorities before work could begin, and the present church was started by Hugh de Lacy in 1100. Building went slowly and was not finally completed until the 14th century. The abbey stands, surrounded by lawns, in the attractive little market-place at the heart of the town.

Leave on the A19, SP 'York', and cross the River Ouse by a wooden toll bridge. Pass through Barlby and at the end turn right on to the A163, SP 'Market Weighton', then right again across the railway. Later cross the River Derwent for Bubwith and continue to Holme-upon-Spalding-Moor.

HOLME-UPON-SPALDING-MOOR, Humberside
Lonely Beacon Hill, crowned by Holme Church, looks out over the surrounding flat plain, once a marshland where travellers were guided by the welcome sight of the church tower. Monks kept a nightly vigil, tolling the church bell as a signal to anyone who might be lost. The church is a charming medieval structure, its walls whitewashed inside to show off the beautiful wood furnishings.

At the end of the village turn left, SP 'Bridlington'. In 1¾ miles, at the roundabout, turn left, and 2½ miles farther, at the next roundabout, turn left again on to the A1079, SP 'York'. Pass through Shiptonthorpe to Hayton, then in 1 mile turn right on to the B1247 for Pocklington.

POCKLINGTON, Humberside
This red-roofed little market town sits snugly in the shadow of the Yorkshire Wolds, with many attractive houses along the cheerful streets leading up to the medieval church, sometimes called the Cathedral of the Wolds. A memorial on the church wall commemorates an 18th-century flying man, Tom Pelling, who performed acrobatic tricks on a tightrope slung from the church tower to a nearby inn.

BURNBY HALL GARDENS, Humberside
These beautiful water gardens (OACT) on the outskirts of Pocklington were created by Major Stewart, a world-traveller in the old tradition, who gathered rare plants on his travels and brought home one of the finest collections of water lilies in Europe. Specimens of more than 50 varieties of lily bloom here all summer long. Nearby, in the Stewart Museum, is his collection of hunting trophies.

At the roundabout in Pocklington keep forward, SP 'Malton', then go over the crossroads. Nearly ½ mile farther turn right into Garth Ends, SP 'Millington'. At the next roundabout turn left, then in 1¾ miles keep forward, SP 'Givendale'. This byroad climbs on to the Wolds and passes the hamlet of Great Givendale. Continue for 1¾ miles and turn left on to the A166, SP 'York', to reach Stamford Bridge.

STAMFORD BRIDGE, Humberside
The first of the 2 decisive battles of English history was fought at this quiet village on the River Derwent in 1066. King Harold was threatened by 2 invading forces: across the North Sea were the combined fleets of Tostig of Northumbria and Harold Hardrada of Norway; on the French side of the channel lay the ships of William of Normandy. Both fleets were waiting for a favourable wind to bring them to England, and the Norsemen arrived first, obliging Harold to march his army north to Yorkshire, where he inflicted a crushing defeat on the invaders. In the meantime, however, William had landed in Kent and the Saxon army, exhausted from their long march south, were defeated at the Battle of Hastings and Harold was killed.

Beyond the town cross the River Derwent, then in 5 miles, at the roundabout, take the A1079 for the return to York.

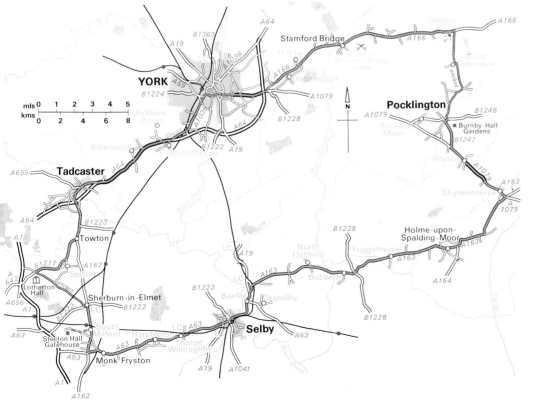

Key to Town Plans

Whitley Bay
North Shields
Newcastle
Sunderland
Carlisle
Washington
Chester-le-Street
Houghton-le-Spring
Durham
Peterlee
Keswick
Billingham
Stockton-on-Tees
Middlesbrough
Bowness-on-Windermere
Kendal
Ripon
Lancaster
Knaresborough
York
Harrogate
Fleetwood
Keighley
Beverley
Blackpool
Bradford
Leeds
Lytham
Hull
Manchester
Liverpool
Manchester Airport
Sheffield
Northwich
Chester
Middlewich

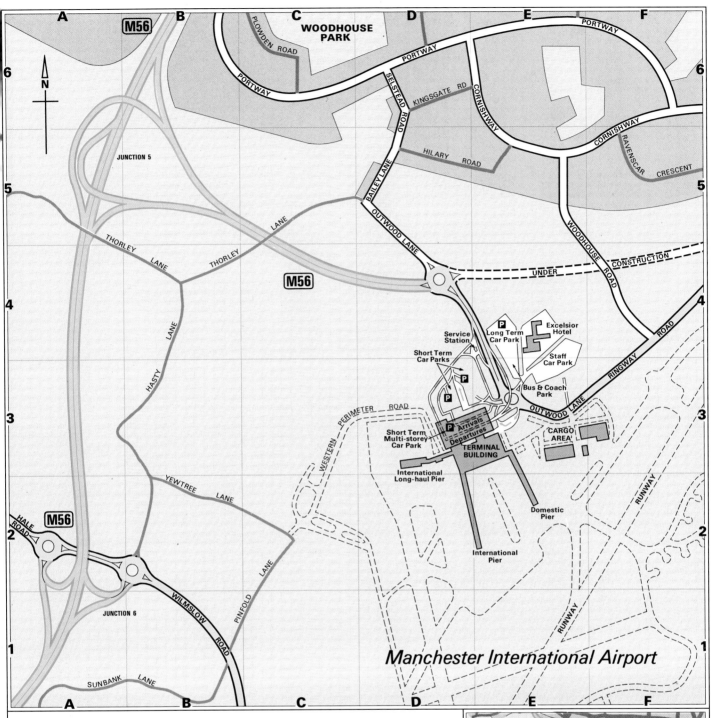

Manchester International Airport

Manchester International Airport

Nine miles south of the city of Manchester lies Manchester International Airport, operating flights to and from the Midlands, the north west, north east, Yorkshire and Wales. As well as flights within Britain, there are regular scheduled services operating to all the major business centres in Europe, the Far East and Australia. Charter and inclusive tour flights also operate from here to destinations world-wide.

The airport has been in use since just before World War II, and enjoys the distinction that its main buildings were opened by HRH Prince Philip. This was not until 1962, when the Prince became the first pilot to park an aircraft alongside the arrivals pier, and the first passenger to use the airport's facilities.

Today Manchester International has a spacious concourse area on the first floor of the terminal.

A bank, post office, bookstall, tobacconist and pharmacy are situated here. At the apron end of the concourse (and lying adjacent to the observation windows) is the Concourse Cafe, a self-service restaurant and bar. Also offering refreshments for travellers and other visitors to the airport is the 200-seat Lancaster restaurant and cocktail lounge, which overlooks International Pier B, and within just two minutes walk the Excelsior Hotel offers 300 bedrooms, a restaurant, a coffee shop and a bar.

The airport is well placed for passengers coming here by both road and rail. It offers easy access to the M56 and to the national motorway network. Greater Manchester Transport buses link the airport to Manchester and to Stockport all the year round, and also make a link to most towns in Greater Manchester during the summer months. Coach services also run to Birmingham, Liverpool, Lancaster, Leeds and Sheffield.

For railway travellers, the nearest station to the airport is Heald Green, which is about two miles away and has two bus services. Frequent trains go to Manchester (Piccadilly) and to Crewe.

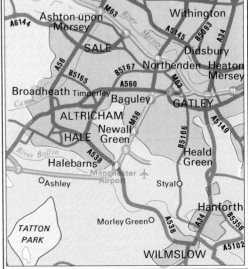

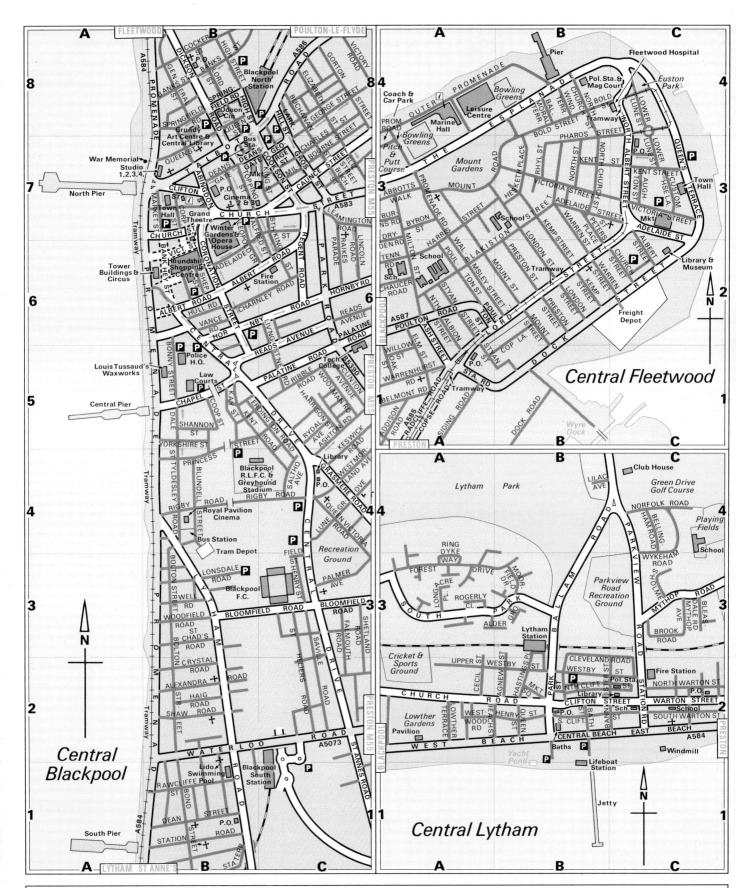

Blackpool

No seaside resort is regarded with greater affection than Blackpool. It is still the place where millions of North Country folk spend their holidays; its famous illuminations draw visitors from all over the world. It provides every conceivable kind of traditional holiday entertainment, and in greater abundance than any other seaside resort in Britain. The famous tower – built in the 1890s as a replica of the Eiffel Tower – the three piers, seven miles of promenade, five miles of illuminations, countless guesthouses, huge numbers of pubs, shops, restaurants and cafes play host to eight million visitors a year.

At the base of the tower is a huge entertainment complex that includes a ballroom, a circus and an aquarium. Other 19th-century landmarks are North Pier and Central Pier, the great Winter Gardens and Opera House and the famous trams that still run along the promenade – the only electric trams still operating in Britain. The most glittering part of modern Blackpool is the famous Golden Mile, packed with amusements, novelty shops and snack stalls. Every autumn it becomes part of the country's most extravagant light show – the illuminations – when the promenade is ablaze with neon representations of anything and everything from moon rockets to the Muppets. Autumn is also the time when Blackpool is a traditional venue for political party conferences.

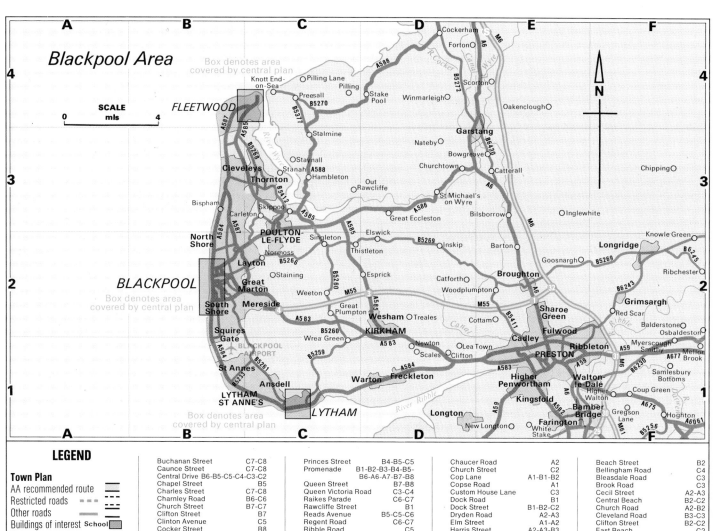

Blackpool Area

Box denotes area covered by central plan

SCALE mls 0 — 4

LEGEND

Town Plan

AA recommended route
Restricted roads
Other roads
Buildings of interest — School
Car parks — P
Parks and open spaces

Area Plan

A roads
B roads
Locations — Wrea Green O
Urban area

Street Index with Grid Reference

Blackpool

Abingdon Street	B7
Adelaide Street	B6-B7-C7
Albert Road	B6-C6
Alexandra Road	B2
Alfred Street	B7-C7-C6
Ashton Road	C4-C5
Bank Hey Street	B6-B7
Banks Street	B8
Bloomfield Road	B3-C3
Blundell Street	B4
Bolton Street	B2-B3-B4
Bond Street	B1-B2
Bonny Street	B5-B6
Buchanan Street	C7-C8
Caunce Street	C7-C8
Central Drive	B6-B5-C5-C4-C3-C2
Chapel Street	B5
Charles Street	C7-C8
Charnley Road	B6-C6
Church Street	B7-C7
Clifton Street	B7
Clinton Avenue	C5
Cocker Street	B2
Cookson Street	B8-B7-C7
Coop Street	B5
Coronation Street	B5-B6-B7
Corporation Street	B7
Crystal Road	B2
Dale Street	B4-B5
Deansgate	B7-C7
Dean Street	B1
Dickson Road	B7-B8
Erdington Road	B5-C5-C4
Elizabeth Street	C7-C8
Falmouth Road	C2-C3
Field Street	C3
General Street	B8
George Street	C7-C8
Gorton Street	C8
Grasmere Road	C4
Grosvenor Street	C7
Haig Road	B2
Harrison Street	C5
Henry Street	C3
High Street	B8
Hornby Road	B6-C6
Hull Road	B6
Kay Street	B5
Kent Road	B5-C5-C4
Keswick Road	C4-C5
King Street	C7
Larkhill Street	C8
Leamington Road	C7
Leopold Grove	B7-B6-C6
Lincoln Road	C6-C7
Livingstone Road	C5-C6
Lonsdale Road	B3
Lord Street	B8
Lune Grove	C4
Lytham Road	B1-B2-B3-B4
Market Street	B7
Milbourne Street	C7-C8
Palatine Road	B5-C5-C6
Palmer Avenue	C3
Park Road	C5-C6-C7

Princes Street	B4-B5-C5
Promenade	B1-B2-B3-B4-B5-B6-A6-A7-B7-B8
Queen Street	B7-B8
Queen Victoria Road	C3-C4
Raikes Parade	C6-C7
Rawcliffe Street	B1
Reads Avenue	B5-C5-C6
Regent Road	C6-C7
Ribble Road	C5
Rigby Road	B4-C4
Rydal Avenue	C5
St Annes Road	C1-C2
St Chad's Road	B3
St Heliers Road	C2-C3
Salthouse Avenue	C4
Saville Road	C2-C3
Shannon Street	B5
Shaw Road	B2
Sheppard Street	B6
Shetland Road	C2-C3
South King Street	C6-C7
Springfield Road	B8
Station Road	B1
Station Terrace	B1
Talbot Road	B7-B8-C8
Topping Street	B7
Tyldesley Road	B4
Vance Road	B6
Victoria Street	B6
Victory Road	C8
Waterloo Road	B2-C2
Wellington Road	B3
Westmorland Avenue	C4
Woodfield Road	B3
Woolman Road	C5
Yorkshire Street	B5

Fleetwood

Abbots Walk	A3
Adelaide Street	B3-C3-C2
Addison Road	A1
Albert Street	C2-C3
Ash Street	A1-A2
Aughton Street	C3
Balmoral Terrace	B4
Belmont Road	A1
Blakiston Street	A2-B2-B3
Bold Street	B4-C4
Burns Road	A3
Byron Street	A3

Chaucer Road	A2
Church Street	C2
Cop Lane	A1-B1-B2
Copse Road	A1
Custom House Lane	C3
Dock Road	B1
Dock Street	B1-B2-C2
Dryden Road	A2-A3
Elm Street	A1-A2
Harris Street	A2-A3-B3
Hesketh Place	B3
Kemp Street	B2-B3
Kent Street	B3-C3
London Street	B2-B3
Lord Street	A1-A2-B2-C2-C3
Lower Lune Street	C3-C4
Milton Street	A2-A3
Mount Road	A3-B3
Mount Street	A2-B2
North Albert Street	C3-C4
North Albion Street	A1-A2
North Church Street	B3-B4
North Street	B3
Oak Street	A1
Outer Promenade	A4-B4
Pharos Street	B3-C3-C4
Poulton Road	A2
Poulton Street	A2
Preston Street	B2
Promenade Road	A3-A4
Queen's Terrace	C3-C4
Radcliffe Road	A1
Rhyl Street	B3
St Peters Place	B2-B3
Siding Road	A1
Station Road	A1
Styan Street	A2-A1-B1
Tennyson Road	A2
The Esplanade	A3-A4-B4
Victoria Street	B3-C3
Walmsley Street	A3-A2-B2
Warrenhurst Road	A1
Warren Street	B3-B2-C2
Willow Street	A1
Windsor Terrace	B4

Lytham

Agnew Street	B2-B3
Alder Grove	A3-B3
Ballam Road	B2-B3-B4-C4
Bath Street	B2

Beach Street	B2
Bellingham Road	C4
Bleasdale Road	C3
Brook Road	C3
Cecil Street	A2-A3
Central Beach	B2-C2
Church Road	A2-B2
Cleveland Road	B3-C3
Clifton Street	B2-C2
East Beach	C2
Forest Drive	A3-B3
Hastings Place	B2-B3
Henry Street	B2
Lilac Avenue	B4
Longacre Place	A3
Lowther Terrace	A2
Market Square	B2
Moorfield Drive	B3
Mythop Avenue	C3
Mythop Road	C3
Norfolk Road	C4
North Clifton Street	B2-C2
North Warton Street	C2
Park Street	B2
Parkview Road	C2-C3-C4
Queen Street	B2
Ring Dyke Way	A3
Rogerly Close	A3
South Clifton Street	B2-C2
South-Holme	C3
South Park	A3-B3
South Warton Street	C2
Station Road	C2
Upper Westby Street	A2-B2
Warton Street	C2
West Beach	A2-B2
Westby Street	B2-C2
Westwood Road	A2
Wykeham Road	C3-C4

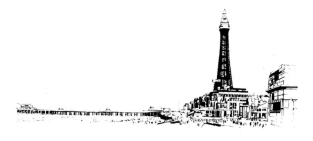

BLACKPOOL

Three piers, seven miles of promenade packed with entertainments galore and seemingly endless sandy beaches spread out beneath Blackpool's unmistakable tower which stands 518ft high in Britain's busiest and biggest holiday resort.

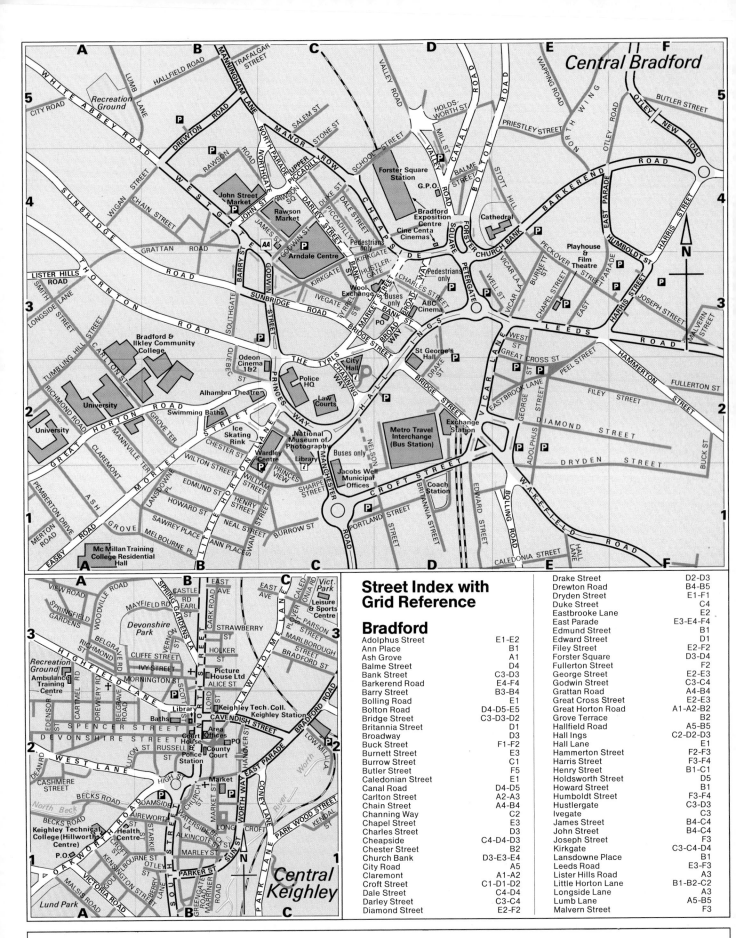

Central Bradford

(map)

Central Keighley

(map)

Street Index with Grid Reference

Bradford

Adolphus Street	E1-E2
Ann Place	B1
Ash Grove	A1
Balme Street	D4
Bank Street	C3-D3
Barkerend Road	E4-F4
Barry Street	B3-B4
Bolling Road	E1
Bolton Road	D4-D5-E5
Bridge Street	C3-D3-D2
Britannia Street	D1
Broadway	D3
Buck Street	F1-F2
Burnett Street	E3
Burrow Street	C1
Butler Street	F5
Caledonian Street	E1
Canal Road	D4-D5
Carlton Street	A2-A3
Chain Street	A4-B4
Channing Way	C2
Chapel Street	E3
Charles Street	D3
Cheapside	C4-D4-D3
Chester Street	B2
Church Bank	D3-E3-E4
City Road	A5
Claremont	A1-A2
Croft Street	C1-D1-D2
Dale Street	C4-D4
Darley Street	C3-C4
Diamond Street	E2-F2
Drake Street	D2-D3
Drewton Road	B4-B5
Dryden Street	E1-F1
Duke Street	C4
Eastbrooke Lane	E2
East Parade	E3-E4-F4
Edmund Street	B1
Edward Street	D1
Filey Street	E2-F2
Forster Square	D3-D4
Fullerton Street	F2
George Street	E2-E3
Godwin Street	C3-C4
Grattan Road	A4-B4
Great Cross Street	E2-E3
Great Horton Road	A1-A2-B2
Grove Terrace	B2
Hallfield Road	A5-B5
Hall Ings	C2-D2-D3
Hall Lane	E1
Hammerton Street	F2-F3
Harris Street	F3-F4
Henry Street	B1-C1
Holdsworth Street	D5
Howard Street	B1
Humboldt Street	F3-F4
Hustlergate	C3-D3
Ivegate	C3
James Street	B4-C4
John Street	B4-C4
Joseph Street	F3
Kirkgate	C3-C4-D4
Lansdowne Place	B1
Leeds Road	E3-F3
Lister Hills Road	A3
Little Horton Lane	B1-B2-C2
Longside Lane	A3
Lumb Lane	A5-B5
Malvern Street	F3

Bradford

Wool and Bradford are almost synonymous, such was its importance in the 19th century as a central market after the Industrial Revolution brought steam power to the trade. Like many small market towns that exploded into industrial cities almost overnight, Bradford's architecture is a mish-mash of grand civic buildings, factories and crowded housing. Among the former, the Wool Exchange is impressive, with its ornate tower adorned with stone busts of 13 famous men, and the massive town hall, also topped by a tower, 200ft high. Few traces remain of the town's past but one obvious exception is the cathedral. Set on a rise, its detailed carvings – particularly the 20 angels that support the nave roof – catch the eye.

Bradford boasts several parks – notably Lister Park where there is a boating lake, an open-air swimming pool, a botanical garden and a scented garden for the blind – and Bowling Park, on the other side of town. Cartwright Hall, named after the inventor of the power loom, stands in Lister Park. It now houses Bradford's permanent art collection.

Keighley The Brontë sisters used to walk from Haworth to this pleasant 19th-century town for their shopping sprees. Nowadays, the restored Keighley and Worth Valley Railway is a great attraction and passengers can travel to Oxenhope.

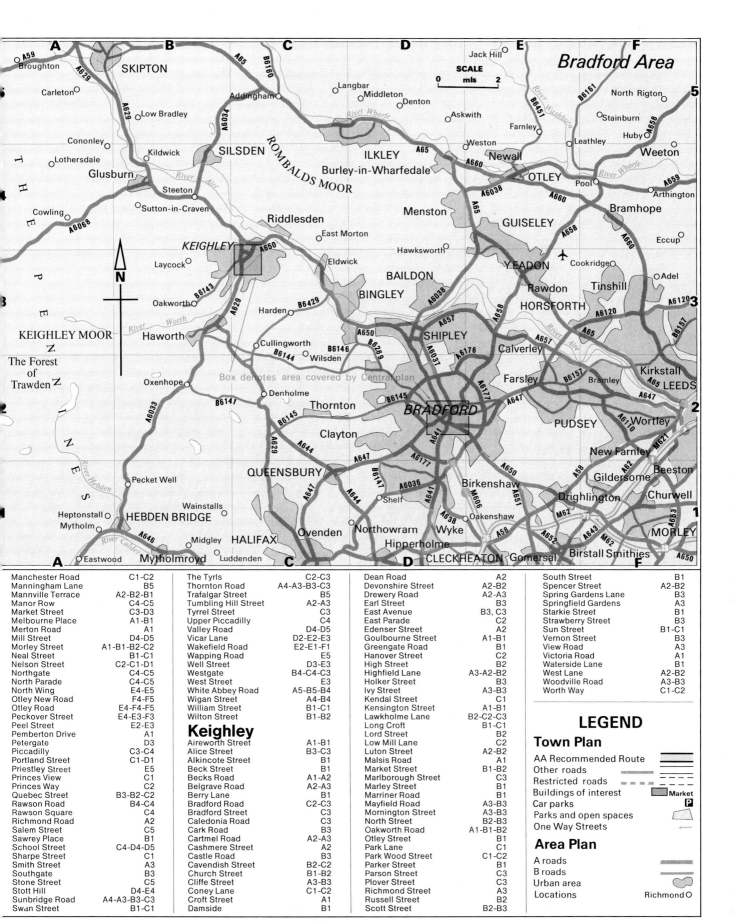

SCALE
0   mls   2

Manchester Road	C1-C2	The Tyrls	C2-C3	Dean Road	A2
Manningham Lane	B5	Thornton Road	A4-A3-B3-C3	Devonshire Street	A2-B2
Mannville Terrace	A2-B2-B1	Trafalgar Street	B5	Drewery Road	A2-A3
Manor Row	C4-C5	Tumbling Hill Street	A2-A3	Earl Street	B3
Market Street	C3-D3	Tyrrel Street	C3	East Avenue	B3, C3
Melbourne Place	A1-B1	Upper Piccadilly	C4	East Parade	C2
Merton Road	A1	Valley Road	D4-D5	Edenser Street	A2
Mill Street	D4-D5	Vicar Lane	D2-E2-E3	Goulbourne Street	A1-B1
Morley Street	A1-B1-B2-C2	Wakefield Road	E2-E1-F1	Greengate Road	B1
Neal Street	B1-C1	Wapping Road	E5	Hanover Street	C2
Nelson Street	C2-C1-D1	Well Street	D3-E3	High Street	B2
Northgate	C4-C5	Westgate	B4-C4-C3	Highfield Lane	A3-A2-B2
North Parade	C4-C5	West Street	E3	Holker Street	B3
North Wing	E4-E5	White Abbey Road	A5-B5-B4	Ivy Street	A3-B3
Otley New Road	F4-F5	Wigan Street	A4-B4	Kendal Street	C1
Otley Road	E4-F4-F5	William Street	B1-C1	Kensington Street	A1-B1
Peckover Street	E4-E3-F3	Wilton Street	B1-B2	Lawkholme Lane	B2-C2-C3
Peel Street	E2-E3			Long Croft	B1-C1
Pemberton Drive	A1	**Keighley**		Lord Street	B2
Petergate	D3	Aireworth Street	A1-B1	Low Mill Lane	C2
Piccadilly	C3-C4	Alice Street	B3-C3	Luton Street	A2-B2
Portland Street	C1-D1	Alkincote Street	B1	Malsis Road	A1
Priestley Street	E5	Beck Street	B1	Market Street	B1-B2
Princes View	C1	Becks Road	A1-A2	Marlborough Street	C3
Princes Way	C2	Belgrave Road	A2-A3	Marley Street	B1
Quebec Street	B3-B2-C2	Berry Lane	B1	Marriner Road	B1
Rawson Road	B4-C4	Bradford Road	C2-C3	Mayfield Road	A3-B3
Rawson Square	C4	Bradford Street	C3	Mornington Street	A3-B3
Richmond Road	A2	Caledonia Road	C3	North Street	B2-B3
Salem Street	C5	Cark Road	B3	Oakworth Road	A1-B1-B2
Sawrey Place	B1	Cartmel Road	A2-A3	Otley Street	B1
School Street	C4-D4-D5	Cashmere Street	A2	Park Lane	C1
Sharpe Street	C1	Castle Road	B3	Park Wood Street	C1-C2
Smith Street	A3	Cavendish Street	B2-C2	Parker Street	B1
Southgate	B3	Church Street	B1-B2	Parson Street	C3
Stone Street	C5	Cliffe Street	A3-B3	Plover Street	C3
Stott Hill	D4-E4	Coney Lane	C1-C2	Richmond Street	A3
Sunbridge Road	A4-A3-B3-C3	Croft Street	A1	Russell Street	B2
Swan Street	B1-C1	Damside	B1	Scott Street	B2-B3

South Street	B1
Spencer Street	A2-B2
Spring Gardens Lane	B3
Springfield Gardens	A3
Starkie Street	B1
Strawberry Street	B3
Sun Street	B1-C1
Vernon Street	B3
View Road	A3
Victoria Road	A1
Waterside Lane	B1
West Lane	A2-B2
Woodville Road	A3-B3
Worth Way	C1-C2

LEGEND

Town Plan

AA Recommended Route	
Other roads	
Restricted roads	
Buildings of interest	Market
Car parks	P
Parks and open spaces	
One Way Streets	

Area Plan

A roads	
B roads	
Urban area	
Locations	Richmond O

BRADFORD
St George's, built with the profits of the wool trade, is one of Bradford's imposing Victorian buildings. It is once again being used for the purpose for which it was intended – a concert hall – and has exceptionally good acoustics.

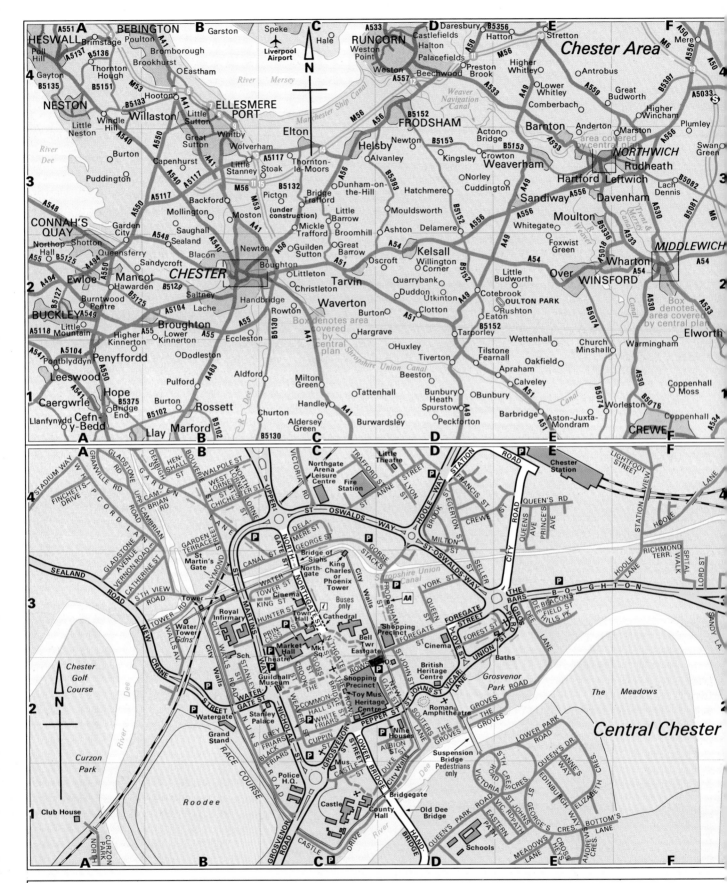

Chester

Chester is the only English city to have preserved the complete circuit of its Roman and medieval walls. On the west side, the top of the walls is now at pavement level, but on the other three sides the walk along the ramparts is remarkable. Two of the old watchtowers contain small museums: the Water Tower, built to protect the old river port, displays relics of medieval Chester; King Charles's Tower, from which Charles I watched the defeat of the Royalist army at the Battle of Rowton Moor in 1645, portrays Chester's role in the Civil War.

Looking down from the top of the Eastgate, crowned with the ornate and gaily-coloured Jubilee Clock erected in 1897, the view down the main street, the old Roman *Via Principalis*, reveals a dazzling display of the black-and-white timbered buildings for which Chester is famous. One of these, Providence House, bears the inscription 'God's Providence is Mine Inheritance', carved in thanks for sparing the survivors of the plague of 1647 that ravaged the city.

On either side of Eastgate, Watergate and Bridge Street are the Rows, a feature unique to Chester, and dating back at least to the 13th century. These covered galleries of shops, raised up at first-floor level, protected pedestrians from weather and traffic. Chester's magnificent cathedral has beautifully carved choir stalls.

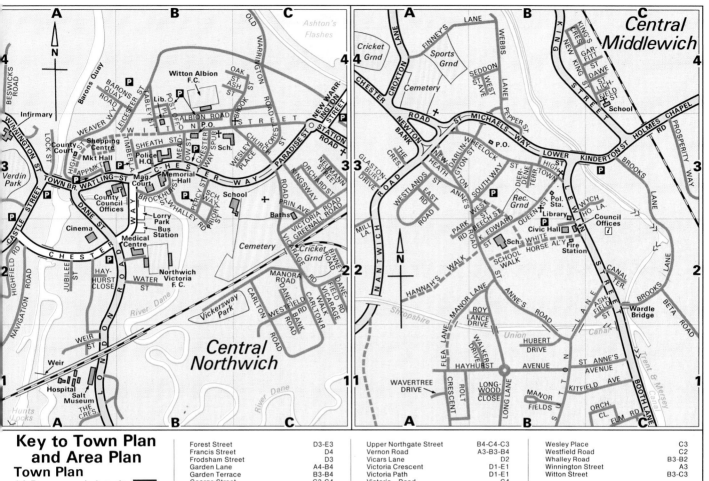

Key to Town Plan and Area Plan

Town Plan

AA Recommended roads	▬▬▬
Other roads	▬▬▬
Restricted roads	▬ ▬ ▬
Buildings of interest	College ▦
One Way Streets	→
Car Parks	🅿
Parks and open spaces	▢
Churches	✝

Area Plan

A roads	▬▬▬
B roads	▬▬▬
Locations	Duddon○
Urban area	◯

Street Index with Grid Reference

Chester

Albion Street	D2
Andrews Crescent	E1
Anne's Way	E2-E1
Beaconsfield Street	E3
Black Friars	C1-C2
Bottom's Lane	E1-F1
Boughton	E3-F3
Bouverie Street	B4
Bridge Street	C2
Brook Street	D4
Cambrian Road	A4-B4
Canal Street	B3-C3
Castle Drive	C1
Castle Street	C1
Catherine Street	A3-B3
Chichester Street	B4-C4
City Road	E3-E4
City Walls Road	B3-B2
Commonhall Street	C2
Crewe Street	D4-E4
Crook Street	C2
Cross Heys	E1
Cuppin Street	C2
Curzon Park North	A1
Dee Hills Park	E3
Dee Lane	E3
Delamere Street	C4
Denbigh Street	B4
Duke Street	D1-D2
Eastern Path	D1-E1
Edinburgh Way	E1
Egerton Street	D4
Elizabeth Crescent	E1-E2
Finchetts Drive	A4
Foregate Street	D3
Forest Street	D3-E3
Francis Street	D4
Frodsham Street	D3
Garden Lane	A4-B4
Garden Terrace	B3-B4
George Street	C3-C4
Gladstone Avenue	A3-A4
Gladstone Road	A4
Gorse Stacks	C4-C3-D3
Goss Street	C2
Granville Road	A4
Grey Friars	C2
Grosvenor Park Road	E3
Grosvenor Road	C1
Grosvenor Street	C1-C2
Groves Road	D2-E2
Handbridge	D1
Henshall Street	B4
Hoole Lane	F3-F4
Hoole Way	D4
Hunter Street	B3-C3
King Street	B3-C3
Lightfoot Street	E4-F4
Lord Street	F3
Lorne Street	B4
Lower Bridge Street	C2-C1-D1
Lower Park Road	D2-E2
Love Street	D3
Lyon Street	D4
Meadows Lane	E1
Milton Street	D4
New Crane Street	A3-B3-B2
Newgate Street	D2
Nicholas Street	C2-C1
Northgate Street	C3-C2
North Lorne Street	C1
Nuns Road	B2-B1-C1
Pepper Street	C2-D2
Princess Street	C3
Prince's Avenue	E4
Queens Avenue	E4
Queen's Drive	E1-E2
Queen's Park Road	D1-E1
Queen's Road	E4
Queen Street	D3
Raymond Street	B3-B4
Richmond Terrace	F4
St Anne Street	C4-D4
St George's Crescent	E1
St Johns Road	E1
St Johns Street	D2
St John Street	D3-D2
St Martins Way	B4-B3-C3-B2-C2
St Oswalds Way	C4-D4-D3
Sealand Road	A3
Seller Street	D3
Souters Lane	D2
South Crescent Road	D2-E2-E1
South View Road	A3-B3
Spital Walk	F4-F3
Stadium Way	A4
Stanley Road	B2
Station Road	D4-E4
Station View	F4
The Bars	E3
The Groves	D2-E2
The Rows	C2
Tower Road	B4
Trafford Street	C4-D4
Union Street	D2-D3-E3
Upper Cambrian Road	A4-B4-B3

Upper Northgate Street	B4-C4-C3
Vernon Road	A3-B3-B4
Vicars Lane	D2
Victoria Crescent	D1-E1
Victoria Path	D1-E1
Victoria Road	C4
Walls Avenue	B3-B2
Walpole Street	B4
Watergate Street	B2-C2
Water Tower Street	B3-C3
Weaver Street	C2
West Lorne Street	B4
White Friars	C2
Whipcord Lane	A4-B4
York Street	D3

Northwich

Albion Road	B3
Apple Market	A3
Ash Street	B4-C4
Barons Quay Road	A4-B4
Beswicks Road	A4
Binney Road	C2
Brockhurst Street	B3
Brook Street	B3-C3-C4
Carlton Road	C2-C1
Castle Street	A2-A3
Chester Way	A2-B2-B3-C3
Chester Way Spur	B3
Church Road	C3
Danebank Road	C2-C1
Danefield Road	C2
Dane Street	A3-A2
Forest Street	C3
Greenall Road	C2-C3
Hayhurst Close	A2
Highfield Road	A2
High Street	A3
Jubilee Street	A2
Kingsway	C3
Leicester Street	B3-B4
Lock Street	A3
London Road	A1-A2-B2
Manora Road	C2
Meadow Bank	B3
Navigation Road	A1-A2
Neumann Street	C3
New Warrington Street	C3-C4
Oak Street	B4-C4
Old Warrington Road	C4-C3
Orchard Street	C3
Paradise Street	C3
Percy Street	B3
Post Office Place	B4-B3
Princes Avenue	C3
Priory Street	B2-B3
School Way	B3
Sheath Street	B3
Station Road	C3
The Crescent	A1
Tabley Street	B4-B3
Timber Lane	B3
Town Bridge	A3
Vicarage Road	C2
Vicarage Walk	C2
Victoria Road	C2-C3
Water Street	B2
Watling Street	A3-B3
Weaver Way	A3-B3-B4
Weir Street	A1

Wesley Place	C3
Westfield Road	C2
Whalley Road	B3-B2
Winnington Street	A3
Witton Street	B3-C3

Middlewich

Ashfield Street	C2
Beech Road	B2-B3
Beta Road	C2-C1
Booth Lane	C1
Brooks Lane	C3-C2
Canal Terrace	C2
Chester Road	A4-A3
Croxton Lane	A4
Darlington Street	A3-B3
Dawe Street	C4
Dierdene Terrace	B3
East Road	A3
Elm Road	C1
Finney's Lane	A4-B4
Flea Lane	A1
Garfitt Street	B4-C4
Glastonbury Drive	A3
Hannah's Walk	A2-B2
Hayhurst Avenue	A1-B1
High Town	B3
Holmes Chapel Road	C3-C4
Hubert Drive	B1
Kinderton Street	B3-C3
King Edward Street	B2
King's Crescent	B4-C4
King Street	B4-C4-C3
Kitfield Avenue	B1-C1
Lewin Street	B3-B2-C2-C1
Lichfield Street	C4
Long Lane	B1
Longwood Close	B2
Lower Street	B3
Manor Fields	B1
Manor Lane	A2-B2
Mill Lane	A2
Nantwich Road	A1-A2-A3
New King Street	B4-C4
Newton Bank	A4-A3
Newton Heath	A3
Orchard Close	C1
Park Road	A2-B2
Pepper Street	B4-B3
Prosperity Way	C3
Queen Street	B2-B3
Rolt Crescent	A1-B1
Roy Lance Drive	B2
St Anne's Avenue	B1-C1
St Anne's Road	A3-B3-B2-B1
St Michaels Way	A3-B3
School Walk	B2
Seddon Street	B4
Southway	B3
Sutton Lane	B1-B2-C2
The Crescent	A3
Walker Drive	B1
Wavertree Drive	A1
Webbs Lane	B4
West Avenue	B4
Westlands Road	A3-A2
West Street	A3
Wheelock Street	A3-B3
White Horse Alley	B2
Wych House Lane	B3-C3

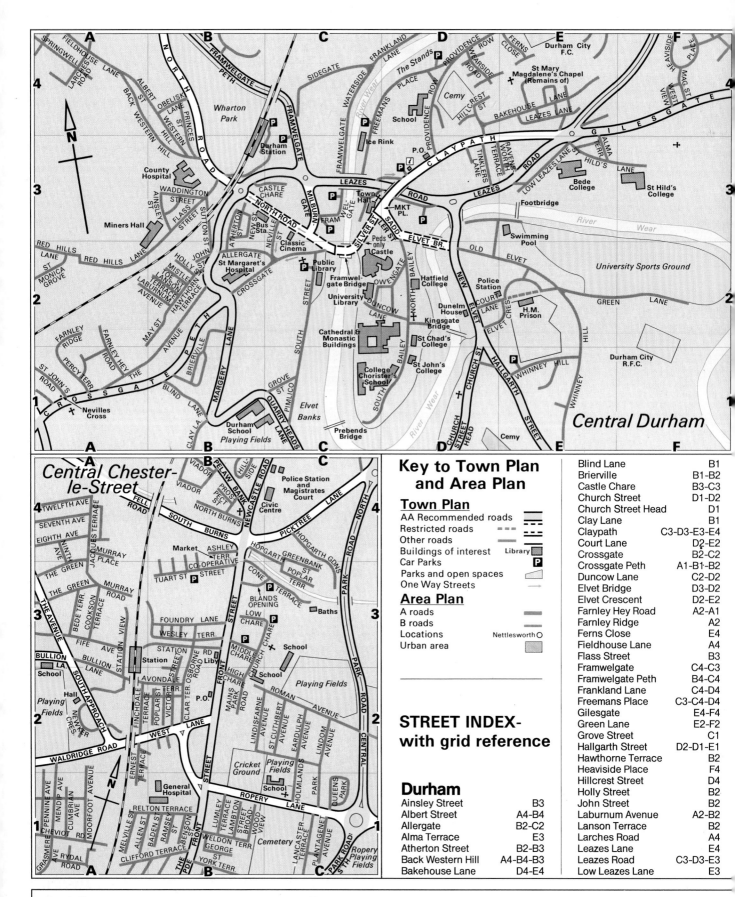

Central Durham

Central Chester-le-Street

Durham

The castle and the cathedral stand side by side high above the city like sentinels, dramatically symbolising the military and religious power Durham wielded in the past. Its origins date from about 995 when the remains of St Cuthbert arrived from Lindisfarne and his shrine was a popular centre of pilgrimage. Soon after that early fortifications were built, later replaced by a stone castle which became the residence of the Prince-Bishops of Durham – powerful feudal rulers appointed by the King. Today the city's university, the oldest in England after Oxford and Cambridge, occupies the castle and most of the buildings around peaceful, secluded Palace Green. The splendid Norman cathedral, sited on the other side of the Green, is considered to be one of the finest in Europe. Its combination of strength and size, tempered with grace and beauty, is awe-inspiring.

Under the shadow of these giants the old city streets, known as vennels, ramble down the bluff past the 17th-century Bishop Cosin's House and the old grammar school, to the thickly-wooded banks of the Wear. Here three historic bridges link the city's heart with the pleasant Georgian suburbs on the other side of the river.

Although Durham is not an industrial city, it has become the venue for the North-East miners' annual Gala Day in July.

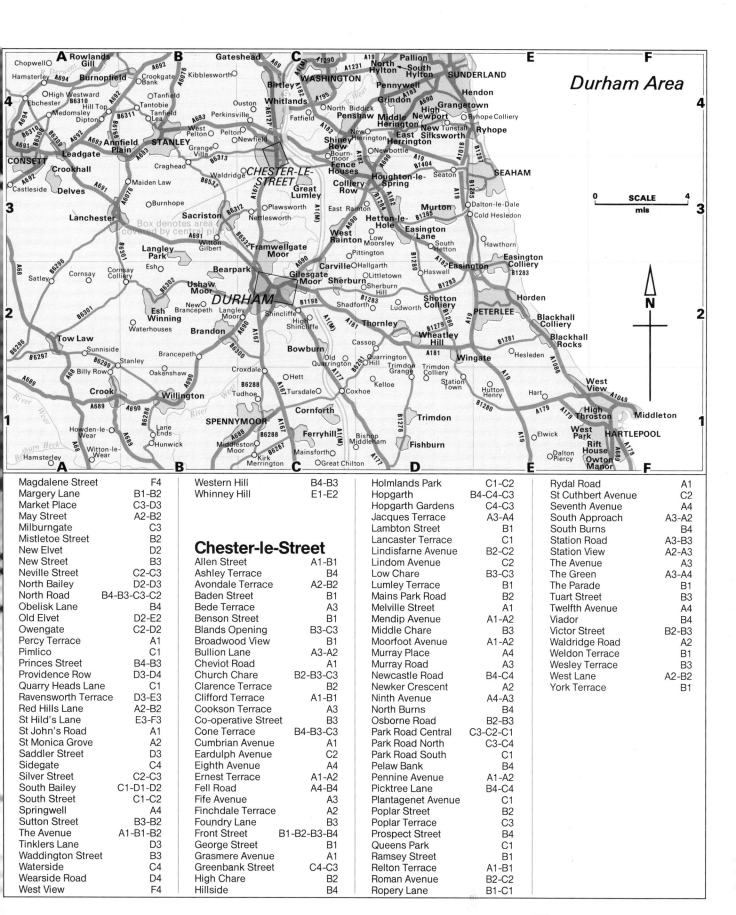

Durham Area

SCALE 0 — 4 mls

N

Magdalene Street	F4	Western Hill	B4-B3	Holmlands Park	C1-C2	Rydal Road	A1

DURHAM
High above the wooded banks of the River Wear, Durham's castle and cathedral crown the steep hill on which the city is built. They share the site with several of the university's attractive old buildings.

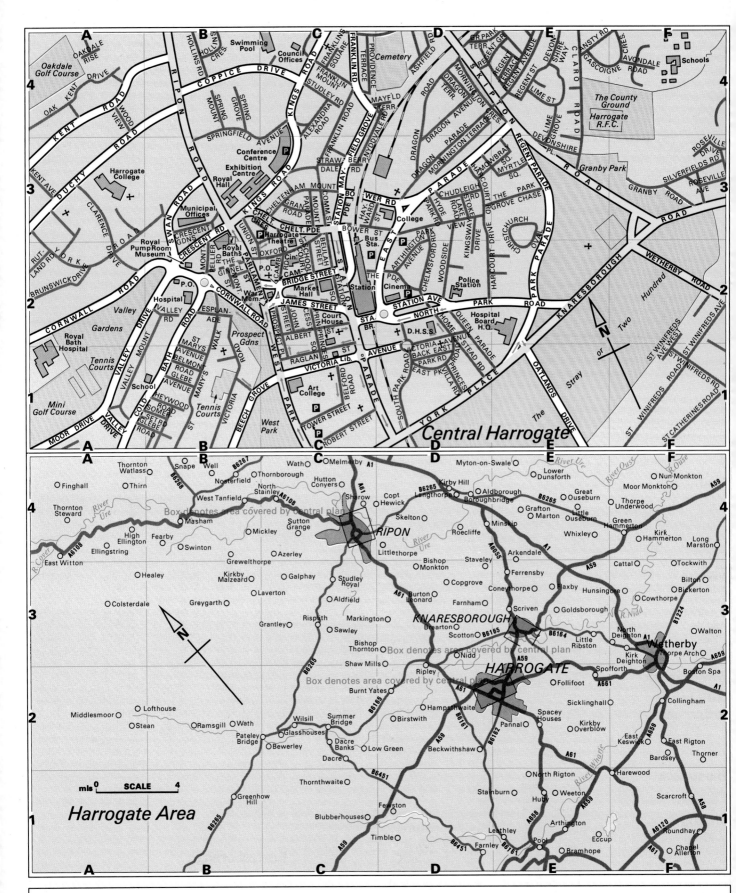

Central Harrogate

Harrogate Area

mls 0 SCALE 4

Harrogate

Dignified Victorian stone buildings and lovely gardens reflect Harrogate's 19th-century popularity as a spa town and its Royal Baths, opened in 1897, became one of the largest hydrotherapy establishments in the world. More recently the town has become a busy conference centre, the main venues being the Royal Hall and the elegant old Assembly Rooms. A glass-covered walkway in Valley Gardens leads to the Sun Pavilion and part of the lovely Harlow Car Gardens is used for experimental horticulture.

Ripon, known as the Gateway to the Dales, stands at the junction of three rivers; the Ure, the Skell and the Laver. Its small cathedral, a delightful 12th-century building occupying the site of an Anglo-Saxon church, has a small museum of church treasures in the original crypt. One corner of the town's rectangular market square is marked by the medieval Wakeman's house, now a local museum and tourist information centre.

Knaresborough Here buildings scramble higgledy-piggledy up a rocky outcrop from the banks of the River Nidd to the town's ruined 14th-century castle. The keep, two baileys and two gatehouses have survived, and there is a museum in the grounds. The town is able to claim two records; it has the oldest linen-mill and the oldest chemist's shop in England.

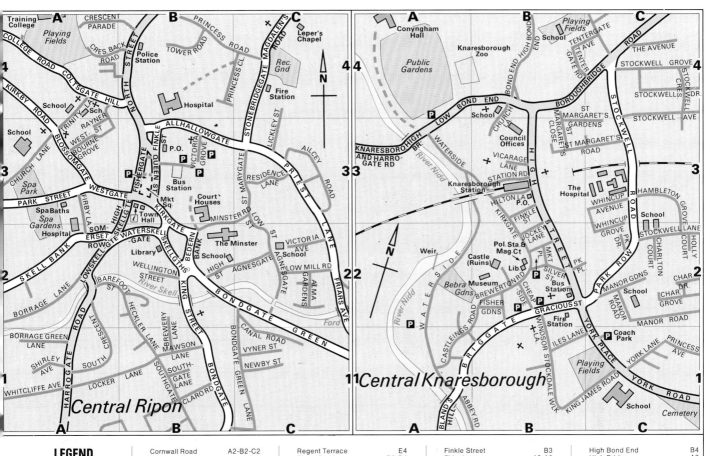

Central Ripon

Central Knaresborough

LEGEND

Town Plan

AA recommended route
Restricted roads
Other roads
Buildings of interest   Station ▣
Car parks   🅿
Parks and open spaces
One way streets ←

Area Plan

A roads
B roads
Locations   Nidd ○
Urban area

Street Index with Grid Reference

Harrogate

Albert Street	C2
Alexandra Road	C4
Ansty Road	E4-F4
Arthington Avenue	D2
Ashfield Road	D4
Avondale Road	F4
BackEast Park Road	D1
Beech Grove	B1-C1
Belford Road	C1
Belmont Road	B1
Beulah Street	C2
Bower Road	C3-D3
Bower Street	C3-D3
Brunswick Drive	A2
Cambridge Road	C2
Cambridge Street	C2
Chelmsford Road	D2-D3
Cheltenham Crescent	B3-C3
Cheltenham Mount	C3
Cheltenham Parade	C3
Christchurch Oval	E2-E3
Chudleigh Road	D3
Clarence Drive	A2-A3
Claro Road	E3-E4
Cold Bath Road	A1-B1-B2
Commercial Street	C3
Coppice Drive	B4-C4
Cornwall Road	A2-B2-C2
Crescent Gardens	B3
Crescent Road	B2-B3
Devonshire Place	E3
Devonshire Way	E4
Dragon Avenue	D3-D4
Dragon Parade	D3-D4
Dragon Road	D3-D4
Dragon Terrace	D4
Duchy Road	A3-A4-B4
East Parade	D2-D3-E3-E4
East Park Road	D1-D2
Esplanade	B2
Franklin Mount	C4
Franklin Road	C3-C4
Franklins Square	C4
Gascoigne Crescent	E4-F4
Glebe Avenue	B1
Glebe Road	A1-B1
Granby Road	F3
Granville Road	C3
Grove Park Terrace	D4-E4
Harcourt Drive	D2-D3
Harcourt Road	D3
Hayward Street	C3-D3
Heywood Road	B1
Hollins Crescent	B4
Hollins Road	B4
Homestead Road	D1-D2
Hyde Park Road	D3
James Street	C2
John Street	C2
Kent Avenue	A3
Kent Road	A3-A4-B4
King's Road	B3-C3-C4
Kingsway Drive	D2-D3
Knaresborough Road	E1-E2-F2-F3
Lime Grove	E3-E4
Lime Street	E4
Mayfield Grove	C3-C4
Mayfield Terrace	C4-D4
Montpellier Road	B2
Montpellier Street	B2
Moor Drive	A1
Mornington Crescent	D4-E4
Mornington Terrace	D3-D4
Mount Parade	C3
Mowbray Square	D3-E3
Myrtle Square	E3
North Park Road	D2-E2
Nyddvale Road	C3-C4-D4
Oakdale Rise	A4
Oak Kent Drive	A4
Oatlands Drive	E1
Oxford Street	B2-C2-C3
Park Chase	E3
Park Parade	E1-E2-E3
Park View	D3
Parliament Street	B3-B2-C2
Princes Square	C1-C2
Princes Street	C2
Princes Villa Road	D1
Prospect Place	C1-C2
Providence Terrace	C4
Queen Parade	D2-D1-E1
Raglan Street	C1-C2
Regent Avenue	E4
Regent Grove	D4-E4
Regent Parade	E3-E4
Regent Street	E4
Regent Terrace	E4
Ripon Road	B3-B4
Robert Street	C1
Roseville Avenue	F3
Roseville Drive	F3
Rutland Road	A2
St Catherine's Road	F1
St Marys Avenue	B1
St Mary's Walk	B1-B2
St Winifreds Avenue	F1-F2
St Winifreds Avenue West	F1-F2
St Winifreds Road	F1
School Court	C2
Silverfields Road	F3
Skipton Road	D4-E4-E3-F3
Somerset Road	A1-B1
South Park Road	D1
Springfield Avenue	B4-B3-C3-C4
Spring Grove	B4
Spring Mount	B4
Station Avenue	D2
Station Bridge	C2
Station Parade	C3-C2-C1-D1
Station Square	C2
Stoke Lake Road	D3
Strawberry Dale Road	C3
Studley Road	C4
Swan Road	B2-B3
The Ginnel	B2
The Grove	D3-E3
The Parade	C2-D2
Tower Street	C1
Union Street	B2-B3
Valley Drive	A1-A2-B2
Valley Mount	A1-B1-B2
Valley Road	B2
Victoria Avenue	C1-D1-D2
Victoria Road	B1-B2
West Park	C1-C2
Wetherby Road	F2
Woodside	D2-D3
Wood View	A4
York Place	D1-E1
York Road	A3-A2-A3-B3

Ripon

Agnesgate	B2-C2
Ailcey Road	C3
Allhallowgate	B3-C3
Alma Gardens	C2
Barefoot Street	A2-B2
Bedern Bank	B2
Blossomgate	A3
Bondgate	B1
Bondgate Green	B2-C2-C1
Bondgate Green Lane	C1-C2
Borrage Green Lane	A1
Borrage Lane	A2
Brewery Lane	B1-B2
Canal Road	C1-C2
Church Lane	A3
Claro Road	B1
College Road	A4
Coltsgate Hill	A4-B4
Crescent Back Road	A4-B4
Crescent Parade	A4-B4
Finkle Street	B3
Firby Lane	A2-A3
Fishergate	B3
Friars Avenue	C1-C2
Harrogate Road	A1-A2
Heckler Lane	B1-B2
High Skellgate	A3-A2-B2-B3
High Street	B2
King Street	B1-B2
Kirkby Road	A3-A4
Kirkgate	B2-B3
Lickley Street	C3-C4
Locker Lane	A1-B1
Low Mill Lane	C2
Lowskellgate	A2
Low Street	C2-C3
Magdalen's Road	C4
Mawson Lane	B1
Minster Road	B2-B3-C3
Newby Street	C1
North Street	B3-B4
Park Street	A3
Priest Lane	C2-C3
Princess Close	B4-C4
Princes Road	B4-C4
Queen Street	B3
Rayner Street	A3-A4
Residence Lane	C3
St Agnesgate	C2
St Marygate	C3
Shirley Avenue	A1
Skell Bank	A2
Skellgarths	B2
Somerset Row	A2
South Crescent	A1-A2
Southgate	B1
Southgate Lane	B1
Stonebridgegate	C3-C4
Tower Road	B4
Trinity Lane	A3-A4
Victoria Avenue	C2
Victoria Grove	B3
Vyner Street	C1
Waterskellgate	A2-B2
Wellington Street	B2
Westbourne Grove	A3
Westgate	A3-B3
Whitcliffe Avenue	A1

Knaresborough

Abbey Road	A1-B1
Bland's Hill	A1
Bond End	B4
Boroughbridge Road	B4-C4
Brewerton Road	B2
Briggate	A1-B1-B2
Castleings Road	A1-B1-B2
Charlton Court	C2
Charlton Drive	C2
Charlton Grove	C2
Cheapside	B2
Church Lane	B3-B4
Finkle Street	B3
Fisher Gardens	B2
Gracious Street	B2
Hambleton Grove	C2-C3
High Bond End	B4
High Bridge	A3
High Street	B2-B3-B4
Hilton Lane	B3
Holly Court	C2
Iles Lane	B1-C1
Jockey Lane	B2-B3
King James Road	B1-C1
Kirkgate	B2-B3
Knaresborough and Harrogate Road	A3
Low Bond End	A3-A4-B4
Manor Gardens	C2
Manor Road	C2
Market Place	B2
Park Drive	C2
Park Place	B2-C2
Park Row	C2
Princess Avenue	C1
St Margaret's Close	B3-B4
St Margaret's Gardens	B3-C3
St Margaret's Road	B3-C3
Silver Street	B2
Station Road	B3
Stockdale Walk	B1
Stockwell Avenue	C4
Stockwell Crescent	C4
Stockwell Drive	C4
Stockwell Grove	C4
Stockwell Lane	C2
Stockwell Road	C2-C3-C4
Tentergate Avenue	B4-C4
Tentergate Road	B4-C4
The Avenue	C4
Vicarage Lane	B3
Waterside	A1-A2-B2-B3-B3
Whincup Avenue	C2-C3
Whincup Grove	C2-C3
Windsor Lane	B1-B2
York Lane	C1
York Place	B2-C2-C1
York Road	C1

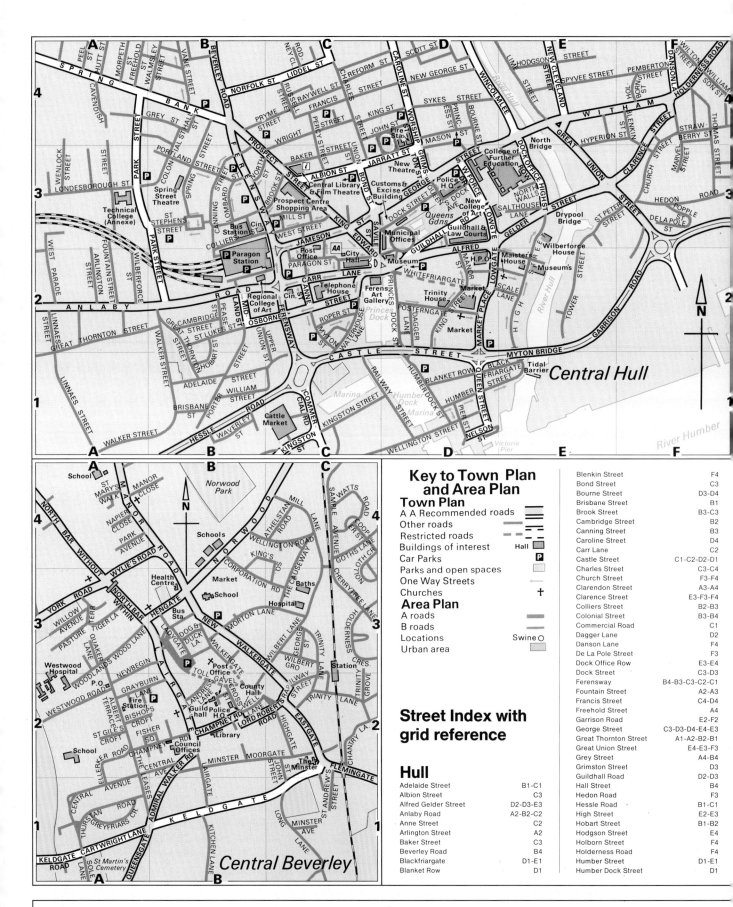

Central Hull

Central Beverley

Key to Town Plan and Area Plan

Town Plan
A A Recommended roads
Other roads
Restricted roads
Buildings of interest — Hall
Car Parks — P
Parks and open spaces
One Way Streets
Churches — +

Area Plan
A roads
B roads
Locations — Swine ○
Urban area

Street Index with grid reference

Hull

Adelaide Street	B1-C1
Albion Street	C3
Alfred Gelder Street	D2-D3-E3
Anlaby Road	A2-B2-C2
Anne Street	C2
Arlington Street	A2
Baker Street	C3
Beverley Road	B4
Blackfriargate	D1-E1
Blanket Row	D1
Blenkin Street	F4
Bond Street	C3
Bourne Street	D3-D4
Brisbane Street	B1
Brook Street	B3-C3
Cambridge Street	B2
Canning Street	B3
Caroline Street	D4
Carr Lane	C2
Castle Street	C1-C2-D2-D1
Charles Street	C3-C4
Church Street	F3-F4
Clarendon Street	A3-A4
Clarence Street	E3-F3-F4
Colliers Street	B2-B3
Colonial Street	B3-B4
Commercial Road	C1
Dagger Lane	D2
Danson Lane	F4
De La Pole Street	F3
Dock Office Row	E3-E4
Dock Street	C3-D3
Ferensway	B4-B3-C3-C2-C1
Fountain Street	A2-A3
Francis Street	C4-D4
Freehold Street	A4
Garrison Road	E2-F2
George Street	C3-D3-D4-E4-E3
Great Thornton Street	A1-A2-B2-B1
Great Union Street	E4-E3-F3
Grey Street	A4-B4
Grimston Street	D3
Guildhall Road	D2-D3
Hall Street	B4
Hedon Road	F3
Hessle Road	B1-C1
High Street	E2-E3
Hobart Street	B1-B2
Hodgson Street	E4
Holborn Street	F4
Holderness Road	F4
Humber Street	D1-E1
Humber Dock Street	D1

Hull

Officially Kingston-upon-Hull, this ancient port was specially laid out with new docks in 1293, on the decree of Edward I, and echoes of the town's past can be seen in the Town Docks Museum. The docks and the fishing industry are synonymous with Hull – it has Britain's busiest deep-sea fishing port – although flour-milling, vegetable oil extraction and petrochemical production are also important. The centre of Hull consists of broad streets and spacious squares and parks, such as Queen's Gardens, laid out on the site of what used to be Queen's Dock. The older part of the town which lies south-east of here between the docks and the River Hull is full of character, with a number of Georgian buildings and places of interest.

Beverley is one of England's most distinguished towns. Between its two principal buildings – the famous Minster and St Mary's Church – are medieval streets and pleasing market squares graced by redbrick Georgian houses built by the landed gentry of the East Riding during the town's heyday as a fashionable resort. The Minster's twin towers soar above the rooftops of the town as a constant reminder that here is one of the most beautiful pieces of Gothic architecture in Europe. The wealth of beauty and detail throughout is immense, but carving in both stone and wood is one of its most outstanding features.

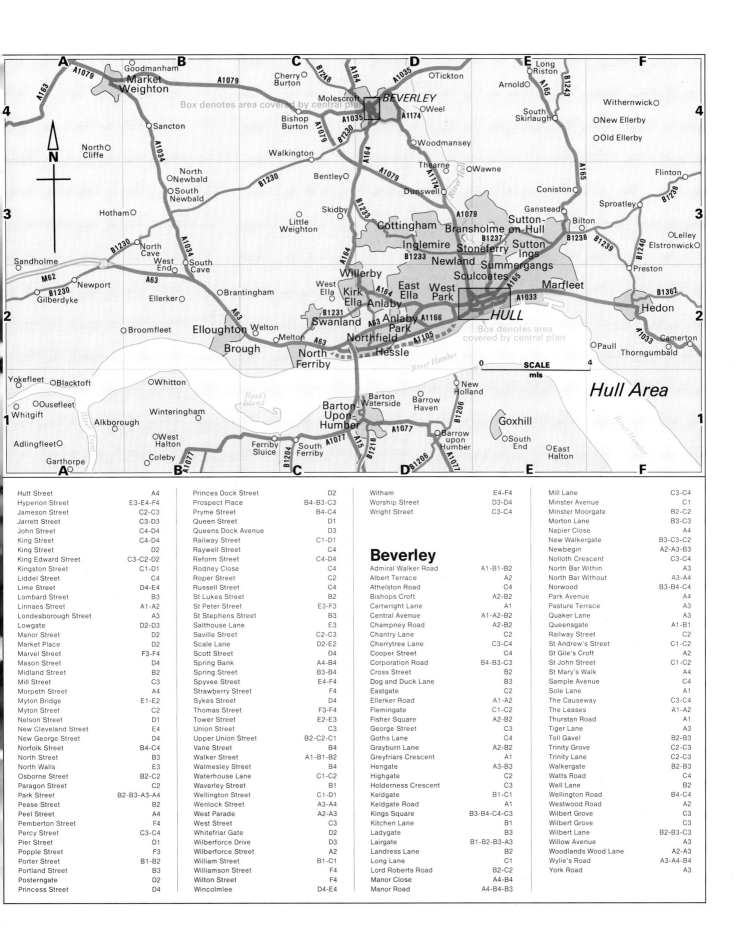

Hull Area

Box denotes area covered by central plan

SCALE
0 ————— 4
mls

Hutt Street	A4	Princes Dock Street	D2
Hyperion Street	E3-E4-F4	Prospect Place	B4-B3-C3
Jameson Street	C2-C3	Pryme Street	B4-C4
Jarrett Street	C3-D3	Queen Street	D1
John Street	C4-D4	Queens Dock Avenue	D3
King Street	C4-D4	Railway Street	C1-D1
King Street	D2	Raywell Street	C4
King Edward Street	C3-C2-D2	Reform Street	C4-D4
Kingston Street	C1-D1	Rodney Close	C4
Liddel Street	C4	Roper Street	C2
Lime Street	D4-E4	Russell Street	C4
Lombard Street	B3	St Lukes Street	B2
Linnaes Street	A1-A2	St Peter Street	E3-F3
Londesborough Street	A3	St Stephens Street	B3
Lowgate	D2-D3	Salthouse Lane	E3
Manor Street	D2	Saville Street	C2-C3
Market Place	D2	Scale Lane	D2-E2
Marvel Street	F3-F4	Scott Street	D4
Mason Street	D4	Spring Bank	A4-B4
Midland Street	B2	Spring Street	B3-B4
Mill Street	C3	Spyvee Street	E4-F4
Morpeth Street	A4	Strawberry Street	F4
Myton Bridge	E1-E2	Sykes Street	D4
Myton Street	C2	Thomas Street	F3-F4
Nelson Street	D1	Tower Street	E2-E3
New Cleveland Street	E4	Union Street	C3
New George Street	D4	Upper Union Street	B2-C2-C1
Norfolk Street	B4-C4	Vane Street	B4
North Street	B3	Walker Street	A1-B1-B2
North Walls	E3	Walmesley Street	B4
Osborne Street	B2-C2	Waterhouse Lane	C1-C2
Paragon Street	C2	Waverley Street	B1
Park Street	B2-B3-A3-A4	Wellington Street	C1-D1
Pease Street	B2	Wenlock Street	A3-A4
Peel Street	A4	West Parade	A2-A3
Pemberton Street	F4	West Street	C3
Percy Street	C3-C4	Whitefriar Gate	D2
Pier Street	D1	Wilberforce Drive	D3
Popple Street	F3	Wilberforce Street	A2
Porter Street	B1-B2	William Street	B1-C1
Portland Street	B3	Williamson Street	F4
Posterngate	D2	Wilton Street	F4
Princess Street	D4	Wincolmlee	D4-E4

Witham	E4-F4	Mill Lane	C3-C4
Worship Street	D3-D4	Minster Avenue	C1
Wright Street	C3-C4	Minster Moorgate	B2-C2
		Morton Lane	B3-C3
		Napier Close	A4

Beverley

Admiral Walker Road	A1-B1-B2	New Walkergate	B3-C3-C2
Albert Terrace	A2	Newbegin	A2-A3-B3
Athelston Road	C4	Nolloth Crescent	C3-C4
Bishops Croft	A2-B2	North Bar Within	A3
Cartwright Lane	A1	North Bar Without	A3-A4
Central Avenue	A1-A2-B2	Norwood	B3-B4-C4
Champney Road	A2-B2	Park Avenue	A4
Chantry Lane	C2	Pasture Terrace	A3
Cherrytree Lane	C3-C4	Quaker Lane	A3
Cooper Street	C4	Queensgate	A1-B1
Corporation Road	B4-B3-C3	Railway Street	C2
Cross Street	B2	St Andrew's Street	C1-C2
Dog and Duck Lane	B3	St Gile's Croft	A2
Eastgate	C2	St John Street	C1-C2
Ellerker Road	A1-A2	St Mary's Walk	A4
Flemingate	C1-C2	Sample Avenue	C4
Fisher Square	A2-B2	Sole Lane	A1
George Street	C3	The Causeway	C3-C4
Goths Lane	C4	The Leases	A1-A2
Grayburn Lane	A2-B2	Thurstan Road	A1
Greyfriars Crescent	A1	Tiger Lane	A3
Hengate	A3-B3	Toll Gavel	B2-B3
Highgate	C2	Trinity Grove	C2-C3
Holderness Crescent	C3	Trinity Lane	C2-C3
Keldgate	B1-C1	Walkergate	B2-B3
Keldgate Road	A1	Watts Road	C4
Kings Square	B3-B4-C4-C3	Well Lane	B2
Kitchen Lane	B1	Wellington Road	B4-C4
Ladygate	B3	Westwood Road	A2
Lairgate	B1-B2-B3-A3	Wilbert Grove	C3
Landress Lane	B2	Wilbert Grove	C3
Long Lane	C1	Wilbert Lane	B2-B3-C3
Lord Roberts Road	B2-C2	Willow Avenue	A3
Manor Close	A4-B4	Woodlands Wood Lane	A2-A3
Manor Road	A4-B4-B3	Wylie's Road	A3-A4-B4
		York Road	A3

HULL
Schemes to cross the Humber estuary were first discussed over 100 years ago, but it was not until 1981 that the mammoth project was sucessfully completed. At 4626ft, the Humber Bridge has the longest main span in the world.

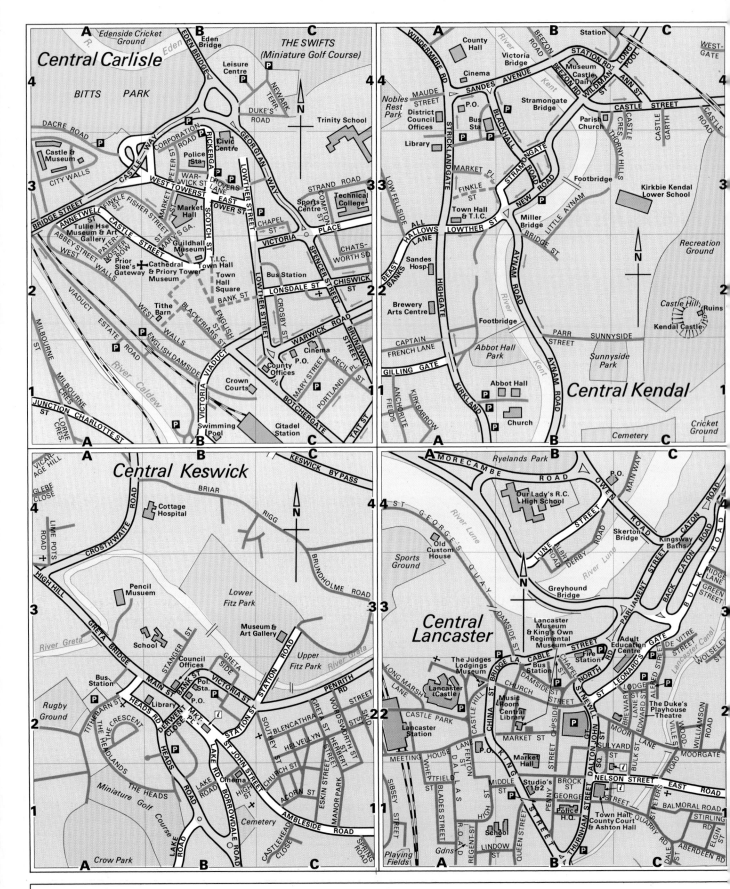

Lake District

Keswick With the River Greta running through it and Skiddaw looming above, this is a charming, quiet market town set amid beautiful scenery at the southern end of Derwentwater. The Fitz Park Museum and Art Gallery houses a collection of manuscripts by the numerous authors and poets who took their inspiration from the Lakeland.

Windermere has remained unspoiled despite the enormous popularity it has won as a holiday resort. Centred around its extensive lake, it stands in a setting which has been exalted by poets and artists for years. Windermere's architecture is mainly Victorian, as a result of the railway coming in the mid-19th century and bringing prosperity to the town. But conservationists campaigned to stop the railway going any further, and so the natural peace of the area was preserved.

Lancaster Dominating the city from its hilltop site, Lancaster Castle was once the headquarters of the Duchy and is still in use today — as a prison. Its late Georgian courtrooms and the beautiful Shire Hall are open to visitors. Close by stands the Priory, an architectural gem, and also of interest is the early 17th-century Judge's Lodgings house, which provided accommodation for assize judges for 150 years. The building now houses a display of dolls, with beautiful

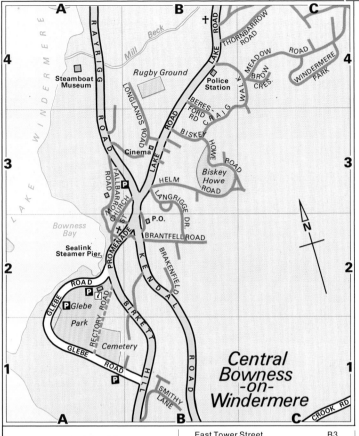

Central Bowness-on-Windermere

LEGEND

AA Recommended roads
Restricted roads
Other roads
Buildings of interest — Library ▢
Car Parks — P
Parks and open spaces
One Way Streets
Churches — ✝

Street Index with Grid Reference

Carlisle

Abbey Street	A2-A3
Annetwell Street	A3
Bank Street	B2-C2
Blackfriars Street	B1-B2
Botchergate	C1
Bridge Street	A3
Brunswick Street	C1-C2
Castle Street	A3-A2-B2
Castle Way	A3-B3-B4
Cecil Street	C1
Chapel Street	C3
Charlotte Street	A1
Chatsworth Square	C2
Chiswick Street	C2
City Walls	A3
Compton Street	C3
Corporation Road	B3-B4
Crosby Street	C1-C2
Dacre Road	A3-A4
Drovers Lane	B3
Duke's Road	B4-C4
East Tower Street	B3
Eden Bridge	B4
English Damside	B1-B2
English Street	B2
Finkle Street	A3
Fisher Street	A3-B3
Georgian Way	B4-B3-C3
Junction Street	A1
Lonsdale Street	C2
Lorne Crescent	A1
Lowther Street	B3-B2-C2
Market Street	B3
Mary Street	C1
Milbourne Crescent	A1
Millbourne Street	A1-A2
Newark Terrace	C4
Paternoster Row	A2-A3
Peter Street	B3
Portland Place	C1
Rickergate	B3
St Mary's Gate	B2-B3
Scotch Street	B2-B3
Spencer Street	C2
Strand Road	C3
Tait Street	C1
Viaduct Estate Road	A2-A1-B1
Victoria Place	C2-C3
Victoria Viaduct	B1
Warwick Road	C1-C2
Warwick Street	B3
West Tower Street	B3
West Walls	A2-B2-B1

Kendall

All Hallows Lane	A2-A3
Anchorite Fields	A1
Ann Street	C4
Aynam Road	B1-B2-B3
Beast Banks	A2
Beezon Road	B4
Blackhall Road	A4-B4-B3
Bridge Street	B3
Captain French Lane	A1
Castle Crescent	C3-C4
Castle Garth	C3-C4
Castle Road	C3-C4
Castle Street	B4-C4
Finkle Street	A3
Gilling Gate	A1
Highgate	A1-A2
Kirkbarrow	A1
Kirkland	A1
Little Aynam	B2-B3
Longpool	C4
Low Fellside	A3
Lowther Street	A3-B3
Market Place	A3
Maude Street	A4
New Road	B3
Parr Street	B1-B2
Sandes Avenue	A4-B4
Station Road	B4
Stramongate	B3
Stricklandgate	A3-A4
Sunnyside	B1-C1
Thorny Hills	B3-C3
Westgate	C4
Wildman Street	B4
Windermere Road	A4

Keswick

Acorn Street	C1
Ambleside Road	C1
Bank Street	B2
Blencathra Street	C2
Borrowdale Road	B1
Briar Rigg	A4-B4-C4
Brundholme Road	C3-C4
Castlehead Close	C1
Church Street	C1
Crosthwaite Road	A3-A4
Derwent Close	B2
Eskin Street	C1-C2
Glebe Close	A4
Greta Bridge	A2-A3
Greta Side	B2
Greta Street	C2
Heads Road	A2-B2-B1
Helvellyn Street	C2
High Hill	A3
Keswick By Pass	C4
Lake Road	B1-B2
Lime Pots Road	A3-A4
Main Street	B2
Manor Park	C1
Market Place	B2
Penrith Road	C2
St Herbert Street	C1-C2
St John Street	B2-B1-C1
Southey Street	C1-C2
Spring Road	C1
Stanger Street	B2-B3
Station Road	C2-C3
Station Street	B2
The Crescent	A2
The Headlands	A1-A2
The Heads	A1-B1
Tithebarn Street	A2
Vicarage Hill	A4
Victoria Street	B2
Wordsworth Street	C1

Lancaster

Aberdeen Road	C1
Albert Road	B3-B4
Alfred Street	C2-C3
Balmoral Road	C1
Black Caton Road	C3-C4
Blades Street	A1
Brewary Lane	C2
Bridge Lane	A2-B2-B3
Brock Street	B1
Bulk Road	C3-C4
Bulk Street	C1-C2
Cable Street	B2-B3
Castle Hill	A2
Castle Park	A2
Caton Road	C4
Chapel Street	B2
Cheapside	B2
China Street	A2
Church Street	B2
Dale Street	C1
Dallas Road	A1-A2
Dalton Square	B1-B2
Damside Street	A3-B3-B2
Derby Road	B3-B4
De Vitre Street	C3
East Road	C1
Edward Street	C2
Elgin Street	C1
Fenton Street	A1-A2
George Street	B1-C1
Great John Street	B2
Green Street	C3
High Street	A1
King Street	A2-B2-B1
Lindow Street	A1-B1
Lodge Street	C2
Long Marsh Lane	A2
Lune Street	B3-B4
Main Way	C4
Market Street	B2
Meeting House Lane	A2
Middle Street	A1-B1
Moorgate	C2
Moor Lane	B2-C2
Morecambe Road	A4-B4
Nelson Street	B1-C1
North Road	B2-B3
Owen Road	B4-C4
Parliament Street	C3-C4
Penny Street	B1-B2
Quarry Road	C1
Queen Street	B1
Regent Street	A1
Ridge Lane	C3
St George's Quay	A3-A4
St Leonard's Gate	B2-C2-C3
St Peter's Road	C1-C2
Sibsey Street	A1
Stirling Road	C1
Stonewell	B2
Sulyard Street	B2-C2
Thurnham Street	B1
Wheatfield Street	A1-A2
Williamson Road	C2
Wolseley Street	C2-C3
Woodville Street	C2

Bowness-on-Windermere

Beresford Road	B3-B4
Birkett Hill	A2-B2-B1
Biskey Howe Road	B3-C3
Brakenfield	B2
Brantfell Road	B2
Brow Crescent	C4
Church Street	A2-A3-B3
Craig Way	B4-C4-B4-B3
Crook Road	C1
Fallbarrow Road	A2-A3
Glebe Road	A2-A1-B1
Helm Road	B3
Kendall Road	B1-B2
Lake Road	B3-B4
Langridge Drive	B2-B3
Longlands Road	B3-B4
Meadow Road	C4
Promenade	A2-B2
Rayrigg Road	A4-A3-B3
Rectory Road	A1-A2
Smithy Lane	B1
Thornbarrow Road	B4-C4
Windermere Park	C4

---

furniture from Gillows and other cabinet makers.

Kendal's motto is "Wool Is My Bread" — a constant reminder that wool was the town's staple trade for over 600 years and brought it the prosperity which it still enjoys today. Flemish weavers started the industry when they settled here in the 14th century, and the town is now a centre for the production of such different products as turbines, carpets, shoes, socks and hornware — although its best known product must be the sustaining Kendal Mint Cake. An interesting local feature are the numerous named and numbered yards which lie tucked away through Kendal's archways and down alleyways, and were once a focus of small industry.

Carlisle Bonnie Prince Charlie proclaimed his father King of England from the steps of Carlisle Cross before marching south to be taken prisoner by the Duke of Cumberland, and Carlisle Castle was the centre of turbulent scenes between English and Scots from Norman times to the Jacobite rebellion. This is the 'Border City', capital of the Border area between England and Scotland. But as well as a past of conflict it can also claim to have some beautiful buildings. Finest of all perhaps is the cathedral; other places of interest are the Guildhall, which is 15th-century, Tullie House (a fine Jacobean building with Victorian extensions), and the city's museum and art gallery, which has a good collection of artefacts from its past.

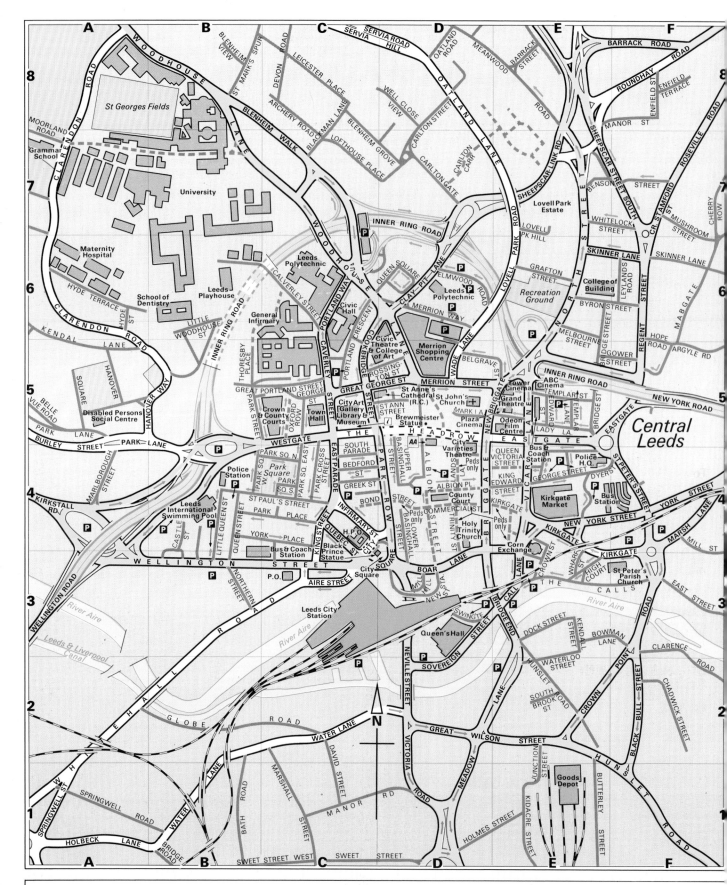

Leeds

In the centre of Leeds is its town hall – a monumental piece of architecture with a 225ft clock-tower. It was opened by Queen Victoria in 1858, and has been a kind of mascot for the city ever since. It exudes civic pride; such buildings could only have been created in the heyday of Victorian prosperity and confidence. Leeds' staple industry has always been the wool trade, but it only became a boom town towards the end of the 18th century, when textile mills were introduced. Today, the wool trade and ready-made clothing (Mr Hepworth and Mr Burton began their work here) are still important, though industries like paper, leather, furniture and electrical equipment are prominent.

Across Calverley Street from the town hall is the City Art Gallery, Library and Museum. Its collections include sculpture by Henry Moore, who was a student at Leeds School of Art. Nearby is the Headrow, Leeds' foremost shopping thoroughfare. On it is the City Varieties Theatre, venue for many years of the famous television programme 'The Good Old Days'. Off the Headrow are several shopping arcades, of which Leeds has many handsome examples. Leeds has a good number of interesting churches; perhaps the finest is St John's, unusual in that it dates from 1634, a time when few churches were built.

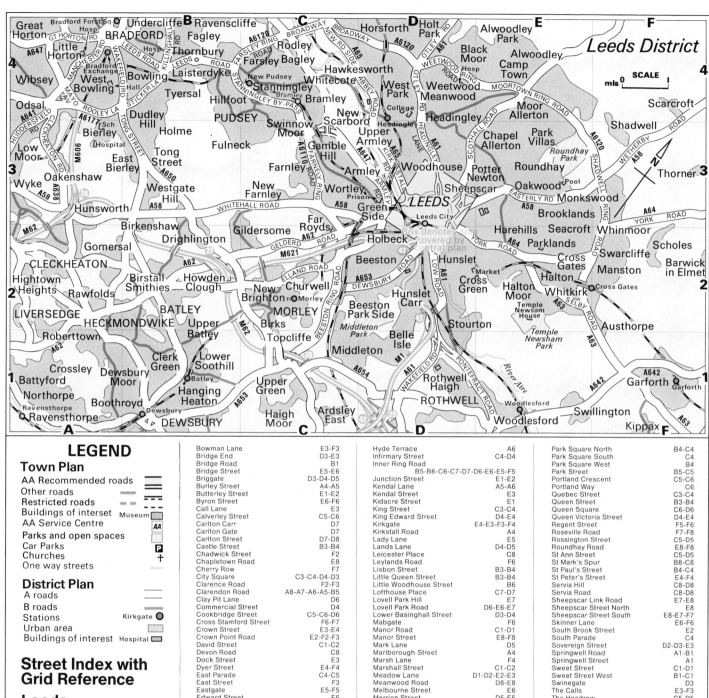

LEGEND

Town Plan

AA Recommended roads	▬
Other roads	▬
Restricted roads	▬ ▬
Buildings of interset	Museum
AA Service Centre	AA
Parks and open spaces	
Car Parks	P
Churches	†
One way streets	→

District Plan

A roads	▬
B roads	▬
Stations	Kirkgate ◉
Urban area	
Buildings of interest	Hospital

Street Index with Grid Reference

Leeds

Aire Street	C3
Albion Place	D4
Albion Street	D3-D4-D5
Archery Road	C7-C8
Argyle Road	F5
Barrack Road	E8-F8
Barrack Street	E8
Bath Road	B1-B2
Bedford Street	C4
Belgrave Street	D5-E5
Belle Vue Road	A5
Benson Street	E7-F7
Black Bull Street	F1-F2-F3
Blackman Lane	C7-C8
Blenheim Grove	C8-C7-D7
Blenheim View	B8
Blenheim Walk	B8-C8-C7
Boar Lane	D3-D4
Bond Street	C4-D4
Bowman Lane	E3-F3
Bridge End	D3-E3
Bridge Road	B1
Bridge Street	E5-E6
Briggate	D3-D4-D5
Burley Street	A4-A5
Butterley Street	E1-E2
Byron Street	E6-F6
Call Lane	E3
Calverley Street	C5-C6
Carlton Carr	D7
Carlton Gate	D7
Carlton Mount	D7-D8
Castle Street	B3-B4
Chadwick Street	F2
Chapeltown Road	E8
Cherry Row	F7
City Square	C3-C4-D4-D3
Clarence Road	F2-F3
Clarendon Road	A8-A7-A6-A5-B5
Clay Pit Lane	D6
Commercial Street	D4
Cookridge Street	C5-C6-D6
Cross Stamford Street	F6-F7
Crown Street	E3-E4
Crown Point Road	E2-F2-F3
David Street	C1-C2
Devon Road	C8
Dock Street	E3
Dyer Street	E4-F4
East Parade	C4-C5
East Street	F3
Eastgate	E5-F5
Edward Street	E5
Elmwood Road	D6
Enfield Street	F8
Enfield Terrace	F8
George Street	C5
George Street	E4
Globe Road	A2-B2-C2
Gower Street	E5-F5
Grafton Street	E6
Great George Street	C5-D5
Great Portland Street	B5-C5
Great Wilson Street	D2-E2
Greek Street	C4-D4
Hanover Square	A5
Hanover Way	A5-B5
High Court	E3
Holbeck Lane	A1-B1
Holmes Street	D1-E1
Hope Road	F5-F6
Hunslett Road	E3-E2-E1-F1-F2
Hyde Street	A6
Hyde Terrace	A6
Infirmary Street	C4-D4
Inner Ring Road	B5-B6-C6-C7-D7-D6-E6-E5-F5
Junction Street	E1-E2
Kendal Lane	A5-A6
Kendal Street	E3
Kidacre Street	E1
King Street	C3-C4
King Edward Street	D4-E4
Kirkgate	E4-E3-F3-F4
Kirkstall Road	A4
Lady Lane	E5
Lands Lane	D4-D5
Leicester Place	C8
Leylands Road	F6
Lisbon Street	B3-B4
Little Queen Street	B3-B4
Little Woodhouse Street	B6
Lofthouse Place	C7-D7
Lovell Park Hill	E7
Lovell Park Road	D6-E6-E7
Lower Basinghall Street	D3-D4
Mabgate	F6
Manor Road	C1-D1
Manor Street	E8-F8
Mark Lane	D5
Marlborough Street	A4
Marsh Lane	F4
Marshall Street	C1-C2
Meadow Lane	D1-D2-E2-E3
Meanwood Road	D8-E8
Melbourne Street	E6
Merrion Street	D5-E5
Merrion Way	D6
Mill Hill	D3
Mill Street	F4
Moorland Road	A7-A8
Mushroom Street	F6-F7
Neville Street	D2-D3
New Briggate	D5-E5
New Station Street	D3
New York Road	F5
New York Street	E4-F4
North Street	E5-E6-E7
Northern Street	B3
Oatland Lane	D8-D7-E7
Oatland Road	D8
Oxford Row	C5
Park Cross Street	C4-C5
Park Lane	A5-B5-B4
Park Place	B4-C4
Park Row	C4-C5-D5-D4
Park Square East	C4
Park Square North	B4-C4
Park Square South	C4
Park Square West	B4
Park Street	B5-C5
Portland Crescent	C5-C6
Portland Way	C6
Quebec Street	C3-C4
Queen Street	B3-B4
Queen Square	C6-D6
Queen Victoria Street	D4-E4
Regent Street	F5-F6
Roseville Road	F7-F8
Rossington Street	C5-D5
Roundhay Road	E8-F8
St Ann Street	C5-D5
St Mark's Spur	B8-C8
St Paul's Street	B4-C4
St Peter's Street	E4-F4
Servia Hill	C8-D8
Servia Road	C8-D8
Sheepscar Link Road	E7-E8
Sheepscar Street North	E8
Sheepscar Street South	E8-E7-F7
Skinner Lane	E6-F6
South Brook Street	E2
South Parade	C4
Sovereign Street	D2-D3-E3
Springwell Road	A1-B1
Springwell Street	A1
Sweet Street	C1-D1
Sweet Street West	B1-C1
Swinegate	D3
The Calls	E3-F3
The Headrow	C5-D5
Templar Lane	E5
Templar Street	E5
Thoresby Place	B5-B6
Trinity Street	D4
Upper Basinghall Street	D4-D5
Vicar Lane	E4-E5
Victoria Road	D1-D2
Wade Lane	D5-D6
Water Lane	B1-B2-C2-D2
Waterloo Street	E2-E3
Well Close View	D8
Wellington Road	A3
Wellington Street	A3-B3-C3
Westgate	B4-B5-C5-C4
Wharf Street	E3-E4
Whitehall Road	A1-A2-B2-B3-C3
Whitelock Street	E7-F7
Woodhouse Lane	A8-B8-B7-C7-C6-D6-D5
York Place	B4-C4
York Street	F4

LEEDS
Offices now occupy the handsome twin-towered Civic Hall which stands in Calverley Street in front of the new buildings of Leeds Polytechnic. This area of the city – the commercial centre – has been extensively redeveloped

Central Liverpool

Liverpool

Although its dock area has been much reduced, Liverpool was at one time second only to London in pre-eminence as a port. Formerly the centrepiece of the docks area are three monumental buildings – the Dock Board Offices, built in 1907 with a huge copper-covered dome; the Cunard Building, dating from 1912 and decorated with an abundance of ornamental carving; and best-known of all, the world-famous Royal Liver Building, with the two 'liver birds' crowning its twin cupolas.

Some of the city's best industrial buildings have fallen into disuse in recent years, and have been preserved as monuments of the industrial age. One has become a maritime museum housing full-sized craft and a workshop where maritime crafts are demonstrated. Other museums and galleries include the Walker Art Gallery, with excellent collections of European painting and sculpture; Liverpool City Libraries, one of the oldest and largest public libraries in Britain, with a vast collection of books and manuscripts; and Bluecoat Chambers, a Queen Anne building now used as a gallery and concert hall. Liverpool has two outstanding cathedrals: the Roman Catholic, completed in 1967 in an uncompromising controversial style; and the Protestant, constructed in the great tradition of Gothic architecture, but begun in 1904 and only recently completed.

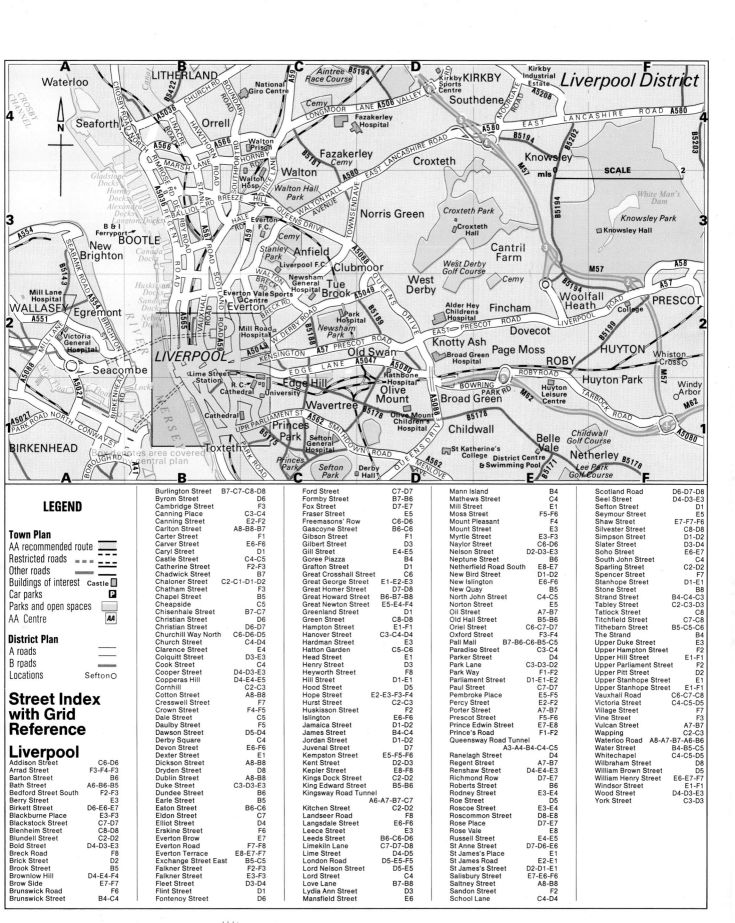

Liverpool District

A580 EAST LANCASHIRE ROAD

LITHERLAND • Orrell • Walton • Fazakerley • Croxteth • KIRKBY • Southdene • Knowsley • PRESCOT • HUYTON

SCALE — mls 0 ... 2

Waterloo • Seaforth • BOOTLE • New Brighton • WALLASEY • Egremont • Seacombe • BIRKENHEAD • LIVERPOOL • Toxteth • Everton • Anfield • Clubmoor • Tue Brook • Norris Green • West Derby • Cantril Farm • Fincham • Dovecot • Page Moss • ROBY • Knotty Ash • Old Swan • Broad Green • Huyton Park • Childwall • Netherley • Belle Vale

LEGEND

Town Plan
AA recommended route	
Restricted roads	
Other roads	
Buildings of interest	Castle
Car parks	P
Parks and open spaces	
AA Centre	AA

District Plan
A roads	
B roads	
Locations	Sefton ○

Street Index with Grid Reference

Liverpool

Addison Street	C6-D6
Arrad Street	F3-F4-F3
Barton Street	B6
Bath Street	A6-B6-B5
Bedford Street South	F2-F3
Berry Street	E3
Birkett Street	D6-E6-E7
Blackburne Place	E3-F3
Blackstock Street	C7-D7
Blenheim Street	C8-D8
Blundell Street	C2-D2
Bold Street	D4-D3-E3
Breck Road	F8
Brick Street	D2
Brook Street	B5
Brownlow Hill	D4-E4-D4
Brow Side	E7-F7
Brunswick Road	F6
Brunswick Street	B4-C4
Burlington Street	B7-C7-C8-D8
Byrom Street	D6
Cambridge Street	F3
Canning Place	C3-C4
Canning Street	E2-F2
Carlton Street	A8-B8-B7
Carter Street	F1
Carver Street	E6-F6
Caryl Street	D1
Castle Street	C4-C5
Catherine Street	F2-F3
Chadwick Street	B7
Chaloner Street	C2-C1-D1-D2
Chatham Street	F3
Chapel Street	B5
Cheapside	C5
Chisenhale Street	B7-C7
Christian Street	D6
Christian Street	D6-D7
Churchill Way North	C6-D6-D5
Church Street	C4-D4
Clarence Street	E4
Colquitt Street	D3-E3
Cook Street	C4
Cooper Street	D4-D3-E3
Copperas Hill	D4-E4-E5
Cornhill	C2-C3
Cotton Street	A8-B8
Cresswell Street	F7
Crown Street	F4-F5
Dale Street	C5
Daulby Street	F5
Dawson Street	D5-D4
Derby Square	C4
Devon Street	E6-F6
Dexter Street	E1
Dickson Street	A8-B8
Dryden Street	D8
Dublin Street	A8-B8
Duke Street	C3-D3-E3
Dundee Street	B6
Earle Street	B5
Eaton Street	B6-C6
Eldon Street	C7
Elliot Street	D4
Erskine Street	F6
Everton Brow	E7
Everton Road	F7-F8
Everton Terrace	E8-E7-F7
Exchange Street East	B5-C5
Falkner Street	F2-F3
Falkner Street	E3-F3
Fleet Street	D3-D4
Flint Street	D1
Fontenoy Street	D6
Ford Street	C7-D7
Formby Street	B7-B6
Fox Street	D7-E7
Fraser Street	E5
Freemasons' Row	C6-D6
Gascoyne Street	B6-C6
Gibson Street	F1
Gilbert Street	D3
Gill Street	E4-E5
Goree Piazza	B4
Grafton Street	D1
Great Crosshall Street	C6
Great George Street	E1-E2-E3
Great Homer Street	D7-D8
Great Howard Street	B6-B7-B8
Great Newton Street	E5-E4-F4
Greenland Street	D1
Green Street	C8-D8
Hampton Street	E1-F1
Hanover Street	C3-C4-D4
Hardman Street	E3
Hatton Garden	C5-C6
Head Street	E1
Henry Street	D3
Heyworth Street	F8
Hill Street	D1-E1
Hood Street	D5
Hope Street	E2-E3-F3-F4
Hurst Street	C2-C3
Huskisson Street	F2
Islington	E6-F6
Jamaica Street	D1-D2
James Street	B4-C4
Jordan Street	D1-D2
Juvenal Street	D7
Kempston Street	E5-F5-F6
Kent Street	D2-D3
Kepler Street	E8-F8
Kings Dock Street	C2-D2
King Edward Street	B5-B6
Kingsway Road Tunnel	A6-A7-B7-C7
Kitchen Street	C2-D2
Landseer Road	F8
Langsdale Street	E6-F6
Leece Street	E3
Leeds Street	B6-C6-D6
Limekiln Lane	C7-D7-D8
Lime Street	D4-D5
London Road	D5-E5-F5
Lord Nelson Street	D5-E5
Lord Street	C4
Love Lane	B7-B8
Lydia Ann Street	D3
Mansfield Street	E6
Mann Island	B4
Mathews Street	C4
Mill Street	E1
Moss Street	F5-F6
Mount Pleasant	F4
Mount Street	E3
Myrtle Street	E3-F3
Naylor Street	C6-D6
Nelson Street	D2-D3-E3
Neptune Street	B6
Netherfield Road South	E8-E7
New Bird Street	D1-D2
New Islington	E6-F6
New Quay	B5
North John Street	C4-C5
Norton Street	E5
Oil Street	A7-B7
Old Hall Street	B5-B6
Oriel Street	C6-C7-D7
Oxford Street	F3-F4
Pall Mall	B7-B6-C6-B5-C5
Paradise Street	C3-C4
Parker Street	D4
Park Lane	C3-D2-D2
Park Way	F1-F2
Parliament Street	D1-E1-E2
Paul Street	C7-D7
Pembroke Place	E5-F5
Percy Street	E2-F2
Porter Street	A7-B7
Prescot Street	F5-F6
Prince Edwin Street	E7-E8
Prince's Road	F1-F2
Queensway Road Tunnel	A3-A4-B4-C4-C5
Ranelagh Street	D4
Regent Street	A7-B7
Renshaw Street	D4-E4-E3
Richmond Row	D7-E7
Roberts Street	B6
Rodney Street	E3-E4
Roe Street	D5
Roscoe Street	E3-E4
Roscommon Street	D8-E8
Rose Place	D7-E7
Rose Vale	E8
Russell Street	E4-E5
St Anne Street	D7-D6-E6
St James's Place	E1
St James Road	E2-E1
St James's Street	D2-D1-E1
Salisbury Street	E7-E6-F6
Saltney Street	A8-B8
Sandon Street	F2
School Lane	C4-D4
Scotland Road	D6-D7-D8
Seel Street	D4-D3-E3
Sefton Street	D1
Seymour Street	E5
Shaw Street	E7-F7-F6
Silvester Street	C8-D8
Simpson Street	D1-D2
Slater Street	D3-D4
Soho Street	E6-E7
South John Street	C4
Sparling Street	C2-D2
Spencer Street	F7
Stanhope Street	D1-E1
Stone Street	B8
Strand Street	B4-C4-C3
Tabley Street	C2-C3-D3
Tatlock Street	C8
Titchfield Street	C7-C8
Tithebarn Street	B5-C5-C6
The Strand	B4
Upper Duke Street	E3
Upper Hampton Street	F2
Upper Hill Street	E1-F1
Upper Parliament Street	F2
Upper Pitt Street	D2
Upper Stanhope Street	E1-F1
Upper Stanhope Street	E1-F1
Vauxhall Road	C6-C7-C8
Victoria Street	C4-C5-D5
Village Street	F7
Vine Street	F3
Vulcan Street	A7-B7
Wapping	C2-C3
Waterloo Road	A8-A7-B7-A6-B6
Water Street	B4-B5-C5
Whitechapel	C4-C5-D5
Wilbraham Street	D8
William Brown Street	D5
William Henry Street	E6-E7-F7
Windsor Street	E1-F1
Wood Street	D4-D3-E3
York Street	C3-D3

LIVERPOOL

The Metropolitan Cathedral of Christ the King is one of Liverpool's most striking landmarks. Crowning the conical roof is a tower of stained glass which throws a pool of coloured light on to the altar below.

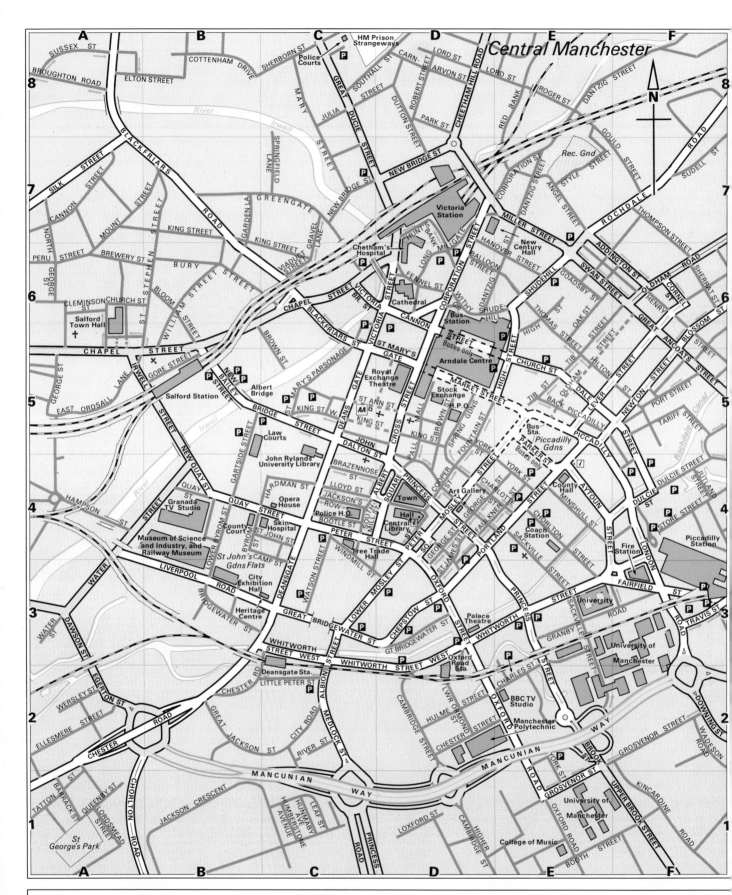

Manchester

The gigantic conurbation called Greater Manchester covers a staggering 60 square miles, reinforcing Manchester's claim to be Britain's second city. Commerce and industry are vital aspects of the city's character, but it is also an important cultural centre – the Halle Orchestra has its home at the Free Trade Hall (a venue for many concerts besides classical music), there are several theatres, a library (the John Rylands) which houses one of the most important collections of books in the world, and a number of museums and galleries, including the Whitworth Gallery with its lovely watercolours.

Like many great cities it suffered badly during the bombing raids of World War II, but some older buildings remain, including the town hall, a huge building designed in Gothic style by Alfred Waterhouse and opened in 1877. Manchester Cathedral dates mainly from the 15th century and is noted for its fine tower and outstanding carved woodwork. Nearby is Chetham's Hospital, also 15th-century and now housing a music school. Much new development has taken place, and more is planned. Shopping precincts cater for the vast population, and huge hotels have provided services up to international standards. On the edge of the city is the Belle Vue centre, a large entertainments complex including concert and exhibition facilities, and a speedway stadium.

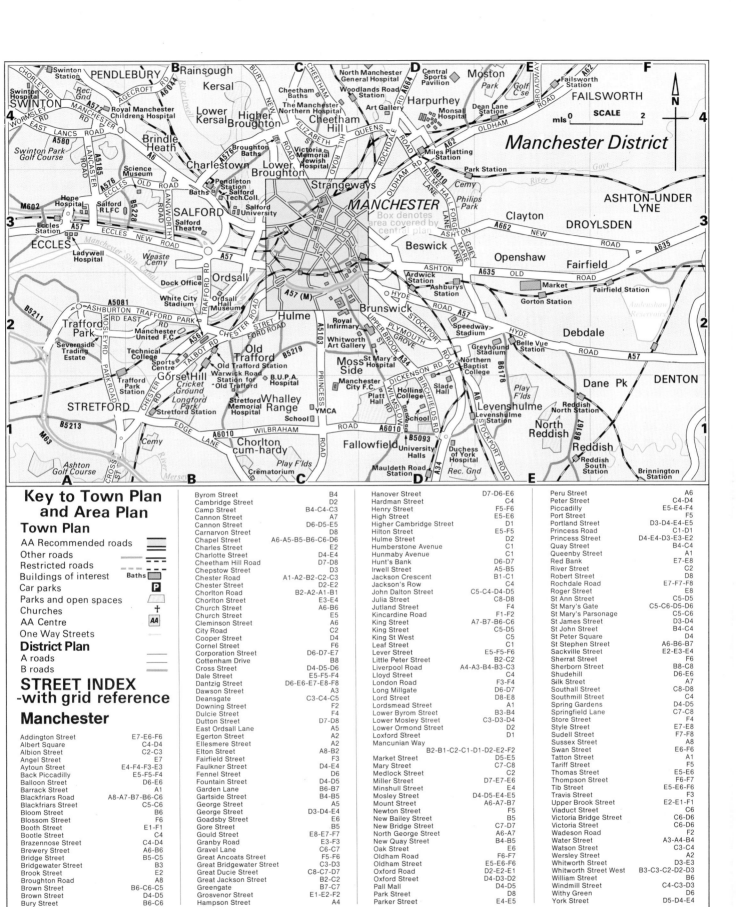

Manchester District

SCALE mls 0 __ 2

FAILSWORTH · ASHTON-UNDER-LYNE · DROYLSDEN · DENTON

Box denotes area covered by central plan

Key to Town Plan and Area Plan

Town Plan
- AA Recommended roads
- Other roads
- Restricted roads
- Buildings of interest — Baths
- Car parks — P
- Parks and open spaces
- Churches — †
- AA Centre — AA
- One Way Streets

District Plan
- A roads
- B roads

STREET INDEX
-with grid reference

Manchester

Street	Grid ref
Addington Street	E7-E6-F6
Albert Square	C4-D4
Albion Street	C2-C3
Angel Street	E7
Aytoun Street	E4-F4-F3-E3
Back Piccadilly	E5-F5-F4
Balloon Street	D6-E6
Barrack Street	A1
Blackfriars Road	A8-A7-B7-B6-C6
Blackfriars Street	C5-C6
Bloom Street	B6
Blossom Street	F6
Booth Street	E1-F1
Bootle Street	C4
Brazennose Street	C4-D4
Brewery Street	A6-B6
Bridge Street	B5-C5
Bridgewater Street	B3
Brook Street	E2
Broughton Road	A8
Brown Street	B6-C6-C5
Brown Street	D4-D5
Bury Street	B6-C6
Byrom Street	B4
Cambridge Street	D2
Camp Street	B4-C4-C3
Cannon Street	A7
Cannon Street	D6-D5-E5
Carnarvon Street	D8
Chapel Street	A6-A5-B5-B6-C6-D6
Charles Street	E2
Charlotte Street	D4-E4
Cheetham Hill Road	D7-D8
Chepstow Street	D3
Chester Road	A1-A2-B2-C2-C3
Chester Street	D2-E2
Chorlton Road	B2-A2-A1-B1
Chorlton Street	E3-E4
Church Street	A6-B6
Church Street	E5
Cleminson Street	A6
City Road	C2
Cooper Street	D4
Cornel Street	F6
Corporation Street	D6-D7-E7
Cottenham Drive	B8
Cross Street	D4-D5-D6
Dale Street	E5-F5-F4
Dantzig Street	D6-E6-E7-E8-F8
Dawson Street	A3
Deansgate	C3-C4-C5
Downing Street	F2
Dulcie Street	F4
Dutton Street	D7-D8
East Ordsall Lane	A5
Egerton Street	A2
Ellesmere Street	A2
Elton Street	A8-B2
Fairfield Street	F3
Faulkner Street	D4-E4
Fennel Street	D6
Fountain Street	D4-D5
Garden Lane	B6-B7
Gartside Street	B4-B5
George Street	A5
George Street	D3-D4-E4
Goadsby Street	E6
Gore Street	B5
Gould Street	E8-E7-F7
Granby Road	E3-F3
Gravel Lane	C6-C7
Great Ancoats Street	F5-F6
Great Bridgewater Street	C3-D3
Great Ducie Street	C8-C7-D7
Great Jackson Street	B2-C2
Greengate	B7-C7
Grosvenor Street	E1-E2-F2
Hampson Street	A4
Hanover Street	D7-D6-E6
Hardman Street	C4
Henry Street	F5-F6
High Street	E5-E6
Higher Cambridge Street	D1
Hilton Street	E5-F5
Hulme Street	D2
Humberstone Avenue	C1
Hunmaby Avenue	C1
Hunt's Bank	D6-D7
Irwell Street	A5-B5
Jackson Crescent	B1-C1
Jackson's Row	C4
John Dalton Street	C5-C4-D4-D5
Julia Street	C8-D8
Jutland Street	F4
Kincardine Road	F1-F2
King Street	A7-B7-B6-C6
King Street	C5-D5
King St West	C5
Leaf Street	C1
Lever Street	E5-F5-F6
Little Peter Street	B2-C2
Liverpool Road	A4-A3-B4-B3-C3
Lloyd Street	C4
London Road	F3-F4
Long Millgate	D6-D7
Lord Street	D8-E8
Lordsmead Street	A1
Lower Byrom Street	B3-B4
Lower Mosley Street	C3-D3-D4
Lower Ormond Street	D2
Loxford Street	D1
Mancunian Way	B2-B1-C2-C1-D1-D2-E2-F2
Market Street	D5-E5
Mary Street	C7-C8
Medlock Street	C2
Miller Street	D7-E7-E6
Minshull Street	E4
Mosley Street	D4-D5-E4-E5
Mount Street	A6-A7-B7
Newton Street	F5
New Bailey Street	B5
New Bridge Street	C7-D7
North George Street	A6-A7
New Quay Street	B4-B5
Oak Street	E6
Oldham Road	F6-F7
Oldham Street	E5-E6-F6
Oxford Road	D2-E2-E1
Oxford Street	D4-D3-D2
Pall Mall	D4-D5
Park Street	D8
Parker Street	E4-E5
Peru Street	A6
Peter Street	C4-D4
Piccadilly	E5-E4-F4
Port Street	F5
Portland Street	D3-D4-E4-E5
Princess Road	C1-D1
Princess Street	D4-E4-D3-E3-E2
Quay Street	B4-C4
Queenby Street	A1
Red Bank	E7-E8
River Street	C2
Robert Street	D8
Rochdale Road	E7-F7-F8
Roger Street	E8
St Ann Street	C5-D5
St Mary's Gate	C5-C6-D5-D6
St Mary's Parsonage	C5-C6
St James Street	D3-D4
St John Street	B4-C4
St Peter Square	D4
St Stephen Street	A6-B6-B7
Sackville Street	E2-E3-E4
Sherrat Street	F6
Sherborn Street	B8-C8
Shudehill	D6-E6
Silk Street	A7
Southall Street	C8-D8
Southmill Street	C4
Spring Gardens	D4-D5
Springfield Lane	C7-C8
Store Street	F4
Style Street	E7-E8
Sudell Street	F7-F8
Sussex Street	A8
Swan Street	E6-F6
Tatton Street	A1
Tariff Street	F5
Thomas Street	E5-E6
Thompson Street	F6-F7
Tib Street	E5-E6-F6
Travis Street	F3
Upper Brook Street	E2-E1-F1
Viaduct Street	C6
Victoria Bridge Street	C6-D6
Victoria Street	C6-D6
Wadeson Road	F2
Water Street	A3-A4-B4
Watson Street	C3-C4
Wersley Street	A2
Whitworth Street	D3-E3
Whitworth Street West	B3-C3-C2-D2-D3
William Street	B6
Windmill Street	C4-C3-D3
Withy Green	D6
York Street	D5-D4-E4

MANCHESTER
The Barton Swing Bridge carries the Bridgewater Canal over the Manchester Ship Canal, which links Manchester with the sea nearly 40 miles away. Completed in 1894, the canal is navigable by vessels up to 15,000 tons.

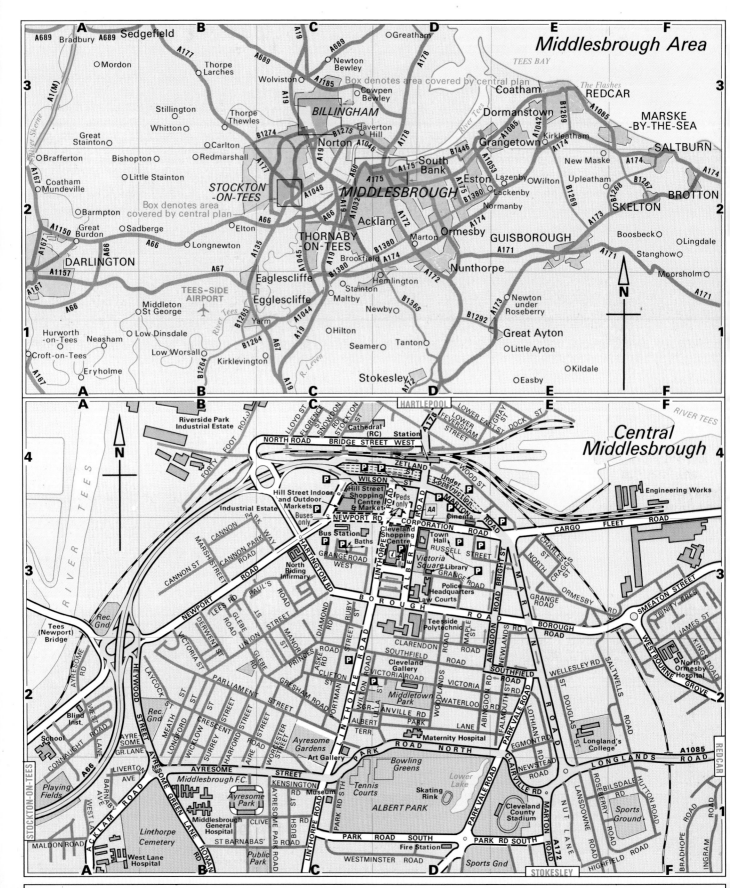

Middlesbrough

Heavy industry dominates Middlesbrough. It has been a centre of iron and steel manufacture since the 1840s although much of the steel-making has moved eastwards to a new works near Redcar. Its rise had begun ten years before, when the Stockton and Darlington Railway purchased land here and turned what had been a quiet riverside village into a busy coal exporting town. Middlesbrough's most notable structure is the Transporter Bridge, built across the Tees in 1911. It is one of only two bridges of its type left in Britain. The town centre is modern with spacious shopping areas and new public buildings. The Dorman Museum covers the region's history and there are two major art galleries.

Stockton has a place in transport history; it was here, on 27 September 1825, that the world's first steam passenger railway service began. The town, also situated on the River Tees, became an engineering and shipbuilding centre and is still an important industrial centre today. It has a town hall of 1763 standing in the middle of one of the widest main streets in England.

Billingham also stands on the Tees, and the river was one of the factors which encouraged various chemical industries to become established here. North Sea oil has given a boost to that industry, and the town centre has been completely rebuilt with every facility.

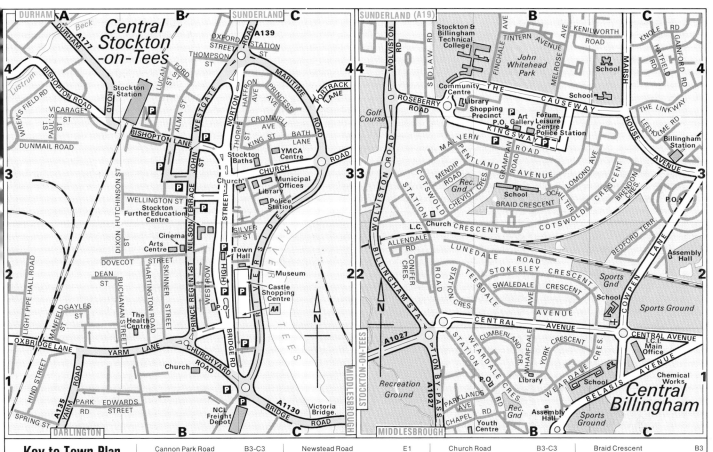

Key to Town Plan and Area Plan

Town Plan

AA Recommended roads
Other roads
Restricted roads
Buildings of interest
Car Parks   **P**
Parks and open spaces
AA Service Centre   **AA**

Area Plan

A roads
B roads
Locations   Aycliffe ○
Urban area

Street Index with Grid Reference

Middlesbrough

Abingdon Road	D2-E2-E3
Acklam Road	A1-B1
Aire Street	B1-B2-C2
Albert Road	D3-D4
Albert Terrace	C2-D2
Aske Road	C2
Ayresome Green Lane	A2-B2-B1
Ayresome Park Road	C1
Ayresome Road	A2
Ayresome Street	B1-C1
Barnaby Avenue	A1
Bilsdale Road	E1-F1
Borough Road	C3-D3-E3
Bradhope Road	F1
Bridge Street West	C4-D4
Bright Street	E3
Bush Street	C1

Cannon Park Road	B3-C3
Cannon Park Way	B3-C3
Cannon Street	B3
Cargo Fleet Road	E3-F3-F4
Charles Street	E3
Clairville Road	E1-E2
Clarendon Road	D2-D3
Clifton Street	C2
Clive Road	B1-C1
Connaught Road	A1-A2
Corporation Road	D4-D3-E3
Craggs Street	E3
Crescent Road	B2-C2-C1
Derwent Street	B2-B3
Diamond Road	C2-C3
Dock Street	E4
Egmont Road	E2
Falmouth Street	E2
Florence Street	C4
Forty Foot Road	B4-C4
Glebe Road	B3-B2-C2
Grange Road	D3-E3
Grange Road West	C3-D3
Granville Road	C2-D2
Gray Street	D4-E4
Gresham Road	C2
Harford Street	B1-B2
Hartinton Road	C3
Heywood Street	A2-B2
Highfield Road	E1-F1
Hutton Road	F1
Ingram Road	F1
James Street	F2-F3
Kensington Road	C1
Kings Road	F2-F3
Lansdowne Road	E1
Laycock Street	C2
Lees Road	B3
Linthorpe Road	C1-C2-C3-D3-D4
Liverton Avenue	A1-B1
Lloyd Street	C4
Longford Street	B1-B2
Longlands Road	E1-F1-F2
Lothian Road	E1-E2
Lower East Street	D4-E4
Lower Feversham Street	D4
Maldon Road	A1
Manor Street	C2-C3
Maple Street	D2-D3
Marsh Street	B3
Marton Road	D4-D3-E3-E2-E1
Meath Street	B2
Newlands Road	E2-E3
Newport Road	B2-B3-C3-C4-D4-D3

Newstead Road	E1
North Road	B4-C4
North Ormesby Road	E3-F3
Nut Lane	E1
Park Lane	D2-E2
Park Road North	C1-C2-D2-E2
Park Road South	C1-D1-E1
Park Vale Road	D1-E1-E2
Parliament Street	B2-C2
Portman Street	C2-C3
Princes Road	C2
Roman Road	B1
Roseberry Road	E1-F1
Ruby Street	C3
Russell Street	D3-E3
St Barnabas' Road	B1-C1
St Douglas Street	E1-E2
St Paul's Road	C3-B3-C3
Saltwells Road	E3-E2-F2
Smeaton Street	F3
Snowdon Road	C4
Southfield Road	C2-D2-E2
Stockton Street	C4
Surrey Street	B1-B2
Sussex Street	D4
Trinity Crescent	F2-F3
Ulla Street	D2
Union Street	B2-C2-C3
Victoria Road	C2-D2-E2
Victoria Street	B2-B3
Waterloo Road	D2-E2
Wellesley Road	E2
West Lane	A1-A2
Westbourne Grove	F2-F3
Westminster Road	C1-D1
Wicklow Street	B1-B2
Wilson Street	C4-D4
Wilton Road	C2-D2
Woodlands Road	D2-D3
Wood Street	D4
Worcester Street	C1-C2
Zetland Street	D4

Stockton-on-Tees

Alma Street	B3-B4
Bath Lane	C3
Bishopton Lane	A3-B3
Bishopton Road	A4-A3
Bridge Road	B2-B1-C1
Buchanan Street	A1-A2
Cannon Park Road	B3-C3
Church Yard Road	B1
Cromwell Avenue	C3
Dean Street	A2
Dixon Street	B2
Dovecot Street	A2-B2
Dunmail Road	A3
Durham Road	A4
Edwards Street	A1-B1
Ford Street	B4
Gayles Street	A2
Haffron Avenue	C3-C4
Hartington Road	B1-B2
High Street	B2-B3
Hind Street	A1
Hutchinson Street	B3
John Street	B3
King Street	B3
Light Pipe Hall Road	A1-A2
Lucan Street	B4
Manfield Street	A1-A2
Maritime Road	C3-C4
Nelson Terrace	B2-B3
Norton Road	B3-B4-C4
Oxbridge Lane	A1
Oxford Street	B4-C4
Park Road	A1
Portrack Lane	C4
Prince Regent Street	B1-B2
Princess Avenue	C4
Riverside	C1-C2-C3
St Paul's Street	A3-A4
Silver Street	B2-C2
Skinner Street	B1-B2
Spring Street	A1
Station Street	C4
Thompson Street	B4
Thorpe Street	C3
Vicarage Street	A4
Wellington Street	B3
Westbourne Street	A1-B1
Westgate	B3-B4
West Row	B2
Wren's Field Road	A3-A4
Yarm Lane	A1-B1-B2
Yarm Road	A1

Billingham

Allendale Road	A2
Bedford Terrace	C2-C3
Belasis Avenue	B1-C1
Billingham Station By-pass	A1-A2
Braid Crescent	B3
Brendon Crescent	C3
Central Avenue	A2-B2-B1-C1-C2
Chapel Road	A1-B1
Cheviot Crescent	A3-B3
Conifer Crescent	A2
Cotswold Crescent	A3-A2-B2-B3-C3
Cowpen Lane	C1-C2-C3
Cumberland Crescent	B1
Finchale Avenue	B4
Gainford Road	C4
Grampian Road	B3
Hatfield Road	C4
Kenilworth Road	B4-C4
Kingsway	A4-A3-B3-B4
Knole Road	C4
Leeholme Road	C3-C4
Lomond Avenue	B3-C3
Lunedale Road	A2-B2
Malvern Road	A3-B3
Marsh House Avenue	C4
Melrose Avenue	B4
Mendip Road	A3
Ochil Terrace	B3
Parklands Avenue	A1-B1
Pentland Avenue	A3-B3-B4-C3-C4
Roseberry Road	A4
Sidlaw Road	A4
Station Crescent	A2
Station Road	A3-A2-A1-B1
Stokesley Crescent	B2-C2
Swaledale Crescent	B2
Teesdale Avenue	A2-B2-C2
Tintern Avenue	B4
The Causeway	A4-B4-C4
The Linkway	C4
Weardale Crescent	A2-A1-B2-B1-C1
Wharfdale Avenue	B1-B2
Wolviston Road	A2-A3-A4
York Crescent	B1-C1

MIDDLESBROUGH
In 1911 the Transporter Bridge was built to replace the river ferry between Port Clarence and Middlesbrough. It is still used today and a special viewing platform has been built to enable visitors to watch the bridge in operation.

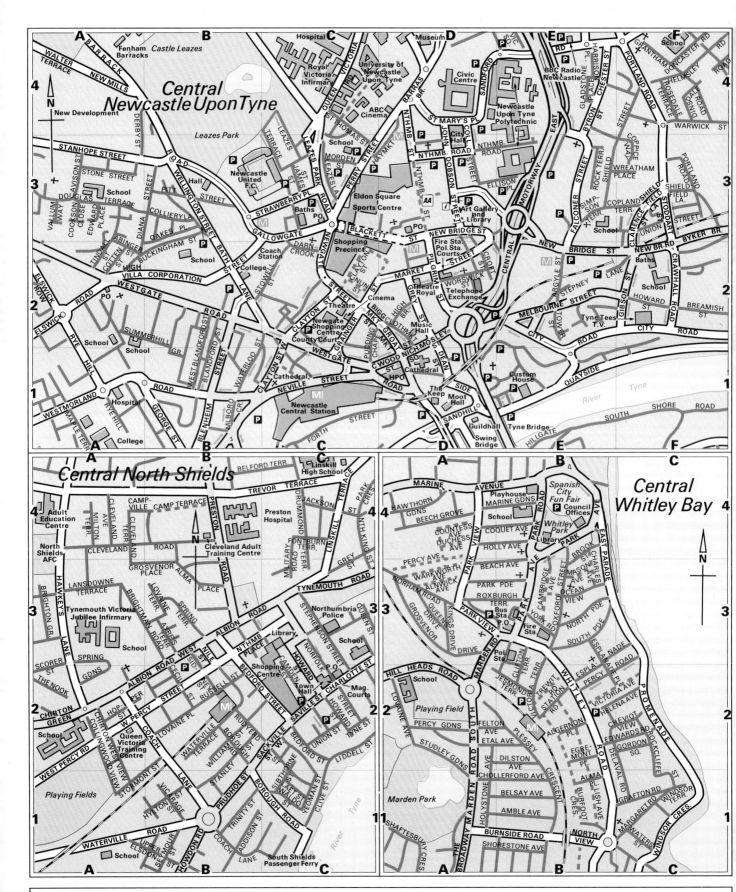

Newcastle

Six bridges span the Tyne at Newcastle; they all help to create a striking scene, but the most impressive is the High Level Bridge, built by Robert Stephenson in 1845-49 and consisting of two levels, one for the railway and one for the road. It is from the river that some of the best views of the city can be obtained. Grey Street is Newcastle's most handsome thoroughfare. It dates from the

time, between 1835 and 1840, when much of this part of the city was replanned and rebuilt. Elegant façades curve up to Grey's Monument. Close to the Monument is the Eldon Centre, combining sports facilities and shopping centre to form an integrated complex which is one of the largest of its kind in Europe. Newcastle has many museums. The industrial background of the city is traced in the Museum of Science and Engineering, while the Laing Art Gallery and Museum covers painting,

costumes and local domestic history. The Hancock Museum has an exceptional natural history collection and the John George Joicey Museum has period displays in a 17th-century almshouse. In Black Gate is one of Britain's most unusual museums – a collection of over 100 sets of bagpipes. Within the University precincts are three further museums. Of the city's open spaces, Town Moor is the largest. At nearly 1,000 acres it is big enough to feel genuinely wild.

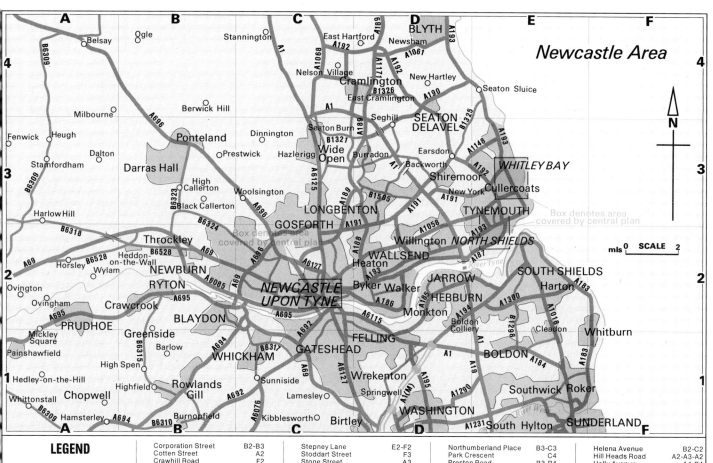

Newcastle Area

BLYTH

WHITLEY BAY

Box denotes area covered by central plan

mls 0 SCALE 2

LEGEND

Town Plan

AA recommended route
Restricted roads
Other roads
Buildings of interest — Hall
Car parks — P
Parks and open spaces
Metro stations — M
One way streets

Area Plan

A roads
B roads
Locations — Craghead ○
Urban area

Street Index with Grid Reference

Newcastle

Abinger Street	A2
Argyle Street	E2
Avison Street	A3
Barrack Road	A4-B4-B3
Barras Bridge	D4
Bath Lane	B2-C2
Bigg Market Street	C2-D2
Blackett Street	C3-D3-D2
Blandford Street	B1-B2
Blenheim Street	B1-B2
Breamish Street	F2
Buckingham Street	A2-B2-B3
Byker Bridge	F2-F3
Byran Street	E3-E4
Central Motorway	E1-D1-D2-E2-E3-E4
Chester Street	E4
City Road	E1-E2-F2
Clarance Street	F2-F3
Clayton Street	C2
Clayton Street West	B1-C1-C2
Clothmarket	D2
College Street	D3-D4
Colliery Lane	B3
Collingwood Street	C1-D1
Cookson Close	A3
Copland Terrace	E3-F3
Coppice Way	F3
Corporation Street	B2-B3
Cotten Street	A2
Crawhill Road	F2
Croft Street	D2
Darn Crook	C2-C3
Dean Street	D1-D2
Derby Street	A3-A4
Diana Street	A2-A3-B3
Dinsdale Road	F4
Doncaster Road	F4
Douglas Terrace	A3-B3
Edward Place	A3
Ellison Place	D3-E3
Elswick Road	A2
Elswick Row	A2
Falconer Street	E3
Forth Street	C1-D1
Gallowgate	B3-C3
George Street	A1-B1
Gibson Street	F2
Gladstone Place	E4
Grainger Street	C1-C2-D2
Grantham Road	F4
Grey Street	D2
Great Market	D1-D2
Harrison Place	E4
Haymarket	D3-D4
Helmsley Road	F4
High Bridge	D2
High Villa	A2
Hillgate	E1
Howard Street	F2
John Dobson Street	D3-D4
Leazes Lane	C3
Leazes Park Road	C3-C4
Leazes Terrace	C3-C4
Maple Terrace	A1
Market Street	D2
Marlborough Crescent	B1
Melbourne Street	E2-F2
Morden Street	C3
Moseley Street	D1-D2
Neville Street	C1
New Bridge Road	F2-F3
New Bridge Street	D3-E3-E2-F2
Newgate Street	C2
New Mills	A4
Northumberland Street	D4-D3-E4
Nun Street	C2
Oakes Place	A2-B2-B3
Perry Street	C3-D3-D4
Pilgrim Street	D2
Pitt Street	B3
Portland Road	F3-F4
Pudding Chape	C1-C2
Quayside	D1-E1-F1-F2
Queen Victoria Road	C4
Rock Terrace	E3
Rosedale Terrace	F4
Rye Hill	A1-A2
St James Street	C3
St Mary's Place	D4
St Nicholas Square	D1-D2
St Thomas Street	C3-C4
Sandford Road	D4-E4
Sandhill	D1
Shield Street	E3-F3-F4
Sheildfield Lane	F3
Side	D1
Simpson Terrace	E3
South Shore Road	E1-F1
Stanhope Street	A3-B3
Stepney Lane	E2-F2
Stoddart Street	F3
Stone Street	A3
Stowell Street	B2-C2
Strawberry Place	B3-C3
Summerhill Grove	A2-B2-B1
Tindall Street	A2
Tower Street	E2
Union Street	F3
Vallum Way	A3
Victoria Square	E4
Walter Terrace	A4
Warwick Street	F4
Waterloo Street	B1-B2-C2
Wellington Street	B3
Westgate Road	A2-B2-C2-C1-D1
Westmorland Road	A1-B1
West Blandford Street	B1-B2
Worswick Street	D2
Wreatham Place	E3-F3

North Shields

Addison Street	B1
Albion Road	B3-C3
Albion Road West	A2-B2-B3
Alma Place	B3
Ayre's Terrace	B3
Bedford Street	B3-B2-C2
Belford Terrace	B4-C4
Borough Road	B2-B1-C1
Brightman Road	A3-B3
Brighton Grove	A3
Camden Street	C2-C3
Camp Terrace	B4
Campville	A4-B4
Cecil Street	B2
Charlotte Street	C2-C3
Chirton Green	A2
Chirton West View	A1-A2
Cleveland Avenue	A4
Cleveland Road	A4-B4
Cleveland Terrace	A3-A4
Clive Street	C1-C2
Coach Lane	A2-B2-B1
Collingwood View	A1-A2
Drummond Terrace	C3-C4
Fontbarn Terrace	C4
Grey Street	C3-C4
Grosvenor Place	A3-B3
Hawkey's Lane	A2-A3-A4
Hopper Street	A2
Howard Street	C2-C3
Howdon Road	B1
Hylton Street	A1-B1
Jackson Street	C4
Laet Street	C1
Lansdowne Terrace	A3
Liddell Street	C2
Linskill Terrace	C3-C4
Lovaine Place	B2
Lovaine Terrace	B3
Military Road	C3-C4
Milton Terrace	A4
Nile Street	B3
Norfolk Street	C2-C3
North King Street	C3-C4
Northumberland Place	B3-C3
Park Crescent	C4
Preston Road	B3-B4
Prudhoe Street	B1-B2
Queen Street	C3
Rudyard Street	B2-C2-C1
Russell Street	B2
Sackville Street West	B2-C2
Saville Street	C2
Scorer Street	A2-A3
Seymour Street	B1
Sibthorne Street	C1-C2
Sidney Street	B2-B3
Spring Gardens	A2-A3
Spring Terrace	B3
Stanley Street	B1-B2
Stephenson Street	C2-C3
Stormont Street	A1-A2-B2
The Nook	A2
Trevor Terrace	B4-C4
Trinity Street	B1
Tyne Street	C2
Tynemouth Road	C3
Union Street	C2
Upper Elsdon Street	A1-B1
Vicarage Street	B1
Waldo Street	C1
Waterville Road	A1-B1
Waterville Terrace	B2
West Percy Road	A1-A2
West Percy Street	A2-B2-B3
William Street	B2-C2
Yeoman Street	C1-C2

Whitley Bay

Algernon Place	B2
Alma Place	B1
Alnwick Avenue	A3
Amble Avenue	A1-B1
Beach Avenue	A3-B3-B4
Beech Grove	A4
Belsay Avenue	A1-B1
Brook Street	B3-B4
Burfoot Crescent	B1
Burnside Road	A1-B1
Cambridge Avenue	B3-B4
Charles Avenue	B3-B4
Cheviot View	B2-C2
Chollerford Avenue	A1-B1
Clifton Terrace	B2-B3
Coquet Avenue	A4-B4
Countess Avenue	A4
Delaval Road	B2-C2-C1
Dilston Avenue	A2-B2
Duchess Avenue	A4
East Parade	B3-B4
Edwards Road	B2-C2
Egremont Place	B2
Esplanade	B2-B3-C3
Esplanade Place	B3-B2-C2
Etal Avenue	A2-B2
Felton Avenue	A2-B2
Gordon Square	C2
Grafton Road	C1
Grosvenor Drive	A3
Hawthorne Gardens	A4
Helena Avenue	B2-C2
Hill Heads Road	A2-A3-A2
Holly Avenue	A4-B4
Holystone Avenue	A1-A2
Jesmond Terrace	A2-B2
Kings Drive	A3
Lish Avenue	B1
Lovaine Avenue	A2
Marden Road	A2-A3-B3
Marden Road South	A1-A2
Margaret Road	C1
Marine Avenue	A4-B4
Marine Gardens	A4-B4
Mason Avenue	B3
Norham Road	A3
North Parade	B3
North View	B1
Ocean View	B3
Oxford Street	B3-B4
Park Avenue	B3-B4
Park Parade	A3-B3
Park Road	B4
Park View	A3-A4
Percy Avenue	A3-A4
Percy Gardens	A2
Percy Road	B2-C2-C3
Plessey Crescent	A2-B2-B1
Promenade	C1-C2-C3
Queens Drive	A3
Rockcliffe Street	C1-C2
Roxburgh Terrace	A3-B3
Shaftesbury Crescent	A1
Shorestone Avenue	A1-B1
South Parade	B3
Station Road	B2
Studley Gardens	A1-A2
The Broadway	A1
Trewit Road	B2
Victoria Avenue	B2-C2
Victoria Terrace	B2-B3
Warkworth Avenue	A3
Waters Street	C1
Whitley Road	B1-B2-B3
Windsor Crescent	C1
Windsor Terrace	C1
York Road	B3

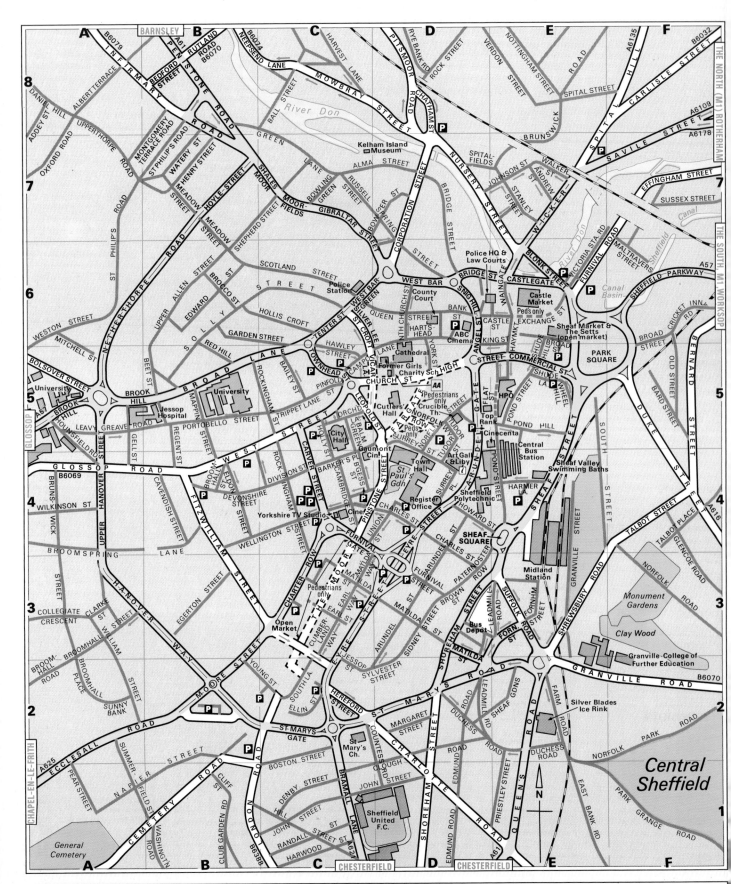

Sheffield

Cutlery – which has made the name of Sheffield famous throughout the world – has been manufactured here since at least as early as the time of Chaucer. The god of blacksmiths, Vulcan, is the symbol of the city's industry, and he crowns the town hall, which was opened in 1897 by Queen Victoria. At the centre of the industry, however, is Cutlers' Hall, the headquarters of the Company of Cutlers. This society was founded in 1624 and has the right to grant trade marks to articles of a sufficiently high standard. In the hall is the company's collection of silver, with examples of craftsmanship dating back every year to 1773. A really large collection of cutlery is kept in the city museum. Steel production, a vital component of the industry, was greatly improved when the crucible process was invented here in 1740. At Abbeydale Industrial Hamlet, 3½ miles south-west of the city centre, is a complete restored site open as a museum and showing 18th-century methods of steel production. Sheffield's centre, transformed since World War II, is one of the finest and most modern in Europe. There are no soot-grimed industrial eyesores here, for the city has stringent pollution controls and its buildings are carefully planned and set within excellent landscaping projects. Many parks are set in and around the city, and the Pennines are within easy reach.

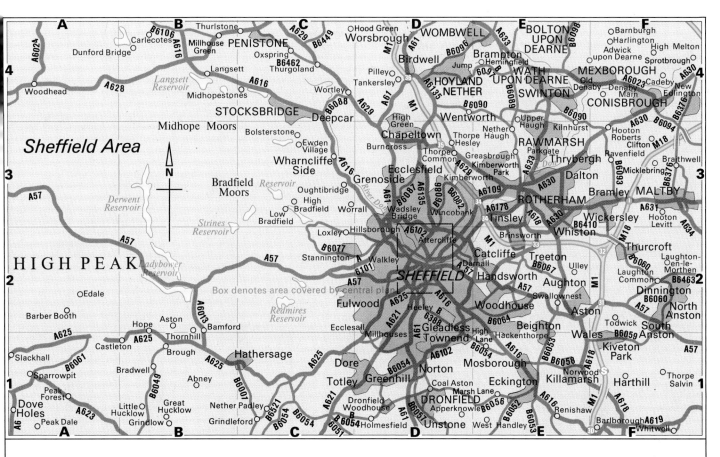

LEGEND

Town Plan

AA Recommended roads
Other roads
Restricted roads
Buildings of interest
AA Centre **AA**
Car Parks **P**
Parks and open spaces

Area Plan

A roads
B roads
Locations Oakworth O
Urban area

Street Index with grid reference

Sheffield

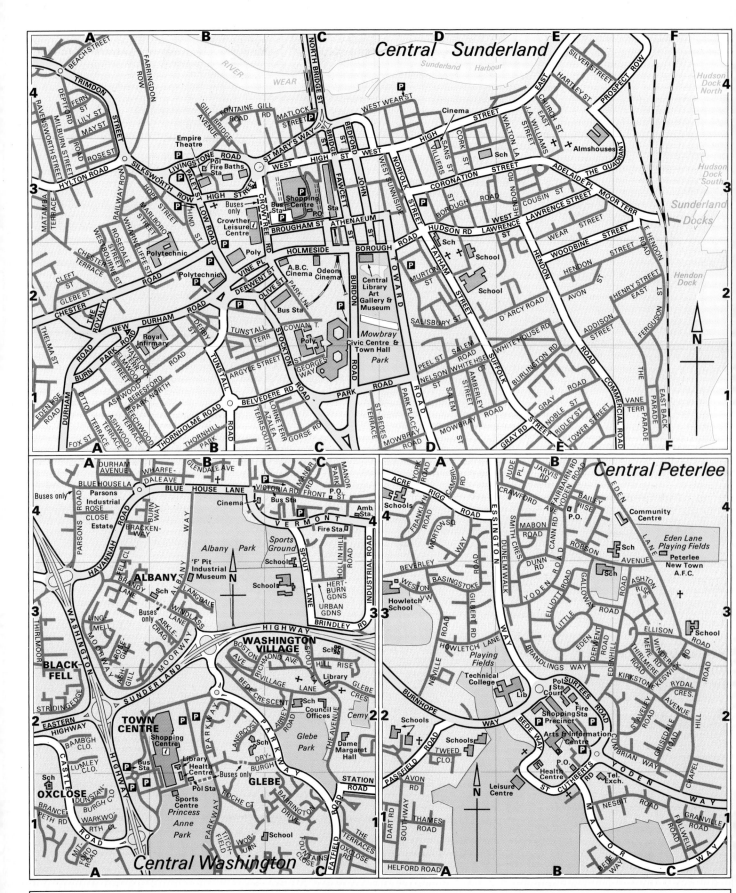

Sunderland

Renowned for its shipbuilding industry, Sunderland is also an important coal port. Its name is derived from the fact that it was 'sundered' from a monastery founded on the far bank of the River Wear in 674. Wearmouth Bridge, originally built in 1796, but replaced in 1929, was one of the first cast-iron bridges in the country. A modern Civic Centre and three museums feature among the town's amenities. Nearby are the fine beaches of Roker and Seaburn.

Peterlee, built to attract industry in the 1950s, is one of Durham's most successful New Towns. It is named after Peter Lee, who started work down the mines at the age of ten, and rose to become president of the Miners' Union. An unexpected but welcome feature of the town is Castle Eden Dene – a three-mile stretch of natural woodland kept as a nature reserve.

Washington is another New Town burgeoning in this industrial corner of north-east England. In the original village stands 17th-century Washington Old Hall, the former home of George Washington's ancestors. Now in the care of the National Trust, it has been fully restored in period style. Another far cry from industry is the Wildfowl Trust's 103-acre park on the north bank of the Wear, where visitors can observe a comprehensive collection of the world's waterfowl in landscaped surroundings.

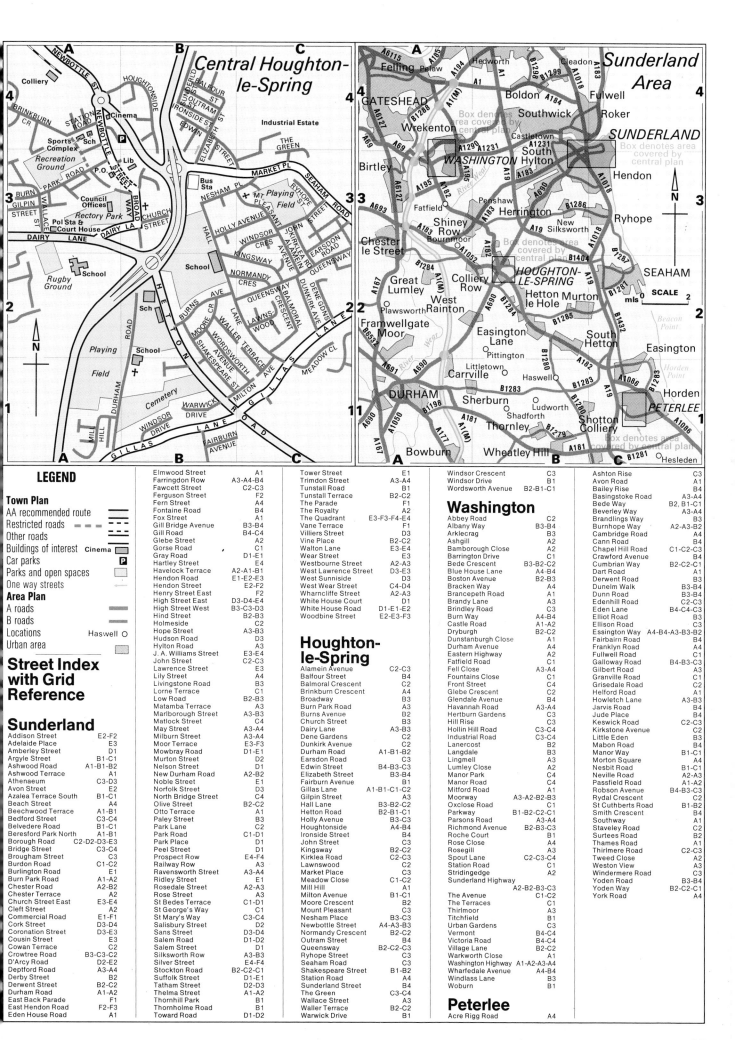

Central Houghton-le-Spring

Industrial Estate

Sunderland Area

SUNDERLAND

SCALE

LEGEND

Town Plan

AA recommended route
Restricted roads
Other roads
Buildings of interest — Cinema
Car parks — P
Parks and open spaces
One way streets

Area Plan

A roads
B roads
Locations — Haswell O
Urban area

Street Index with Grid Reference

Sunderland

Addison Street	E2-F2
Adelaide Place	E3
Amberley Street	D1
Argyle Street	B1-C1
Ashwood Road	A1-B1-B2
Ashwood Terrace	A1
Athenaeum	C3-D3
Avon Street	E2
Azalea Terrace South	B1-C1
Beach Street	A4
Beechwood Terrace	A1-B1
Bedford Street	C3-C4
Belvedere Road	B1-C1
Beresford Park North	A1-B1
Borough Road	C2-D2-D3-E3
Bridge Street	C3-C4
Brougham Street	C3
Burdon Road	C1-C2
Burlington Road	E1
Burn Park Road	A1-A2
Chester Road	A2-B2
Chester Terrace	A2
Church Street East	E3-E4
Cleft Street	A2
Commercial Road	E1-F1
Cork Street	D3-D4
Coronation Street	D3-E3
Cousin Street	E3
Cowan Terrace	C2
Crowtree Road	B3-C3-C2
D'Arcy Road	D2-E2
Deptford Road	A3-A4
Derby Street	B2
Derwent Street	B2-C2
Durham Road	A1-A2
East Back Parade	F1
East Hendon Road	F2-F3
Eden House Road	A1
Elmwood Street	A1
Farringdon Row	A3-A4-B4
Fawcett Street	C2-C3
Ferguson Street	F2
Fern Street	A4
Fontaine Road	B4
Fox Street	A1
Gill Bridge Avenue	B3-B4
Gill Road	B4-C4
Glebe Street	A2
Gorse Road	C1
Gray Road	D1-E1
Hartley Street	E4
Havelock Terrace	A2-A1-B1
Hendon Road	E1-E2-E3
Hendon Street	E2-F2
Henry Street East	F2
High Street East	D3-D4-E4
High Street West	B3-C3-D3
Hind Street	B2-B3
Holmeside	C2
Hope Street	A3-B3
Hudson Road	D3
Hylton Road	A3
J. A. Williams Street	E3-E4
John Street	C2-C3
Lawrence Street	E3
Lily Street	A4
Livingstone Road	B3
Lorne Terrace	C1
Low Road	B2-B3
Matamba Terrace	A3
Marlborough Street	A3-B3
Matlock Street	C4
May Street	A3-A4
Milburn Street	A3-A4
Moor Terrace	E3-F3
Mowbray Road	D1-E1
Murton Street	D2
Nelson Street	D1
New Durham Road	A2-B2
Noble Street	E1
Norfolk Street	D3
North Bridge Street	C4
Olive Street	B2-C2
Otto Terrace	A1
Paley Street	B3
Park Lane	C2
Park Road	C1-D1
Park Place	D1
Peel Street	D1
Prospect Row	E4-F4
Railway Street	A3
Ravensworth Street	A3-A4
Ridley Street	E1
Rosedale Street	A2-A3
Rose Street	A3
St Bedes Terrace	C1-D1
St George's Way	C1
St Mary's Way	C3-C4
Salisbury Street	D2
Sans Street	D3-D4
Salem Road	D1-D2
Salem Street	D1
Silksworth Row	A3-B3
Silver Street	E4-F4
Stockton Road	B2-C2-C1
Suffolk Street	D1-E1
Tatham Street	D2-D3
Thelma Street	A1-A2
Thornhill Park	B1
Thornholme Road	B1
Toward Road	D1-D2
Tower Street	E1
Trimdon Street	A3-A4
Tunstall Road	B1
Tunstall Terrace	B2-C2
The Parade	F1
The Royalty	A2
The Quadrant	E3-F3-F4-E4
Vane Terrace	F1
Villiers Street	D3
Vine Place	B2-C2
Walton Lane	E3-E4
Wear Street	E3
Westbourne Street	A2-A3
West Lawrence Street	D3-E3
West Sunniside	D3
West Wear Street	C4-D4
Wharncliffe Street	A2-A3
White House Court	D1
White House Road	D1-E1-E2
Woodbine Street	E2-E3-F3

Houghton-le-Spring

Alamein Avenue	C2-C3
Balfour Street	B4
Balmoral Crescent	C2
Brinkburn Crescent	A4
Broadway	B3
Burn Park Road	A3
Burns Avenue	B2
Church Street	B3
Dairy Lane	A3-B3
Dene Gardens	C2
Dunkirk Avenue	C2
Durham Road	A1-B1-B2
Earsdon Road	C3
Edwin Street	B4-B3-C3
Elizabeth Street	B3-B4
Fairburn Avenue	B1
Gillas Lane	A1-B1-C1-C2
Gilpin Street	A3
Hall Lane	B3-B2-C2
Hetton Road	B2-B1-C1
Holly Avenue	B3-C3
Houghtonside	A4-B4
Ironside Street	B4
John Street	C3
Kingsway	B2-C2
Kirklea Road	C2-C3
Lawnswood	C2
Market Place	C3
Meadow Close	C1-C2
Mill Hill	A1
Milton Avenue	B1-C1
Moore Crescent	B2
Mount Pleasant	C3
Nesham Place	C3
Newbottle Street	A4-A3-B3
Normandy Crescent	B2-C2
Outram Street	B4
Queensway	B2-C2-C3
Ryhope Street	C3
Seaham Road	C3
Shakespeare Street	B1-B2
Station Road	A4
Sunderland Street	B4
The Green	C3-C4
Wallace Street	A3
Waller Terrace	B2-C2
Warwick Drive	B1
Windsor Crescent	C3
Windsor Drive	B1
Wordsworth Avenue	B2-B1-C1

Washington

Abbey Road	C2
Albany Way	B3-B4
Arklecrag	B3
Ashgill	A2
Bamborough Close	A2
Barrington Drive	C1
Bede Crescent	B3-B2-C2
Blue House Lane	A4-B4
Boston Avenue	B2-B3
Bracken Way	A4
Brancepeth Road	A1
Brandy Lane	A3
Brindley Road	C3
Burn Way	A4-B4
Castle Road	A1-A2
Dryburgh	B2-C2
Dunstanburgh Close	A1
Durham Avenue	A4
Eastern Highway	A2
Fatfield Road	C1
Fell Close	A3-A4
Fountains Close	C1
Front Street	C4
Glebe Crescent	C2
Glendale Avenue	B4
Havannah Road	A3-A4
Hertburn Gardens	C3
Hill Rise	C3
Hollin Hill Road	C3-C4
Industrial Road	C3-C4
Lanercost	B2
Langdale	B3
Lingmell	A3
Lumley Close	A2
Manor Park	C4
Manor Road	C4
Mitford Road	A1
Moorway	A3-A2-B2-B3
Oxclose Road	C1
Parkway	B1-B2-C2-C1
Parsons Road	A3-A4
Richmond Avenue	B2-B3-C3
Roche Court	B1
Rose Close	A4
Rosegill	A3
Spout Lane	C2-C3-C4
Station Road	C1
Stridingedge	A2
Sunderland Highway	A2-B2-B3-C3
The Avenue	C1-C2
The Terraces	C1
Thirlmoor	A3
Titchfield	B1
Urban Gardens	C3
Vermont	B4-C4
Victoria Road	B4-C4
Village Lane	B2-C2
Warkworth Close	A1
Washington Highway	A1-A2-A3-A4
Wharfedale Avenue	A4-B4
Windlass Lane	B3
Woburn	B1

Peterlee

Acre Rigg Road	A4
Ashton Rise	C3
Avon Road	A1
Bailey Rise	B4
Basingstoke Road	A3-A4
Bede Way	B2, B1-C1
Beverley Way	A3-A4
Brandlings Way	B3
Burnhope Way	A2-A3-B2
Cambridge Road	A4
Cann Road	B4
Chapel Hill Road	C1-C2-C3
Crawford Avenue	B4
Cumbrian Way	B2-C2-C1
Dart Road	A1
Derwent Road	B3
Dunelm Walk	B3-B4
Dunn Road	B3-B4
Edenhill Road	C2-C3
Eden Lane	B4-C4-C3
Elliot Road	B3
Ellison Road	C3
Essington Way	A4-B4-A3-B3-B2
Fairbairn Road	B4
Franklyn Road	A4
Fullwell Road	C1
Galloway Road	B4-B3-C3
Gilbert Road	A3
Granville Road	C1
Grisedale Road	C2
Helford Road	A1
Howletch Lane	A3-B3
Jarvis Road	B4
Jude Place	B4
Keswick Road	C2-C3
Kirkstone Avenue	C2
Little Eden	B3
Mabon Road	B4
Manor Way	B1-C1
Morton Square	A4
Nesbit Road	B1-C1
Neville Road	A2-A3
Passfield Road	A1-A2
Robson Avenue	B4-B3-C3
Rydal Crescent	C2
St Cuthberts Road	B1-B2
Smith Crescent	B4
Southway	A1
Staveley Road	C2
Surtees Road	B2
Thames Road	A1
Thirlmere Road	C2-C3
Tweed Close	A3
Weston View	A3
Windermere Road	C3
Yoden Road	B3-B4
Yoden Way	B2-C2-C1
York Road	A4

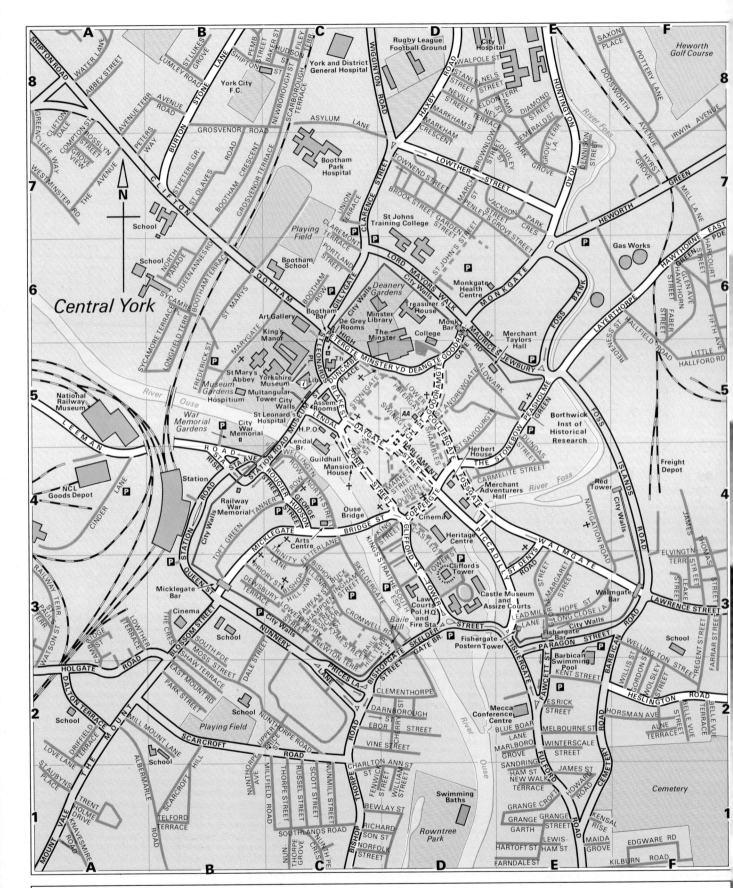

York

York Minster, unquestionably the city's outstanding glory, is considered to be one of the greatest cathedral churches in Europe. It is especially famous for its lovely windows which contain more than half the medieval stained glass in England.

Great medieval walls enclose the historic city centre and their three-mile circuit offers magnificent views of the Minster, York's numerous fine buildings, churches and the River Ouse. The ancient streets consist of a maze of alleys and lanes, some of them so narrow that the overhanging upper storeys of the houses almost touch. The most famous of these picturesque streets is The Shambles, formerly the butchers' quarter of the city, but now colonised by antique and tourist shops. York flourished throughout Tudor, Georgian and Victorian times and handsome buildings from these periods also feature throughout the city.

The Castle Museum gives a fascinating picture of York as it used to be and the Heritage Centre interprets the social and architectural history of the city. Other places of exceptional note in this city of riches include the Merchant Adventurer's Hall; the Treasurer's House, now owned by the National Trust and filled with fine paintings and furniture; the Jorvik Viking Centre, where there is an exciting restoration of the original Viking settlement at York, and the National Railway Museum.

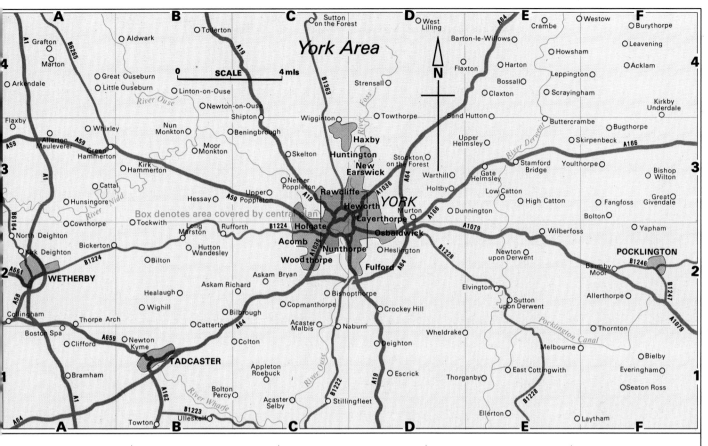

Key to Town Plan and Area Plan

Town Plan

AA Recommended roads
Other roads
Restricted roads
Buildings of interest Station
Churches
Car Parks
Parks and open spaces
AA Service Centre
One Way Streets

Area Plan

A roads
B roads
Locations Fangfoss○
Urban area

Street Index with Grid Reference

York

Abbey Street	A8
Albemarle Road	A2-A1-B1
Aldwark	D5-E5
Alne Terrace	F2
Amber Street	E8
Ann Street	D1
Asylum Lane	C8-C7-D7
Avenue Road	B8
Avenue Terrace	A7-A8-B8
Baile Hill Terrace	C2-C3-D3
Baker Street	C8
Barbican Road	E2-F2-F3-E3
Belle Vue Street	F2
Belle Vue Terrace	F2
Bewlay Street	C1-D1
Bishopgate Street	C2-D2-D3
Bishophill Junior	C3
Bishophill Senior	C3
Bishop Thorpe Road	C1-C2
Blake Street	C5
Blossom Street	B2-B3
Blue Boar Lane	E2
Bootham	B6-C6
Bootham Crescent	B7-C7-C8
Bootham Row	C6
Bootham Terrace	B6
Bridge Street	C4-D4
Brook Street	D7
Brownlow Street	D7-E7-E8
Buckingham Street	C3
Burton Stone Lane	B7-B8
Cambridge Street	A2-A3
Carmelite Street	D4-E4-E5
Castlegate	D3-D4
Cemetery Road	E1-E2
Charlton Street	C1-D1
Cherry Street	D2
Church Street	D5
Cinder Lane	A4
Claremont Terrace	C6-C7
Clarence Street	C6-C7-D7
Clementhorpe	C2-D2
Clifford Street	D3-D4
Clifton	A8-A7-B7
Clifton Dale	A7-A8
Colliergate	D4-D5
Compton Street	A7-A8
Coppergate	D4
Cromwell Road	C3-D3
Dale Street	B2-B3
Dalton Terrace	A2
Darnborough Street	C2-D2
Daygate	C5-C4-D4-D5
Deangate	D5
Dennison Street	E7
Dewsbury Terrace	B3-C3
Diamond Street	E8
Dodsworth Avenue	E8-F8-F7
Driffield Terrace	A2
Dudley Street	D7-E7
Duncombe Place	C5
Dundas Street	E4-E5
East Parade	F6-F7
East Mount Road	B2
Ebor Street	C2-D2
Edgware Road	F1
Eldon Terrace	D8-E8
Elvington Terrace	F3
Emerald Street	E7-E8
Escrick Street	E2
Faber Street	F6
Fairfax Street	C3
Farndale Street	E1
Farrar Street	F2-F3
Fawcett Street	E2-E3
Fenwick Street	C1-D1
Fetter Lane	C3-C4
Fifth Avenue	F5-F6
Filey Terrace	C8
Fishergate	E2-E3
Foss Bank	E5-E6
Fossgate	D4
Foss Islands Road	E4-E5-F5-F4
Frederick Street	B5
Fulford Road	E1-E2
Garden Street	D7
George Hudson Street	C4
George Street	E3-E4
Gillygate	C6
Glen Avenue	F5
Goodramgate	D5-D6
Gordon Street	F2
Grange Croft	E1
Grange Garth	E1
Grange Street	E1

Greencliffe Way	A7-A8
Grosvenor Road	B8-C8
Grosvenor Terrace	B6-B7-C7-C8
Grove Terrace Lane	E7-E8
Grove View	A7
Hallfield Road	F5-F6
Hampden Street	C3
Harcourt Street	F6
Harloft Street	E1
Hawthorne Green	F6
Hawthorn Street	F6
Haxby Road	D7-D8
Heslington Road	E2-F2
Heworth Green	E6-E7-F7
High Ousegate	D4
High Petergate	C5-C6
Holgate Road	A2-A3-B3
Hope Street	E3
Horsman Avenue	E2-F2
Howard Road	E1
Hudson Street	C8
Huntington Road	E6-E7-E8
Hyrst Grove	F7
Irwin Avenue	F7-F8
Jackson Street	D7-E7
James Street	E4
James Street	F3-F4
Jewbury	E5
Kensal Rise	E1
Kent Street	E2
Kilburn Road	E1-F1
Kings Straithe	C4-D4-D3
King Street	C4-D4
Knavesmire Road	A1
Kyme Street	C3
Lawrence Street	F3
Layerthorpe	E5-E6-F6
Lead Mill Lane	E3
Leake Street	F3
Leeman Road	A5-A4-B5-B4
Lendal Coney Street	C5-C4-D4
Lewisham Street	E1
Little Hallford Road	F5
Long Close Lane	E3-F3
Longfield Terrace	B5-B6
Lord Mayors Walk	C6-D6
Lumley Road	B8
Love Lane	A1-A2
Lower Petergate	D5
Lower Priory Street	C3
Lowther Street	D7-E7
Lowther Terrace	A3
Maida Grove	E1
March Street	D7
Margaret Street	E3
Market Street	D4
Markham Crescent	D7-D8
Markham Street	D7-D8
Marlborough Grove	E2
Marygate	B5-B6-C6
Melbourne Street	E2
Micklegate	B3-B4-C4
Millfield Road	C1-C2
Mill Lane	F7
Mill Mount Lane	A2-B2
Minster Yard	C5-D5
Monkgate	D6-E6
Moss Street	B2-B3
Mount Vale	A1
Museum Street	C5

Navigation Road	E4-E3-F3
Nelson Street	D8-E8
Neville Street	D8
Neville Terrace	D8-E8
Newborough Street	C8
New Street	C4-C5
Newton Terrace	C2-C3
New Walk Terrace	E1
Norfolk Street	C1-D1
North Parade	B6
North Street	C4
Nunmill Street	C1-C2
Nunnery Lane	B3-C3-C2
Nunthorpe Avenue	B1-B2
Nunthorpe Grove	C1
Nunthorpe Road	B2-C2
Paragon Street	E3-F3
Park Crescent	E7
Park Grove	E7-E8
Park Street	B2
Parliament Street	D4-D5
Peasholme Green	E5
Pembroke Street	B8
Penley's Grove Street	D7-E7-E6
Peters Way	A7-B7-B8
Piccadilly	D4-D3-E3-E4
Portland Street	C6
Pottery Lane	F8
Prices Lane	C2
Priory Street	B3-C3
Queen Annes Road	B6
Queen Street	B3
Railway Terrace	A3
Redness Street	F5-F6
Regent Street	F2-F3
Richardson Street	C1-D1
Rosslyn Street	A7
Rougier Street	C4
Russel Street	C1-C2
St Andrewgate	D5
St Aubyns Place	A1
St Denys Road	E3-E4
St Johns Street	D6-D7
St Leonards Place	D5-D6
St Lukes Grove	B8
St Marys	B6
St Maurices	D6-D5-E5
St Olaves Road	B7-B8
St Pauls Terrace	A3
St Peters Grove	B7
St Saviourgate	D4-D5-E5
Sandringham Street	E1
Saxon Place	E8-F8
Scarborough Terrace	C8
Scarcroft Hill	B1-B2
Scarcroft Road	A2-B2-C2-C1
Scott Street	C1-C2
Shambles	D4-D5
Shaw Terrace	B2-B3
Shipton Road	A8
Shipton Street	B8-C8
Skeldergate	C4-C3-D3
Skeldergate Bridge	D3
South Esplanade	D3
Southlands Road	C1
South Parade	B2-B3
Stanley Street	D8
Station Avenue	B4
Station Rise	B4
Station Road	B3-B4-C4-C5

Stonegate	C5-D5
Swinegate	D5
Sycamore Place	B6
Sycamore Terrace	A5-B5-B6
Tanner Row	B4-C4
Telford Terrace	B1
The Avenue	A7
The Crescent	B3
The Mount	A1-A2-B2
The Stonebow	D4-E4-E5
Thomas Street	F3-F4
Thorpe Street	C1-C2
Toft Green	B3-B4
Tower Street	D4-D3-E3
Townend Street	D7
Trent Holme Drive	A1
Trinity Lane	C3-C4
Union Terrace	C7
Upper Price Street	B2-C2
Victor Street	C3
Vine Street	C2-D2
Walmgate	D4-E4-E3-F3
Walpole Street	D8-E8
Water Lane	A8
Watson Street	A2-A3
Wellington Row	C4
Wellington Street	F2-F3
Westminster Road	A7
William Street	D1
Willis Street	F2-F3
Winterscale Street	E2
Wolsley Street	F2

97

Legend to Atlas

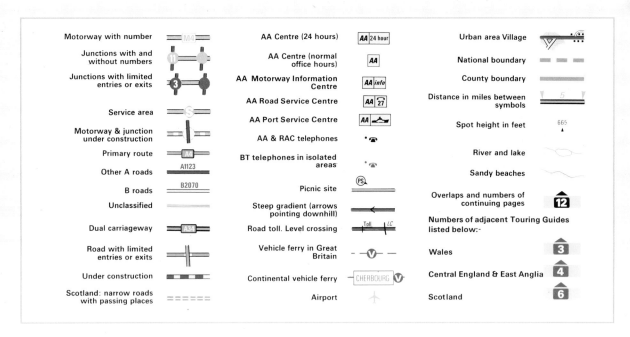

Motorway with number	AA Centre (24 hours)	Urban area Village
Junctions with and without numbers	AA Centre (normal office hours)	National boundary
Junctions with limited entries or exits	AA Motorway Information Centre	County boundary
Service area	AA Road Service Centre	Distance in miles between symbols
Motorway & junction under construction	AA Port Service Centre	Spot height in feet
Primary route	AA & RAC telephones	River and lake
Other A roads	BT telephones in isolated areas	Sandy beaches
B roads	Picnic site	Overlaps and numbers of continuing pages
Unclassified	Steep gradient (arrows pointing downhill)	Numbers of adjacent Touring Guides listed below:-
Dual carriageway	Road toll. Level crossing	Wales
Road with limited entries or exits	Vehicle ferry in Great Britain	Central England & East Anglia
Under construction	Continental vehicle ferry	Scotland
Scotland: narrow roads with passing places	Airport	

Abbey or Cathedral	Coastal Launching Site	Nature Trail
Ruined Abbey or Cathedral	Surfing	Wildlife Park (mammals)
Castle	Climbing School	Wildlife Park (birds)
House and Garden	County Cricket Ground	Zoo
House	Gliding Centre	Forest Drive
Garden	Artificial Ski Slope	Lighthouse
Industrial Interest	Golf Course	Tourist Information Centre
Museum or Collection	Horse Racing	Tourist Information Centre (summer only)
Prehistoric Monument	Show Jumping/Equestrian Centre	Long Distance Footpath
Famous Battle Site	Motor Racing Circuit	AA Viewpoint
Preserved Railway or Steam Centre	Cave	Other Place of Interest
Windmill	Country Park	Boxed symbols indicate tourist attractions in towns
Sea Angling	Dolphinarium or Aquarium	

The National Grid

The National Grid provides a system of reference common to maps of all scales. The grid covers Britain with an imaginary network of 100 kilometre squares. Each square is identified by two letters, *eg* TR. Every 100 kilometre square is then sub-divided into 10 kilometre squares which appear as a network of blue lines on the map pages. These blue lines are numbered left to right [0]-[9] and bottom to top [0]-[9]. These 10 kilometre squares can be further divided into tenths to give a place reference to the nearest kilometre.

Key to Road Maps

Thurso
Wick
Stornoway
Outer Hebrides
Ullapool
Banff
Portree
Inverness
Peterhead
Aberdeen
Fort William
Pitlochry
Oban
Perth
Dundee
Edinburgh
36/37
Largs
Glasgow
Berwick
Peebles
34/35
Campbeltown
Ayr
32/33
Dumfries
30/31
Newcastle upon Tyne
28/29
Stranraer
22/23
Workington
24/25
26/27
Middlesbrough
Isle of Man
Kendal
Scarborough
16/17
Douglas
Lancaster
18/19
20/21
York
Blackpool
Leeds
Hull
10/11
12/13
14/15
Grimsby
Liverpool
Manchester
Sheffield
Caernarfon
2/3
Chester
4/5
6/7
8/9
Lincoln
Stoke
Nottingham
King's Lynn
Shrewsbury
Leicester
Norwich
Great Yarmouth
Peterborough
Aberystwyth
Birmingham
Coventry
Northampton
Worcester
Cambridge
Fishguard
Carmarthen
Hereford
Felixstowe
Gloucester
Pembroke
Swansea
Oxford
Chelmsford
Cardiff
Bristol
Reading
LONDON
Maidstone
Barnstaple
Guildford
Dover
Salisbury
Folkestone
Taunton
Southampton
Brighton
Newhaven
Exeter
Weymouth
Bournemouth
Truro
Plymouth
Scilly Isles

Shetland Islands

Orkney Islands

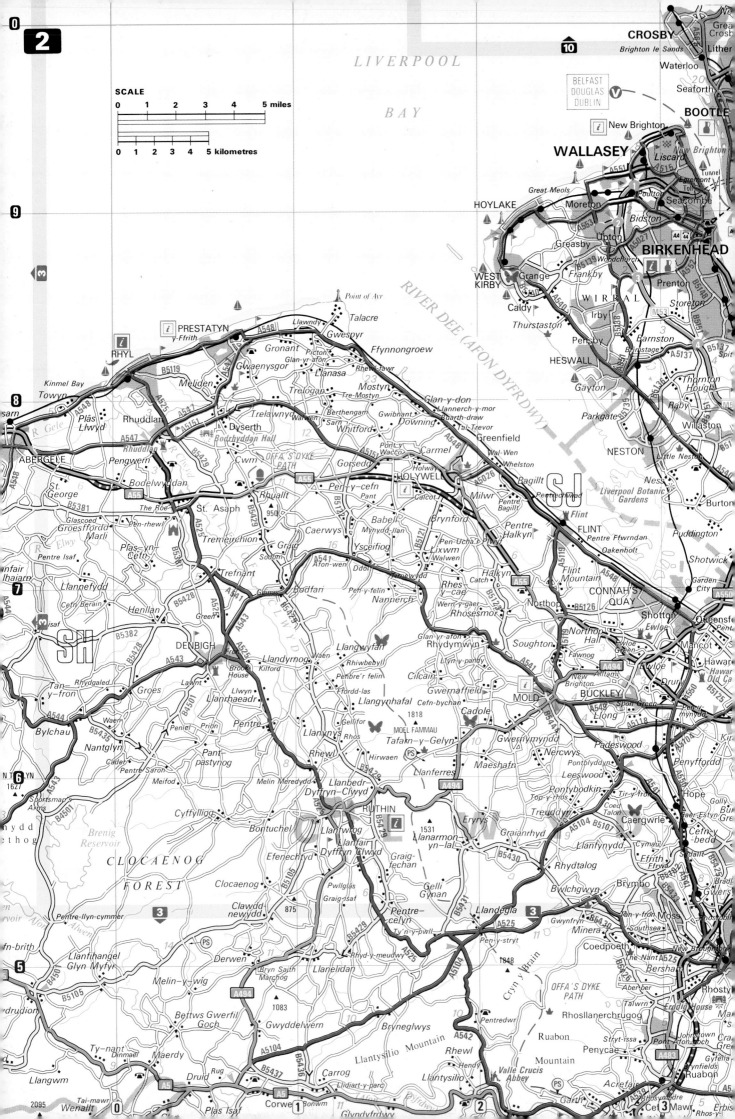

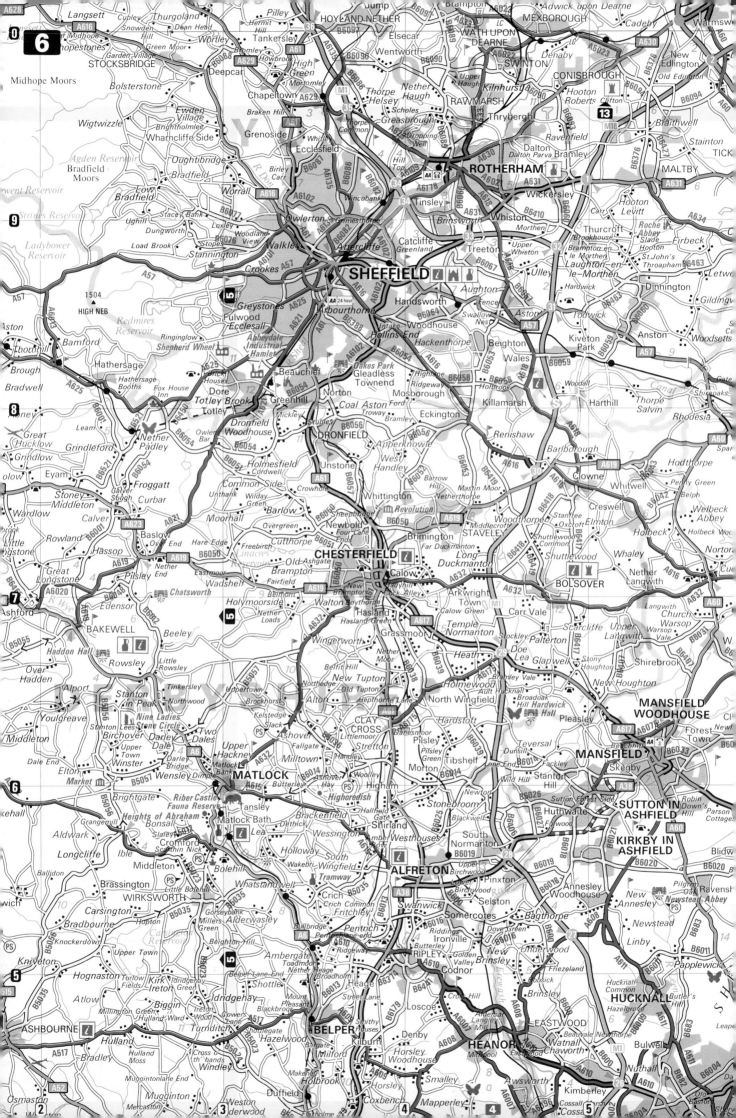

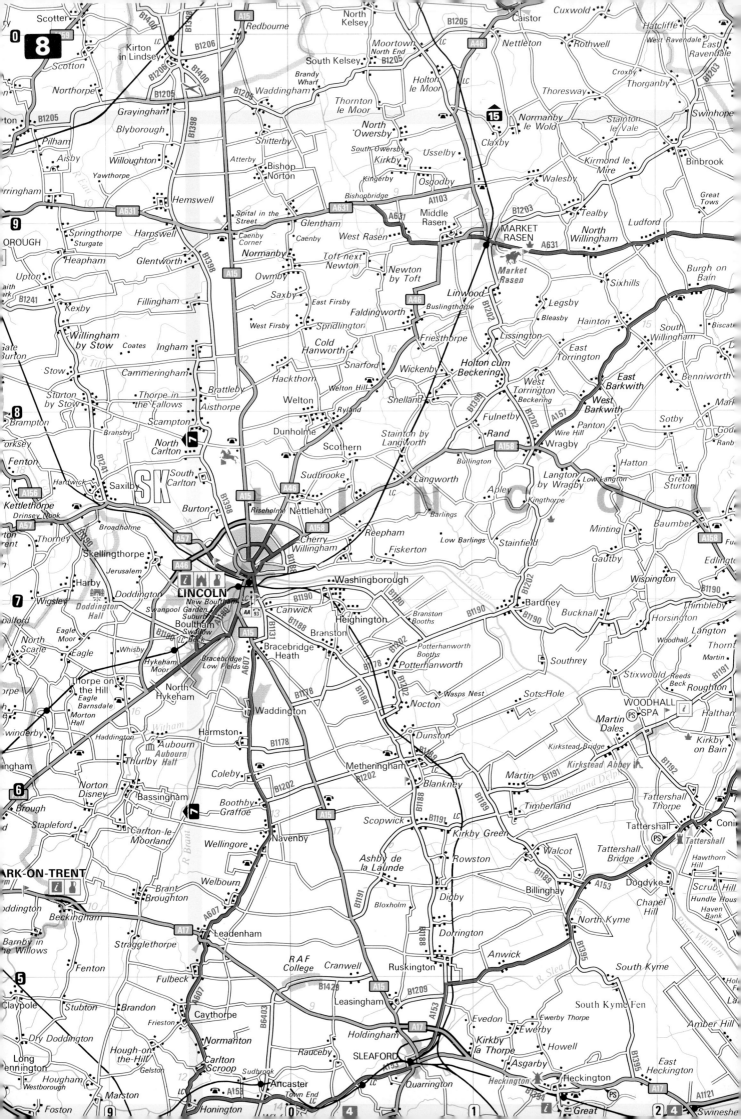

SCALE

0 1 2 3 4 5 miles

0 1 2 3 4 5 kilometres

Waithe · Tetney · North Coates
curt by · North Thoresby · Marshchapel
by · A1031 · Eskham · Donna Nook
B1201 · Fulstow · West End · Grainthorpe
borough · Churchthorpe · A16 · Conisholme · North Somercotes
ham · 15 · Covenham St Bartholomew · Church End · Toby's Hill · Saltfleet
North · Bank Lane · South Somercotes · Saltfleetby St. Clements
Ormsby · Covenham St. Mary · Yarburgh · Skidbrooke
Utterby · Little Grimsby · North End · Saltfleetby St. Peter · Saltfleetby All Saints
Fotherby · Alvingham · Keddington Corner · Cockerington · Theddlethorpe St. Helen
Elkington · Keddington · B1200 · Grimoldby · Theddlethorpe All Saints
LOUTH · River Head · Stewton · Manby · Meers Bridge
A157 · Little Welton · A16 · Legbourne · Little Carlton · MABLETHORPE
Hallington · A153 · PS · North Reston · Great Carlton · Trusthorpe
Raithby · Little Cawthorpe · Gayton le Marsh · A1104 · Strubby · Thorpe · Sutton-on-Sea
Withcall · Maltb · South Reston · Withern · Maltby le Marsh · Sandilands
Tathwell · Haugham · Muckton · Authorpe · Tothill · Woodthorpe · Beesby · Sutton le Marsh
Cadwell Park · Cawkwell · Maidenwell · Burwell · Belleau · Claythorpe · Aby · Saleby · Markby · Asserby · Huttoft
Scamblesby · Farforth · Oxcombe · Ruckland · Walmsgate · White Pit · Thoresthorpe · Asserby Turn · Anderby Creek
Belchford · Little London · South Ormsby · Calceby · Rigsby · Bilsby · Anderby
Tetford · South Thoresby · Driby · Thurlby · Farlesthorpe · Mumby · Authorpe Row
Fulletby · Brinkhill · Well · ALFORD · Cumberworth · Helsey · Hogsthorpe · Chapel St. Leonards
West Ashby · Salmonby · Harrington · Ulceby Cross · Ulceby · Claxby · Willoughby · Mawthorpe Collection · Sloothby · Slackholme End
Greetham · Ashby Puerorum · Bag Enderby · Aswardby · Langton · Dalby · Skendleby · Hasthorpe · Habertoft · Addlethorpe
Low Toynton · Hagworthingham · Partney · Scremby · Welton le Marsh · Orby Marsh · Ingoldmells
High Toynton · Scrafield · Lusby · Sausthorpe · Raithby · Grebby · Candlesby · Orby · Ingoldmells Point
Hameringham · Mavis Enderby · Spilsby · Ashby by Partney · Hundel Hill · Gunby Hall · Winthorpe · Seathorne
Mareham on the Hill · Asgarby · Hundleby · Halton Holegate · Monksthorpe · Bratoft · Burgh le Marsh
Scrivelby · Hareby · Old Bolingbroke · Keal · Toynton All Saints · Halton Fenside · Great Steeping · Irby in the Marsh · SKEGNESS
Moorby · Miningsby · Keal Cotes · Toynton St. Peter · Firsby · Croft · Seacroft
East Kirkby · Kirkby Fenside · Toynton Fen Side · Little Steeping · Thorpe St. Peter
Revesby · Hagnaby · Fendike Corner · Havenhouse Station · Wainfleet All Saints · Gibraltar
Wilksby · Stickford · Wainfleet Bank · Key's Toft
Mareham le Fen · New Bolingbroke Fen Side · Midville · New Leake · Eastville · Friskney · Friskney Eaudike
Medlam · Stickney · Small End
Carrington West Houses · Lade Bank · Snowden's Bridge
Northlands · Sibsey Fen Side · Sibsey · Leake Common Side · Wrangle Lowgate
Frithville · B1183 · A16 · Old Leake · Wrangle · Hall End
Fishtoft Drove · High Ferry · Leverton · Leake Hurn's End
Frith Bank · Leverton Lucasgate
Brothertoft · Cowbridge · West End · Benington · Halltoft End · Butterwick · Benington Sea End
BOSTON · Boston West · Hubbert's Bridge · Burton Corner · Willoughby Hills · Brand End · Freiston
AA · A52 · Wyberton West · Skirbeck · Harbour · Freiston Shore

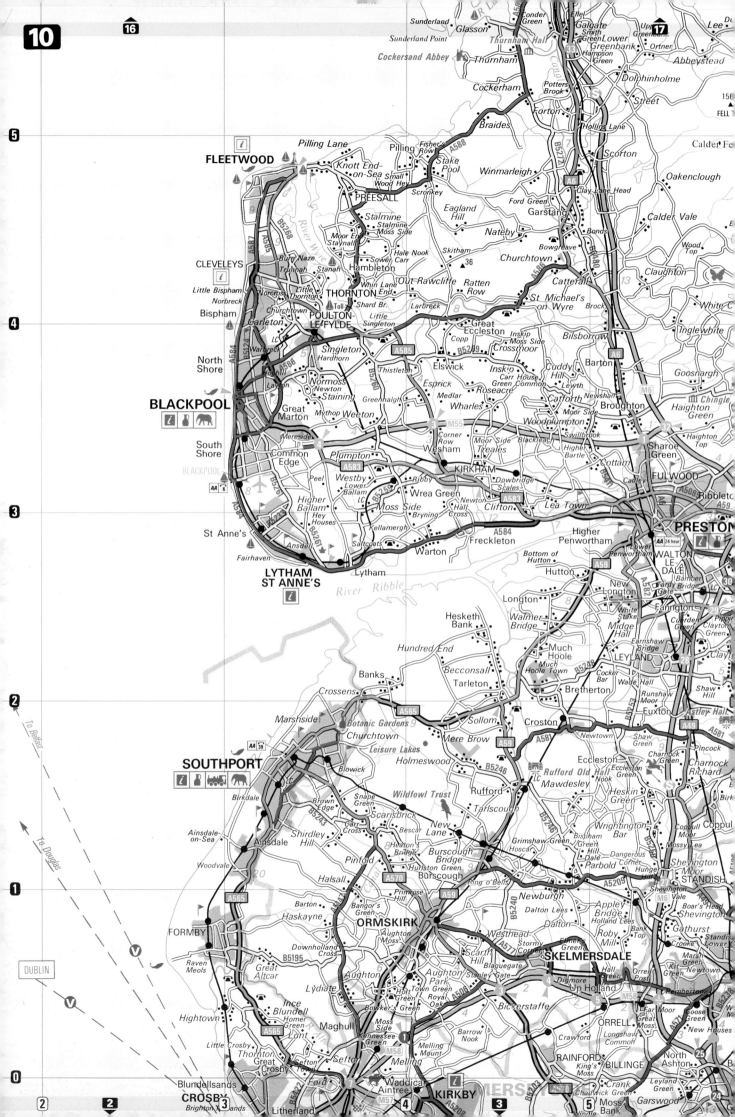

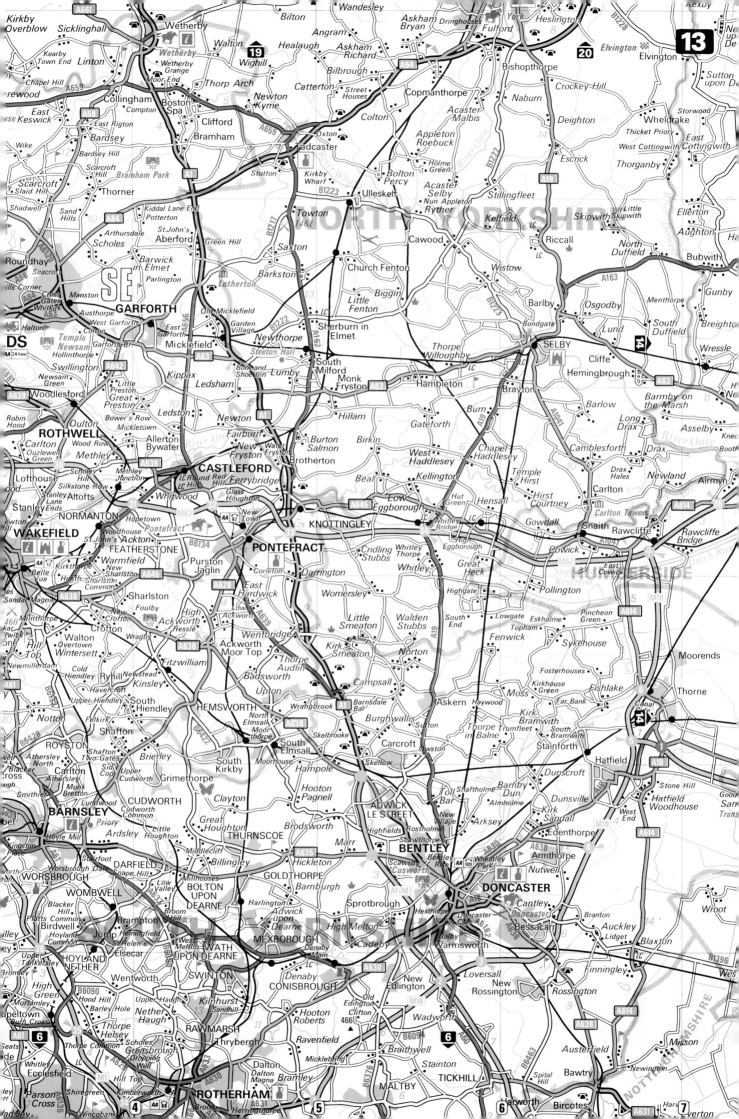

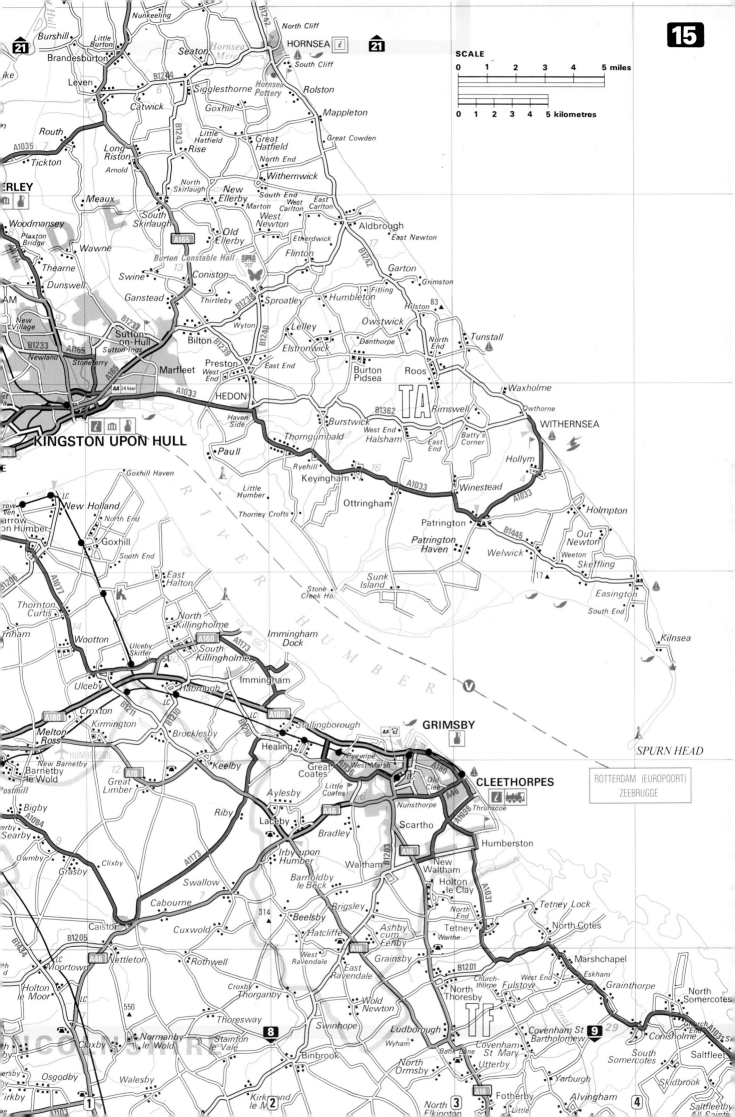

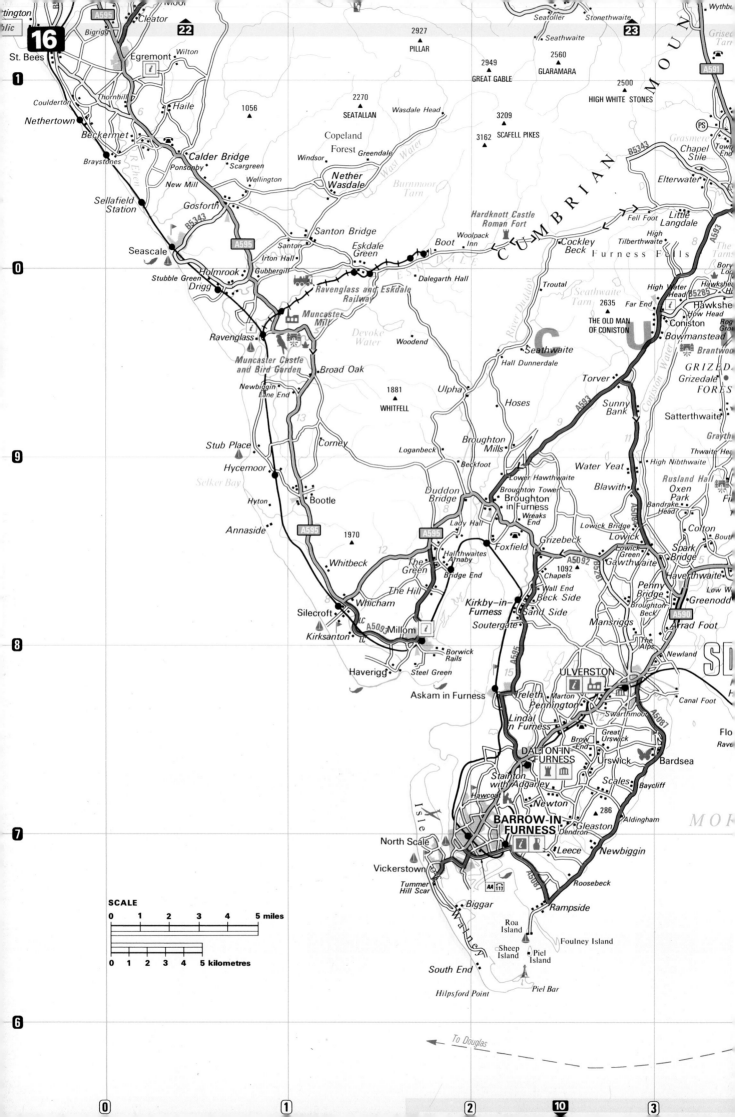

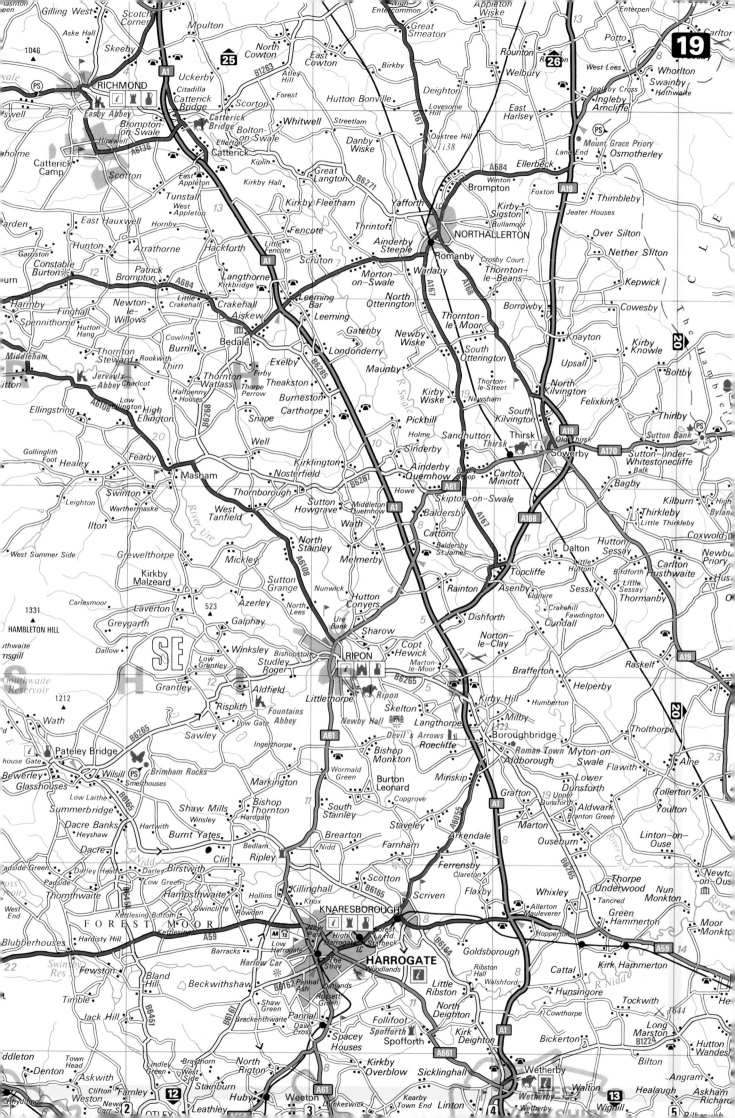

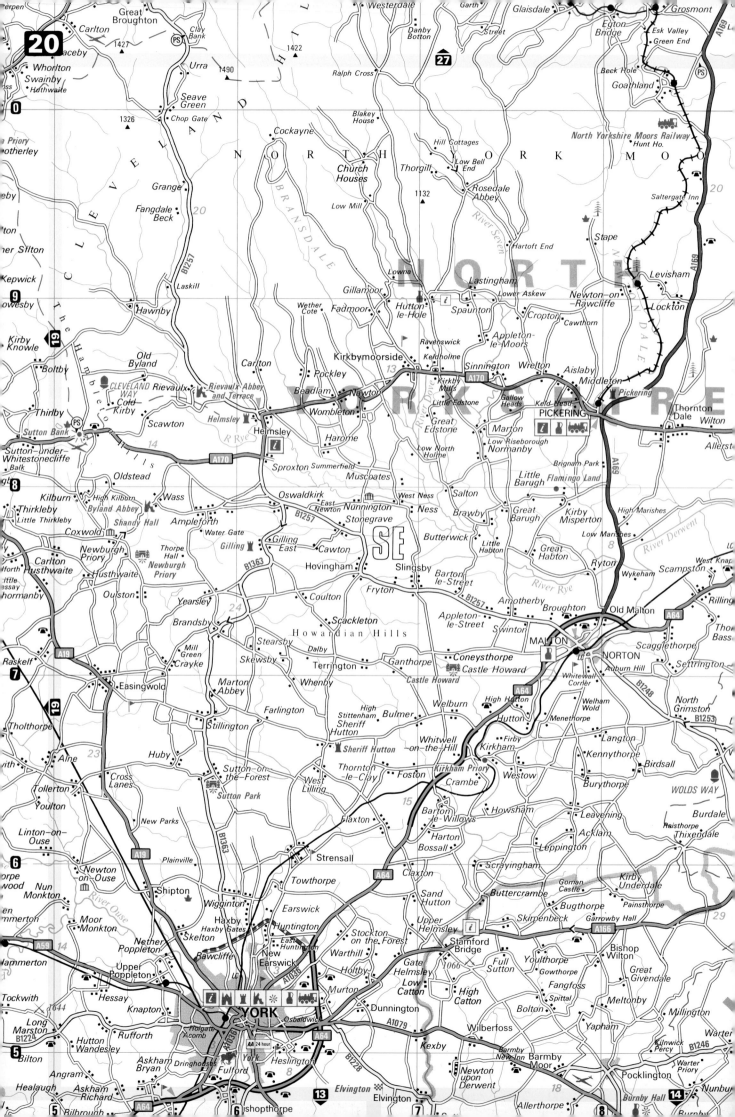

Raw
Robin Hood's Bay
Fylingthorpe
27
Old Peak or South Cheek
Low Flask
Ravenscar
Flask Inn
Falcon Inn
Staintondale
20
Harwood Dale
A171
Cloughton Newlands
Cloughton Wyke
Cloughton
Bickley
Langdale End
Burniston
Cromer Point
Silpho
Suffield
Hackness
SCALBY
CLEVELAND WAY
Newby
Wrench Green
Everley
Barrowcliff
SCARBOROUGH
Falsgrave
Oliver's Mount
AA
Sawdon
Hutton Buscel
Ayton
A170
A165
Osgodby
Eastfield
Cayton Bay
High Killerby
Snainton
A170
Ruston
Wykeham
Irton
Seamer
LC
Cayton
B1261
The Wyke
Gristhorpe
Brompton
Lebberston
LC
FILEY
Flixton
Folkton
LC
Filey Bay
edingham
Westfield
Willerby
A1039
Muston
West Flotmanby
LC
Staxton
Sherburn
Ganton
PS
Hunmanby
Holiday Camp
TA
A64
East Heslerton
Potter Brompton
Fordon
A165
Reighton
West Heslerton
Speeton
Crab Rocks
B1249
Wold Newton
B1229
Buckton
Bempton
Foxholes
Burton Fleming
North Moor
Flamborough
Weaverthorpe
Butterwick
Grindale
West Huntow
Flamborough Head
Linton
East Lutton
Thwing
Little Argam
B1255
West Lutton
Helperthorpe
Octon
Boynton
Sewerby
Sewerby Hall
Kirby Grindalythe
B1253
Langtoft
Rudston
BRIDLINGTON
Sledmere
Cowlam Manor
Low Caythorpe
BRIDLINGTON BAY
Cottam
Bessingby
Carnaby
Hilderthorpe
Sledmere
B1252
Kilham
Haisthorpe
Carnaby
B1251
B1249
Ruston Parva
Burton Agnes Hall
Thornholme
North Kingsfield
Burton Agnes
South Kingsfield
Fraisthorpe
Harpham
Garton-on-the-Wolds
Great Kendale
Lowthorpe
Little Kelk
Gransmoor
A166
Nafferton
Allison Lane End
Barmston
Wetwang
Elmswell
Little Diffield
Great Kelk
Lissett
Ulrome
B1248
GREAT DRIFFIELD
LC
B1249
Wansford
Gembling Lane End
Gembling
West End
B1242
East End
Skipsea
Tibthorpe
Kirkburn
A163
Kelleythorpe
Skerne
Foston on the Wolds
B1249
Skipsea Brough
Southburn
Brigham
Beeford
North Dalton
Hutton
Church End
Upton
A163
Middleton-on-the-Wolds
15
Kilnwick
Watton
Rotsea
North Frodingham
Dunnington
Hutton Cranswick
Hempholme
North End
Bewholme
Atwick
Lund
Beswick
Burshill
Nunkeeling
B1242
North Cliff
Holme on the Wolds
Lockington
14
Brandes Burton
Little Burton
Seaton
HORNSEA
Hornsea Mere
South Cliff
15

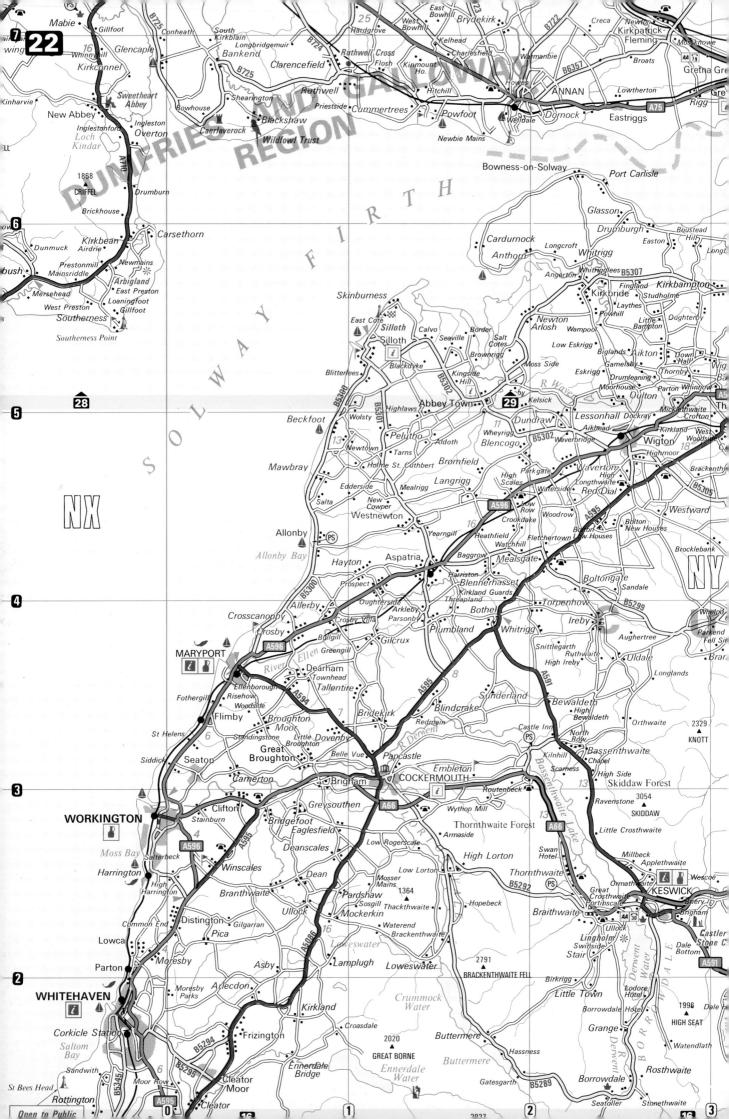

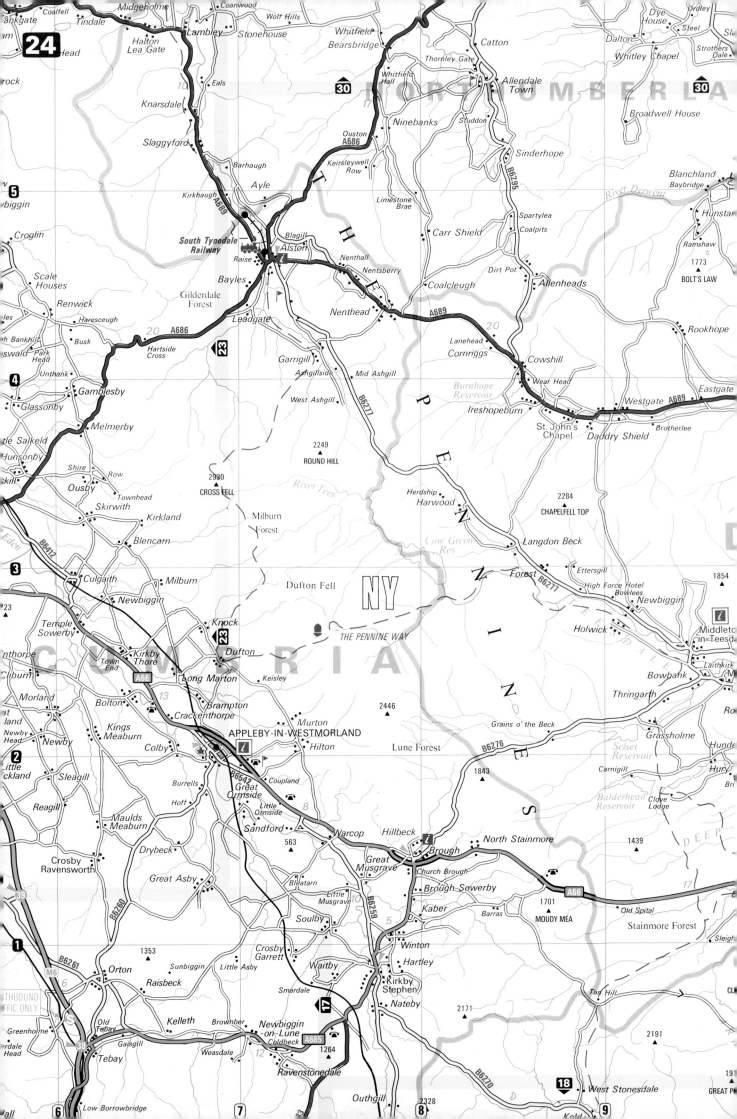

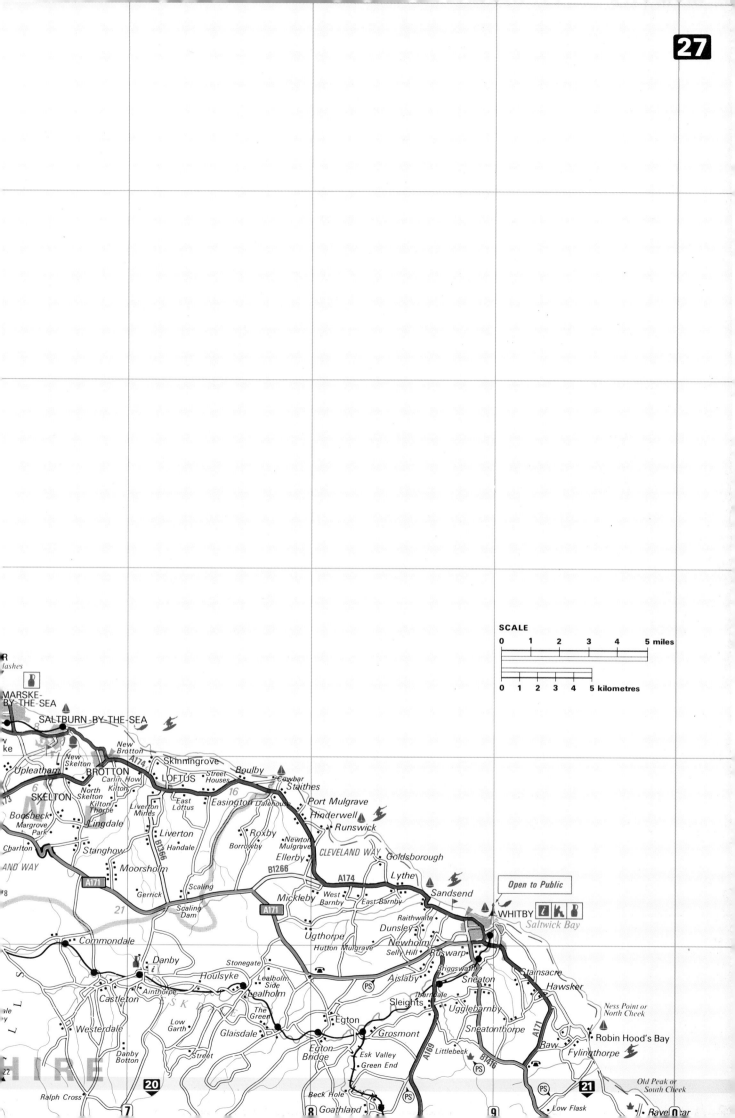

SCALE

0 1 2 3 4 5 miles

0 1 2 3 4 5 kilometres

MARSKE-BY-THE-SEA

SALTBURN-BY-THE-SEA

New Brotton

New Skelton

Upleatham

New Skelton

BROTTON

Skinningrove

Carlin How

LOFTUS

Street Houses

Boulby

Cowbar

Staithes

SKELTON

North Skelton

Kilton

Kilton Thorpe

East Loftus

Easington

Dalehouse

Port Mulgrave

Hinderwell

Boosbeck

Liverton Mines

Handale

Roxby

Newton Mulgrave

Runswick

Margrove Park

Lingdale

Liverton

Borrowby

CLEVELAND WAY

Goldsborough

Charlton

Stanghow

Ellerby

Lythe

AND WAY

Moorsholm

B1366

B1266

A174

Sandsend

A171

Gerrick

Scaling

Mickleby

West Barnby

East Barnby

Open to Public

Scaling Dam

A171

Raithwaite

WHITBY

Saltwick Bay

Commondale

Ugthorpe

Hutton Mulgrave

Dunsley

Newholm

Sell Hill

Ruswarp

Danby

Stonegate

Aislaby

Briggswath

Sneaton

Stainsacre

Houlsyke

Lealholm Side

Lealholm

Hawsker

Ainthorpe

The Green

PS

Sleights

Iburndale

Castleton

ESK DALE

Ugglebarnby

Ness Point or North Cheek

Westerdale

Low Garth

Glaisdale

Egton

Grosmont

Sneatonthorpe

A169

Robin Hood's Bay

Danby Botton

Street

Egton Bridge

Esk Valley

Green End

Littlebeck

B1416

Raw

Fylingthorpe

Ralph Cross

20

Beck Hole

8 Goathland

9

PS

21

Old Peak or South Cheek

Low Flask

Raven

28

SCALE

0   1   2   3   4   5 miles

0 1 2 3 4 5 kilometres

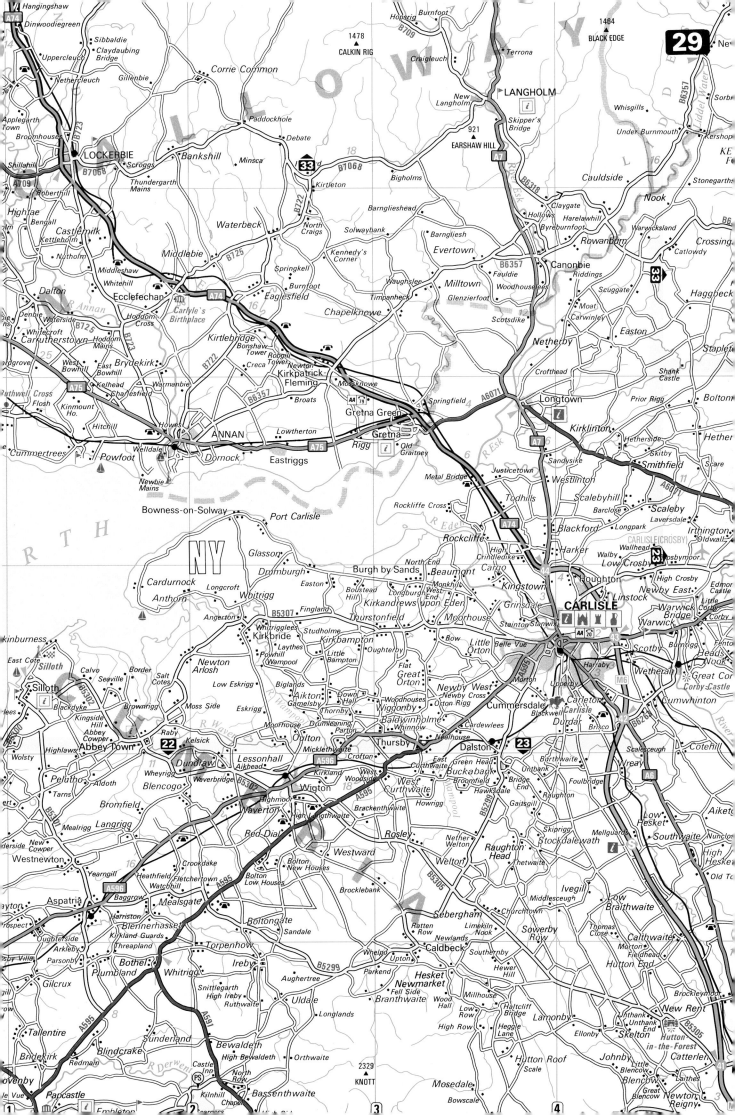

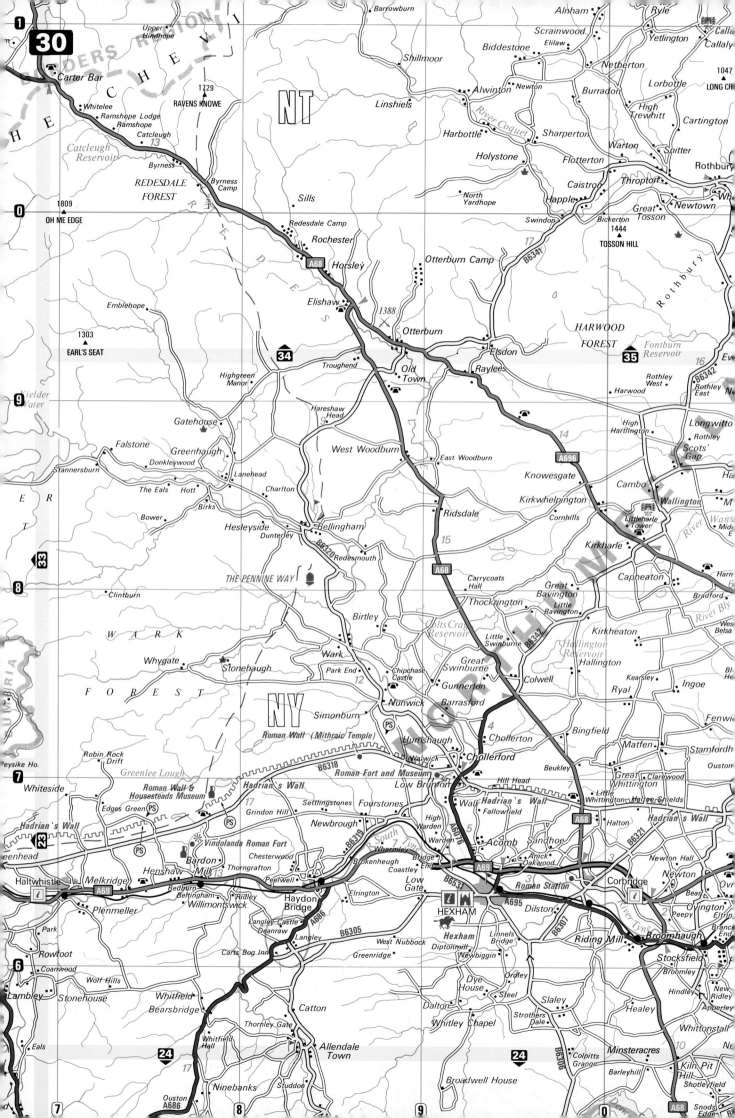

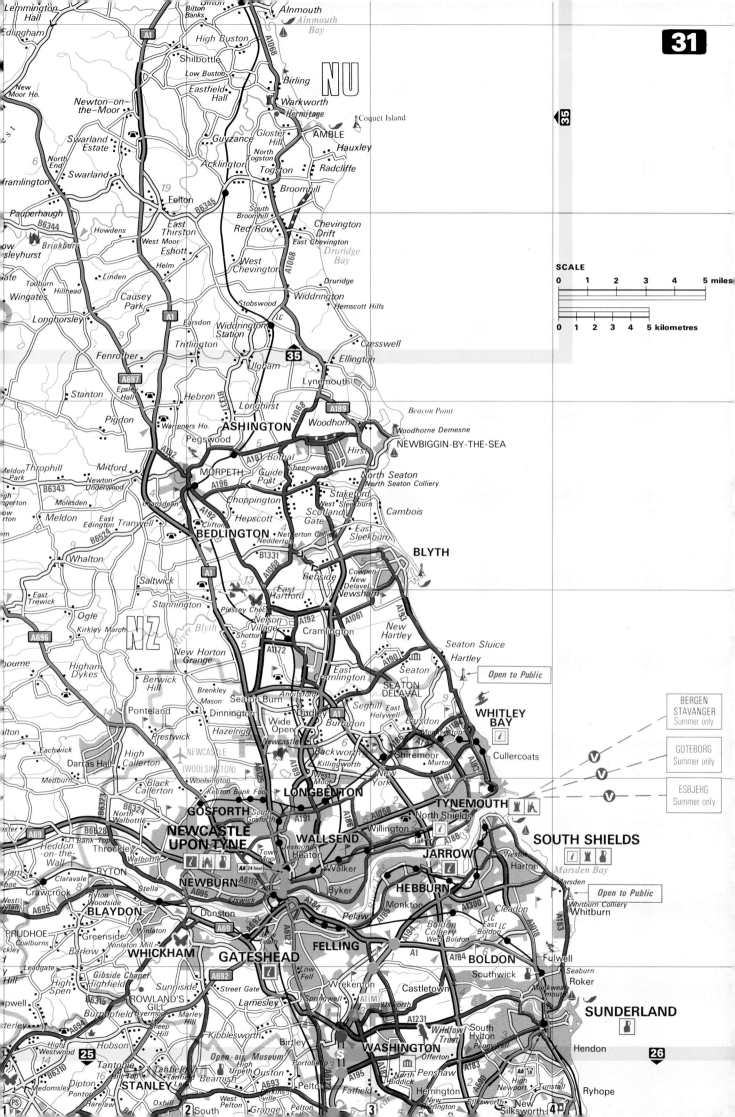

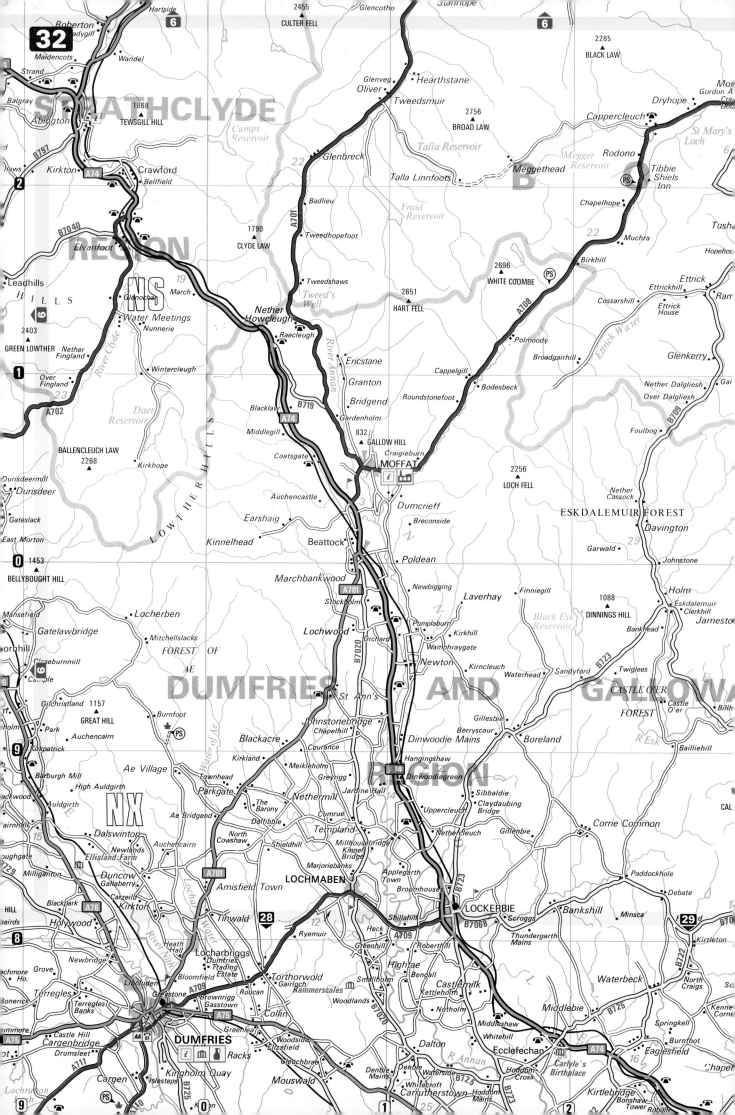

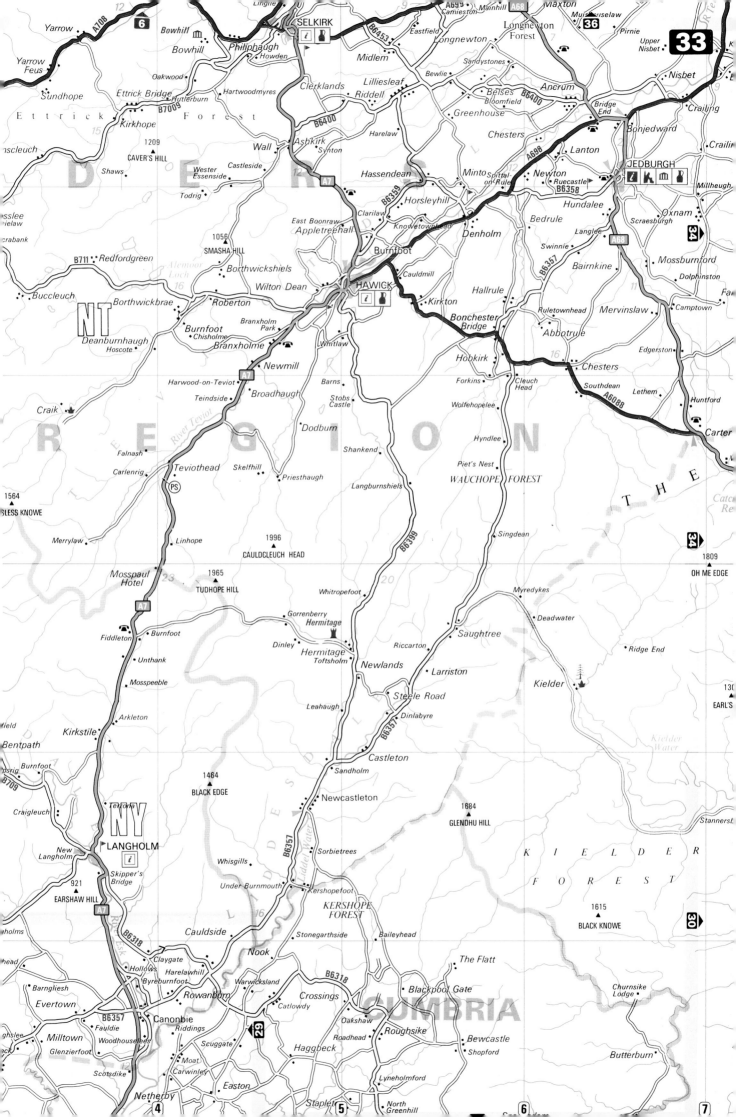

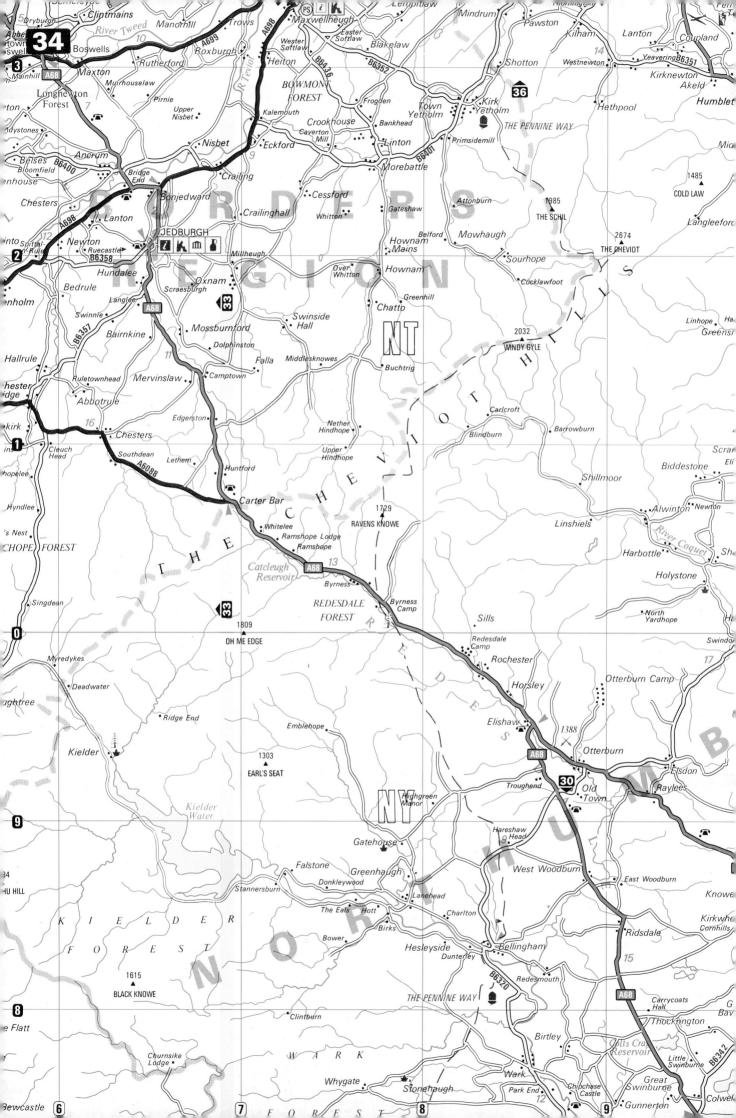

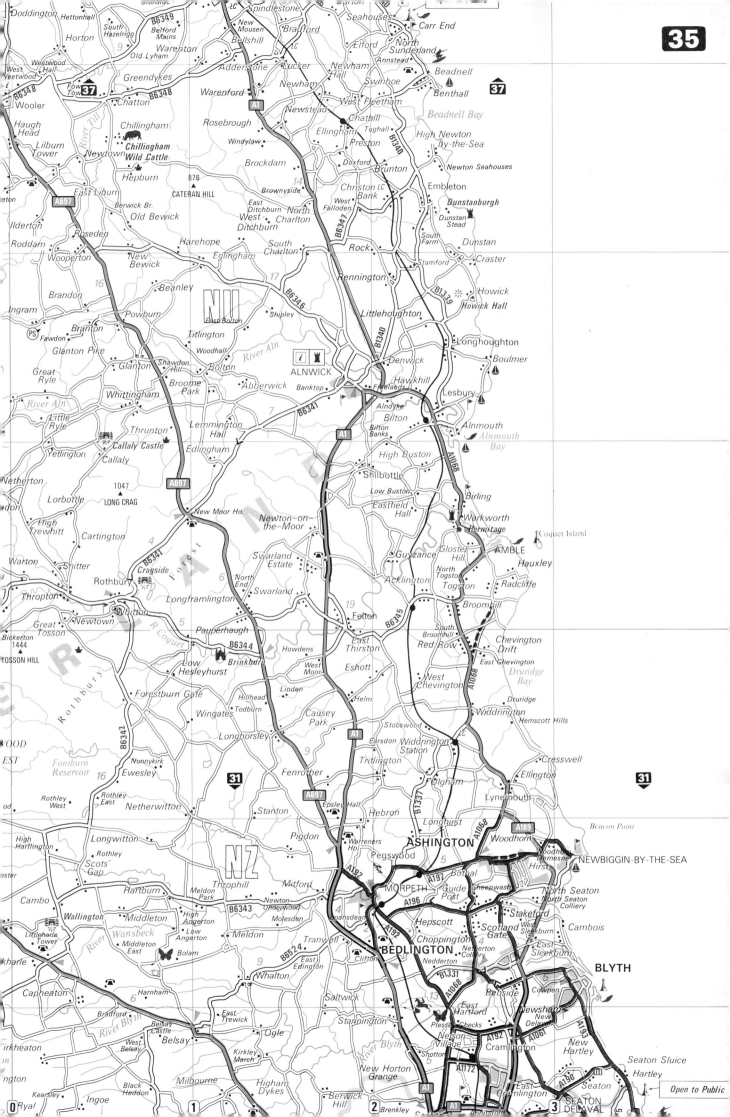

SCALE

| 0 | 1 | 2 | 3 | 4 | 5 miles |

| 0 | 1 | 2 | 3 | 4 | 5 kilometres |

ST ABB'S HEAD

Northfield

St Abbs

Whitecross
Acredale
Cairncross
Biglawburn
EYEMOUTH
Gunsgreenhill

Reston
Ayton
Burnmouth

Prenderguest
usewaybank
Whitering

B6355
Edington
Foulden
Lamberton
Clappers
1333
Conundrum
Foulden
Newton
Meadowhill
Hutton
High Letham
ndykes
Paxton
B6461
Hutton
Mains
Sunwick
BERWICK-UPON-TWEED

gatehead
Loanend
Tweedmouth
Spittal

ne
6461
Fishwick
East Ord

Horndean
Horncliffe
West Longridge
Borewell
kirk
Thorntonpark
Murton
Scremerston
Norham
Thornton
Unthank
70
Norham
Newburn
West
Allerdean
Cheswick

West
Newbi
Shoreswood
Shoresdean
Ancroft
Goswick

CAUSEWAY
FLOODED
AT HIGH TIDE

45
Grindon
Felkington
New
Haggerston
Haggerston
Beal
HOLY ISLAND

Shellacres
Grindonrigg
Berrington
15

wizel Bridge
h Park
Duddo
West Mains
Fenhamhill
Holy
Island
Castle
Heaton
Bowsden
Kentstone
Fenham
Lindisfarne Priory
Castle Point

ill
ed
lees
Etal
Kyloe
Fenwick
Burrows Hole

Crookham
Heatherslaw Mill
B6353
Lowick
Buckton

The Lady Waterford Hall
Brownridge
Smeafield
Elwick
Staple
Sound
FARNE ISLANDS

Branxton
Ford
Holburn
Detchant
Ross
Inner
Sound

1513
Kimmerston
Detchant
Low Middleton
Budle
Bamburgh

Flodden
14
Middleton
Easington
Budle
Bay
Bamburgh

Howtel
NORTHUMBERLAND
Hetton Steads
Nesbit
Belford
Waren
Mill
Glororum
Burton

B6352
Milfield
North
Hazelrigg
Sionside
B1342
Spindlestone
Seahouses

Open to Public

Lanton
Fenton
Town
Hettonlaw
Hettonhall
Belford
Mains
Bellshill
New
Mousen
Bradford
Carr End

9
Yeavering
B6351
Coupland
Newtown
Horton
South
Hazelrigg
Warenton
Old Lyham
Elford
North
Sunderland
Annstead

newton
Kirknewton
Bendor
West
twood
Doddington
Weetwood
Hall
Greendykes
Adderstone
Lucker
Newham
Hall
Beadnell

NU

INDEX

As well as the page number of each place name the index also
includes an appropriate atlas page number together with a four figure
map reference (see National Grid explanation on page 98).

In a very few instances place names appear without a map reference.
This is because either they are not shown on the atlas or they lie just
outside the mapping area of the guide. However, each tour does
include a detailed map which highlights the location of all places
mentioned on the route.

A

	page	map	
Abbeydale Industrial Hamlet	55	6	SK 3282
Abbey Town	22	29	NY 1750
Airton	57	18	SD 9059
Aislaby	43	20	SE 7785
Aldborough	63	19	SE 4065
Aldbrough	13	15	TA 2338
Aldford	25	3	SJ 4159
Allendale Town	35	30	NY 8455
Allenheads	35	24	NY 8645
Almscliffe Crag	47		
Alnmouth	3	35	NU 2410
Alnwick	2	35	NU 1912
Amble	3	35	NU 2604
Ambleside	4,31	17	NY 3704
Ampleforth	33	20	SE 5878
Anglezarke Reservoir	59		
Arkengarthdale	44	18	NZ 0002
Arncliffe	56	18	SD 9371
Ashford-in-the-Water	18	5	SK 1969
Ashness Bridge	36		
Astbury	28	4	SJ 8461
Astley Hall	58	10	SD 5718
Austwick	52	18	SD 7667
Axe Edge	29		
Ayton, West and East	49	21	SE 9884

B

	page	map	
Bakewell	18	5	SK 2168
Bamburgh	2	37	NU 1834
Bampton	61	23	NY 5118
Bangor-is-y-Coed	25		
Banks	9,21	23	NY 5664
Barden Tower	56		
Barnard Castle	6,44	25	NZ 0516
Baslow	19	5	SK 2572
Bassenthwaite	37	22	NY 2332
Bassenthwaite Lake	37	22	NY 2130
Beadnell	2	37	NU 2329
Beal	11	37	NU 0642
Bedale	45	19	SE 2688
Beeley	18	5	SK 2667
Belford	3	37	NU 1033
Bellingham	8,41	30	NY 8383
Bellister Castle	20		
Belmont	59	11	SD 6715
Berwick-on-Tweed	10	37	NT 9953
Beverley	12	15	TA 0339
Bewcastle	9	33	NY 5674
Birdoswald	9,21	23	NY 6266
Black Edge	19		
Blackpool	14	10	SD 3035
Blanchland	35	24	NY 9650
Blisdale	32		
Bolton Abbey	56	18	SE 0754
Boot	5	16	NY 1701
Border Forest Park	8		
Boroughbridge	63	19	SE 3966
Borrowdale	36	22	NY 2514
Bowder Stone	36		
Bowes Castle	44	25	NY 9813
Bowes Museum	44		
Bowness-on-Solway	22	29	NY 2262
Bowness-on-Windermere	30	17	SD 4097
Boynton	17	21	TA 1368
Brafferton	63	19	SE 4370
Braithwaite	27,37	22	NY 2323
Braithwaite Hall	45		
Brampton	21	23	NY 5361
Brandsby	63	20	SE 5872
Brantwood	31	16	SD 3296
Bridlington	16	21	TA 1766
Brimham Rocks	46	19	SE 2165
Brinkburn Priory	3,40	35	NZ 1298
Brompton	49	21	SE 9482
Browsholme Hall	15	11	SD 6845
Burgh-by-Sands	22	29	NY 3259
Burnby Hall Gardens	64	14	SE 8247
Burscough	59	10	SD 4310
Burton Agnes	17	21	TA 1063
Burton Constable Hall	12	15	TA 1936

Buttermere	37	22	NY 1717
Buttertubs Pass	53		
Buxton	18,29	4	SK 0673
Byland Abbey	33	20	SE 5578

C

	page	map	
Caldbeck	37	23	NY 3239
Calderbridge	27	16	NY 0405
Caldron Snout	7		
Capesthorne Hall	29	4	SJ 8473
Cark	31	17	SD 3676
Carlisle	20,22	29	NY 3955
Carnforth	38	17	SD 4970
Carrawbrough	9,34		
Cartmel	31	17	SD 3778
Castell Dinas Bran	25		
Castle Howard	63	20	SE 7271
Castlerigg Stone Circle	37	22	NY 2923
Castleton	55	5	SK 1582
Catterick	45	19	SE 2397
Catterick Bridge	45	19	SE 2299
Chapel-en-le-Frith	55	5	SK 0580
Chatsworth House	19	5	SK 2670
Chester	24	3	SJ 4066
Cheviot Hills, The	11	34	NT 81
Chillingham	3	35	NU 0625
Chirk	25		
Chirk Castle	25		
Chollerford	9,34	30	NY 9170
Chorley	58	10	SD 5817
Clapham	39,52	17	SD 7469
Clappersgate	5,30	16	NY 3603
Cleveland Hills	32	20	SE 59
Clitheroe	15	11	SD 7441
Cloud, The	28		
Cockermouth	23,26	22	NY 1230
Coldstream	11	36	NT 8539
Congleton	28	4	SJ 8562
Coniston	31	16	SD 3097
Coniston Water	31	16	SD 3094
Corby Castle	20	23	NY 4754
Cornhill-on-Tweed	10	37	NT 8639
Cotherstone	7	25	NZ 0119
Cottingham	12	15	TA 0532
Cowan Bridge	38	17	SD 6476
Coxwold	33	20	SE 5377
Cragside Estate	40		
Craster	2	35	NU 2519
Crosby-on-Eden	21		
Cross Keys Inn	53		
Crosthwaite	36	17	SD 4491
Croston	58	10	SD 4818
Cumbrian Mountains	4	16	NY 20

D

	page	map	
Daddry Shield	7	24	NY 8937
Dalby Forest Drive	49		
Danby	43	27	NZ 7009
Dent	52	17	SD 7087
Dentdale	52		
Derwent Reservoir	54	5	SK 1692
Derwent Water	36	22	NY 2620
Doddington	11	37	NU 0032
Dove Cottage	4		
Dove Holes	19	5	SK 0777
Downholme	44	18	SE 1197
Dunnerdale	51		
Dunnerdale Forest	5		
Dunstanburgh Castle	2	35	NU 2623

E

	page	map	
Eamont Bridge	61	23	NY 5228
Easby Abbey	45	19	NZ 1800
Easingwold	63	20	SE 5269
Eastgate	7	24	NY 9538
East Witton	45	19	SE 1486
Edale	55	5	SK 1285
Egglestone Abbey	6,44	25	NZ 0615
Eglingham	3	35	NU 1019
Egremont	27	16	NY 0110
Elsdon	41	34	NY 9393
Embleton	2	35	NU 2322
Ennerdale Bridge	27	22	NY 0615
Eskdale	5	16	NY 1700
Eskdale Green	50	16	NY 1400
Esthwaite Water	30	17	NY 3697
Eyam	55	5	SK 2176

F

	page	map	
Farndon	25	3	SJ 4154
Farne Islands	2	37	NU 2236
Far Sawrey	30	17	SD 3795
Featherstone Castle	20		
Fell Foot Park	30	17	SD 3886
Fewston	47	19	SE 1954
Filey	16	21	TA 1180
Flamborough	16	21	TA 2270
Flash	29	5	SK 0267
Flodden	11	37	NT 9235
Forest of Bowland	15,39	11	SD 6252
Foster Beck Flax Mill	46		
Fountains Abbey	46	19	SE 2668
Froncysyllte	25		
Frosterly	7	25	NZ 0237
Fylde, The	14		
Fylingdales Early Warning Radar Station	43,48		
Fylingdales Moor	48		
Fylingthorpe	48	27	NZ 9405

G

	page	map	
Gargrave	57	11	SD 9354
Garstang	15	10	SD 4945
Gawsworth	29	4	SJ 8869
Giggleswick	52	18	SD 8163
Gilling East	63	20	SE 6176
Gilsland	9,21	23	NY 6366
Glannaventa	51		
Goathand	43,49	20	NZ 8301
Gordale Scar	57		
Gosforth	50	16	NY 0603
Grange	36	22	NY 2517
Grange-over-Sands	30	17	SD 4077
Grasmere	4	16	NY 3307
Grassington	56	18	SE 0064
Graythwaite Hall Gardens	30	17	SD 3691
Great Driffield	17	21	TA 0257
Greenhead	9,21	23	NY 6665
Greta Bridge	44	25	NZ 0813
Grinton	44	18	SE 0498
Grizedale	30	16	SD 3394

H

	page	map	
Haddon Hall	18	5	SK 2366
Hadrian's Wall	9,21,35	23	NY 6696
Haltwhistle	21,35	23	NY 7064
Hamsterley Forest	6	25	NZ 0328
Hard Knott Castle	5	16	NY 2202
Hard Knott Pass	5		
Hardrow Force	53		
Hardrow Scar	53		
Harrogate	47	19	SE 3055
Hartburn	41	31	NZ 0886
Hathersage	54	5	SK 2381
Haverthwaite	31	17	SD 3483
Hawes	53	18	SD 8789
Haweswater Reservoir	61	23	NY 4815
Hawkshead	30	16	SD 3598
Hawsker	48	27	NZ 9207

Y